Growing Up Happy

Produced by
The Philip Lief Group, Inc.

Doubleday

New York   London   Toronto   Sydney   Auckland

Growing Up Happy

Captain Kangaroo
Tells Yesterday's Children
How to Nurture Their Own

by

Bob Keeshan

PUBLISHED BY DOUBLEDAY
a division of Random House, Inc.

A hardcover edition of this book was published in 1989 by Doubleday

www.doubleday.com

Book design by Anne Ling
Original jacket photograph of Bob Keeshan by Deborah Feingold
"Captain Kangaroo" photograph courtesy of CBS

Produced by The Philip Lief Group, Inc.

The Library of Congress has cataloged the hardcover edition as:
Keeshan, Robert.
    Growing up happy : Captain Kangaroo tells yesterday's children how to nurture their own / by Bob Keeshan.
        p.   cm.
    "Produced by the Philip Lief Group, Inc."
    Includes index.
    ISBN 0-385-24909-8
    1. Child rearing—United States.   I. Philip Lief Group.
    II. Title.
    HQ769.K345   1989
    649'.1—dc20   89-32502
                                                                CIP

Grateful acknowledgment is made for permission to reprint the lyrics to the following songs:
"My Blue Heaven." Copyright © 1927 (Renewed 1955) Donaldson Publishing Co. and George Whiting Publishing Co.
"Young at Heart." Copyright © 1954 (Renewed 1983) June's Tunes.
"The Planting Song," words and music by Stan Davis. Copyright © 1977 Saugatuck Productions.

Trade Paperback ISBN: 978-0-385-51444-6

This book is dedicated to
Michael, Laurie and Maeve,
who taught their father
about a very special love,
and to
Britton, Derek, Alex, Connor MacNary,
Kaelan and Connor Matthew,
who continue the education
of their grandfather

Acknowledgments

I acknowledge with my gratitude the enormous contribution made by Carol Bergman, who sat with me through endless hours, helping me to recall events long past through perceptive questioning. Her expertise and her helpful research made this book richer in detail.

My editor Nancy Kalish was always understanding as well as demanding, in the best sense of the word. Her skillfully negotiated changes have improved this book. Most of all, her great enthusiasm for the project was a continual encouragement for me.

I am grateful to Philip Lief, who "bird-dogged" this project for several years. I express my thanks to my good friend Dick Welsh, whose frequent question "Where's the book?" contributed greatly to its completion.

I thank Nancy Evans of Doubleday, whose comments and questions were more valuable because they came from an understanding mother who also happens to be my publisher.

Doubleday's Casey Fuetsch provided insights and suggestions which greatly added to the usefulness of this book. Bill Barry's comments were very helpful, especially concerning how to "interpret" a child.

Jacqueline Deval, Ellen Archer and Jill Roberts graciously shepherded me and the book through the process, sometimes mysterious to the uninitiated, of getting the book to the reader.

For last, I leave my thanks to Jeanne Keeshan, whose nurturing skills are detailed on these pages. The results of those skills and her love can be seen in three very nice adults, our children.

Contents

Preface   1

Chapter 1:   A Mother's Smile   3

Chapter 2:   A Father's Dream   14

Chapter 3:   Childhood's End   22

Chapter 4:   From the Halls of Montezuma   31

Chapter 5:   A Funny Thing Happened on My Way to
              Law School   38

Chapter 6:   Confessions of a Visionary   44

Chapter 7:   A Little Honk Here, A Little Squirt There   51

Chapter 8:   Wedding Bells   58

Chapter 9:   No More Clowning Around   64

Chapter 10:   100 Percent Unemployed   73

Chapter 11:   Reprise, Bring on the Clown   79

Chapter 12.   To Grandfather's House We Go   90

Chapter 13:   Captain 'Roo   96

Chapter 14:   Years of Growth   105

Chapter 15:   The Farmer in the Jeans   111

Chapter 16:   Shooting Up on Violence   119

Chapter 17:   The Etymologist   125

Chapter 18:   Bow-Wow, Tweet Tweet and Roar Roar   137

Chapter 19:   Boys and Girls—Girls and Boys   143

Chapter 20:   Our Rose of Texas   150

Chapter 21:   It's About Time   155

Chapter 22:   I Can Do It Myself   162

Chapter 23:   Who, What, Where, When and Why?   168

Chapter 24:   Romeo, Juliet and the Kids   175

Chapter 25:   Way to Go, Gama!   184

Chapter 26:   Please Leave Quietly   191

Chapter 27:   Thump, Thump, Thump Went My
                Heartbeat   199

Chapter 28:   Anarchy Begins at Home   206

Chapter 29:   All in the Family   214

Chapter 30:   Wish List   221

Suggested Reading List   227

Home Video: As Fun and Learning   229

Preface

When I am asked how I got started in television, I jokingly reply, "Just a bad break!" It may not have been all that bad, but it certainly was not planned. How could I plan for a career in an industry that did not exist when I was a boy? I have been in the business for over forty years—television's life span—and I have seen it grow from an infant technology disdained by entertainment and advertising professionals to a medium that entertains, informs, and sells to the world.

Over forty years ago, I created the first Clarabell on "The Howdy Doody Show"—a lovable clown who, along with Howdy, has since become a television icon. I was a young twenty years of age when Clarabell was born, and I had not thought much about television, children or television's possible and potential effects on young people. Then I became a parent and my perspective changed. Shortly afterwards, I went from performing as a rollicking clown to developing my own children's programming, culminating in the creation of "Captain Kangaroo," a program designed to meet the emotional and educational needs of children while attending to the serious business of entertaining them.

Many of the people I meet on my extensive travels around the nation have traveled these forty years with me; mine has been a public journey. Now those people have children and grandchildren, too, who are still watching the Captain, and I have three children and six grandchildren of my own. Amazing! More than three generations of Americans have been touched by Captain Kangaroo.

This book is about my life and my development as a person, a television producer/entertainer, and as an advocate for children. I am still changing and expect to continue to change, and my enthusiasm for the world and all its wonder, especially those young wonders, children, has not diminished over the years.

Much has happened to me in studios and in executive suites so your curiosity about the strange world of television should be satisfied in my recounting of these events. But I have also learned a few things about the difficulties and the joys of raising children in this modern age. If you are now embarking on starting a family and if you have just discovered or rediscovered the Captain on television, I know you will find plenty of useful material in this book. And I hope you will be inspired to use my experiences to augment your parent power in the shaping of a precious life.

If you are an adult with no daily responsibility for children, but who cares about the future, this book will impress you with the need for all of us to help with the successful nurturing of children. When a parent fails in raising a child, everyone pays a very high economic and social cost. Today, we must all be parents to all children. May this book convince you of that need and demonstrate how you can help nurture America's children.

Chapter 1
A Mother's Smile

When I was a boy, my mother and I would make eye contact, and she would give me a smile that would make my day. Her eyes and her smile would say, "I love you, you're terrific." She was the center of my universe, and, like most children, I thought I had the most wonderful mother in the world. I adored her.

Slim and beautiful as a young girl, Margaret Frances Conroy had married my father against her parents' wishes on May 17, 1916, the day after she turned eighteen. Her parents, Irish immigrants, disapproved of her intended because he had only arrived from Ireland as recently as 1905. I suppose that, according to the strange mores of the immigrant community, they thought he was not American enough and therefore showed little promise. They were wrong.

Margaret and Joseph became "serious," as my father shyly described their courtship to me many years later, soon after Margaret had wandered into the grocery store on Manhattan's Amsterdam Avenue where he worked as a clerk. Was it an errand for a loaf of bread, a bottle of milk, a pound of potatoes that led to romance? In an act of defiance uncommon in that era, Margaret Conroy followed her heart into matrimony as soon as she reached the legal age.

Without the support of her family and with most of his family still "on the other side" in Ireland, the newlyweds set up house, first in Manhattan, and then later, as my father became more successful, in Lynbrook, New York, then a sparsely settled Long Island suburb of New York City. As was the custom in those days, my father worked from dawn to dusk providing for his family, while my mother stayed home, rearing the children and tending to the house. They both worked extremely hard. It never occurred to them to do otherwise.

By the time I entered the world on June 27, 1927, my parents had two boys—Jack, born in 1917, and Bill, born in 1920. For a short while, until my sister Catherine joined us in 1930, I was the family baby. My two brothers were out at school during the day, while I stayed home with my mother. Like most toddlers, I felt my mother was devoted only to me. This is a common illusion, of course, and with growth I came to understand that she had been equally devoted to all her children.

Many parents, not understanding the natural self-centered orientation of a toddler, attempt to discipline this "selfishness" out of a young child, inflicting serious and lasting damage in the process. Most children of this age subscribe to the premise, "What's mine is mine and what's yours is mine!" It is a passing state, often distressful to other members of the family, but part of the growing process. It's a mistake to engage in a battle of wills with a self-centered two-year-old. You won't win and you'll feel pretty dumb being outwitted by someone that much smaller and younger. Parenting can be humiliating when you don't keep things in perspective. Lighten up enough to laugh at things as they are. And fortunately, you'll find that, when handled with sensitivity and finesse, toddlers can be gently prodded toward less exasperating behavior.

As a youngster I had many friends and made friends easily, but I was, by and large, a solitary child. I was often alone, but I was not lonely. I would happily spend hour upon hour by myself, working a patch of sand and dirt close by the garage back of our house. This was my Kingdom, perhaps my first Treasure House, a place where I created worlds of wonder, not with fancy interactive toys, but with some sticks, clothespins, and buttons borrowed from my mother's button box. Do modern mothers keep a button box? I think not. For that matter, whatever happened to clothespins? Most contemporary children would wonder at such a contrivance. "You mean you *pinned* the clothes to the rope? Why not just put them in the dryer?" To me, two clothespins stuck together could become the body and wings of an airplane. It required some imagination on my part, but that was the point of the exercise.

The many buttons borrowed from my mother became kings and queens, sea captains, more daring than Errol Flynn, battling fierce pirates of my imagination. There was a large silver button, which I can still see in my mind's eye, that was Pan American's "China Clipper" about to take wing from nearby Flushing Bay and move, at great speed, to far-off Oriental seas. (China, by the way, existed, in my imagination, around and behind the garage, not far from the blue hydrangea bush.)

I could spend solitary hours with my stick and button collections. My brothers thought me a bit daffy and my sister nagged at me to put away my strange playthings and share her play. Perhaps I embarrassed her. To this day, a faraway look will appear in her eyes as she softly comments, "Bobby played with buttons."

But my mother tolerated and even encouraged my excursions into fantasy worlds. A smile from her was like a smile from Clement Moore's Santa Claus. With a smile and a nod of her head she let me know it was all right, that she understood. I think of her often these days as I watch my grandchildren develop. To watch them play, to see them exploring and discovering the world, is a joy. Often, when they allow me to share their play, I rediscover those things which I have taken for granted for too many years. To view the world through the eyes of a child can be a stimulating and refreshing experience for us stodgy adults.

"Without fantasies to give us hope," writes the noted psychologist Bruno Bettelheim in his book *The Uses of Enchantment,* "we do not have the strength to meet the adversities of life. Childhood is a time when fantasies need to be nurtured."

I think it would be a nifty idea to hang a banner above the door of every American family that declares, "Childhood is a time when fantasies need to be nurtured." The banner would remind weary parents trudging home from workday wars that the truly creative and important work of their day is about to begin—the nurturing of their young human beings. I suppose, like most slogans, the banner would go unnoticed a few days after hanging. But a reminder is always needed, for fantasy is critical to child development.

Although my mother was not a highly educated woman, she instinctively understood the importance of fantasy play in a child's development. Too often, today's adults, burdened by their MBA's and other advanced degrees, regard imaginative play as juvenile, a time waster, and feel that, if children are to grow, imagination must be put firmly in its place early on and children brought into the "real world," that dull place where creativity has no friends.

I often remind parents that child's play is work, the serious work of children through which they learn about their environment and how to relate to other children and to grown-ups. It is through this serious work that children develop. If the play is recognized and encouraged by adults as serious work, the child can develop in an orderly and progressive manner. Deprive a child of these tools of development, and growth is as difficult as house-building would be for a carpenter whose hammer and saw have been taken away.

The preservation of illusion is critical to fantasy, yet so many of today's heavy-minded adults seem to take pleasure in destroying the images of imagination. "Now, you know there is no Santa Claus. That's Uncle Charley romping around the Christmas tree in his traditional holiday costume." The disturbing tendency of modern advertisers to use Santa as a huckster is a display of great insensitivity. Even revered historical characters are not safe from the hawkers of modern merchandising. George Washington and the cherry tree, and Abe Lincoln and his log cabin, were cherished in my childhood. Today's child may think of those two presidents as the guys who work the showroom floor selling autos and VCR's during the Presidents' Day sales.

Even Captain Kangaroo has sometimes been the victim of an over-zealous parent. Recently, for example, a young father with his four-year-old daughter in tow recognized me on an airplane. He dragged his daughter to my seat, but when she arrived and he explained that this was Captain Kangaroo, she had no idea what he was talking about. She wanted to believe her father and her eyes searched the cabin for *her* Captain, with bushy white hair, red jacket with white piping, perhaps with Bunny Rabbit or Mister Moose. She even looked out the window hoping to see the Captain sitting on a cloud. The object of her father's attention, however, was a rather ordinary looking guy in a sport jacket with briefcase, a stranger to this child.

I said, nicely, "Please don't disillusion her. You will destroy the fantasy for her and she will never enjoy the Captain again."

I have always worked hard to preserve the illusions of the Captain and other residents of fantasy worlds. My wife, Jeanne, and I were officers of the Preservation of Illusions Society in our children's young days and we fill the same role with our grandchildren today. Our son, Michael, is in his late thirties. I think he has the straight line on Santa Claus, but he doesn't say so, perhaps because he's not sure that *we* know the truth. He's a good guy, protecting us like that. Every Easter I would give the saddle of the front door its annual coat of black paint and then lay newspaper about the house, because the Easter Bunny might step on the wet paint. On Easter morn, leading to each basket left by the Easter Bunny were the newspapers covered with bunny prints in black paint. My daughter Laurie still smiles when she thinks of those bunny prints and can hardly wait for her children to be old enough for her to paint the door saddle at Easter. (Knowing Laurie, she'll probably use pink, her favorite color. Good for her!)

Another example of how we preserved the illusions of the Treasure House in our own home relates to my youngest daughter, Maeve. This sparkling child was four years old when she came to Manhattan with her mother, brother and sister for a visit to the circus. They came to pick up Dad, who was in the Captain's Treasure House finishing a show. Maeve was excited to see the Captain, and we have pictures of her sitting on his lap in serious discussion, as any four-year-old might be. The Captain soon excused himself, went to his dressing room, shed make-up and costume and, in ten minutes, returned to the studio in street clothes ready for a circus visit. Maeve ran into my arms, and with great excitement exclaimed, "Daddy! You should have been here. You just missed the Captain!" Now, that's preserving illusions!

Shortly before I blew out the candles on my sixth birthday cake, my family moved closer to Manhattan, to Forest Hills of tennis fame, which was then a small community of lovely single-family homes. It was there, in our Jewel Street house, that so many things happened to me, the sweet memories of which I still cherish.

The house seemed huge to my six-year-old eyes. (I've been back often. It's not that large, but it was big enough to build some rich childhood experiences.) It had a spacious back yard and a large musty-smelling basement perfect for winter afternoons of playing house or producing plays. It was in this basement that we kept a cast-off windup Victrola complete with horn and scratchy old records of operas and Sousa marches. I mouthed arias with Caruso and paraded to "Stars and Stripes Forever," actions I still perform on television and on stage with symphony orchestras.

There was also a screened in porch where I spent summer hours, especially during rainy days, when, oblivious to any danger, I watched with awe the great bolts of lightning and then counted the seconds before the thunderclaps. We all like to recall the sights and sounds of good times, and I like to add the recollection of smells. I can close my eyes and the damp sweetness of a warm summer day is fresh in my memory. Quiet, lazy, sleepy summer days, the stuff of which Faulkner made southern lore, the stuff of my northern childhood. Singing cicadas with transparent wings; Japanese beetles chewing on choice roses; large bees making their appointed rounds of aster and alyssum; a wasp, attracted to the water, sending us running and screaming from the spray of the cooling hose set upon the slippery grass. As children, we were attuned to nature without considering it anything extraordinary; this was the world in which we lived, and to learn to be in harmony with it was sensible.

Today we live in a messy world in which summer beaches are strewn with medical waste; the treated effluent of our towns and cities stifles ocean residents; acid rain fells more growth than Paul Bunyan could dream of cutting; our air is filled with noxious gases, and our space is closing above our continents, threatening to turn our earth into a huge greenhouse. These conditions result, not from a few single acts, but from a collective carelessness and arrogance. If those who made the many small decisions resulting in our cumulative environmental mess had been more "tuned" to their world, more sensitive to their place in the delicate structure of nature, we might be living in a different and more pleasant world and not on the edge of environmental calamity. I believe this "tuning in" to nature begins at a tender age and is an important aspect of development.

Tuning a child to nature does not involve lectures and visits to museums, although these stimuli are important, on an intellectual level, to an older child. Tuning a child to our shared world should be a collection of emotional experiences—examining a tree leaf, lying on the grass or a city rooftop on a warm summer night wondering about the twinkle of stars, watching a diligent ant drag a crumb several times its weight across a hot pavement, observing water soaking into dry ground and into sand more quickly than it does into clay. Our world is filled with observable phenomena which most adults have forgotten, or worse, have come to regard as unimportant. But appreciating these daily events is important to the development of a nature-sensitive child.

I can lie in bed on a rainy evening and *feel* the rain seeping into the ground in search of thirsty roots. There is a direct line between me and the child of fifty years ago who listened to the beat of raindrops pounding on the driveway and watched in wonder as they made furrows along the row of hollyhocks outside my home. Tuning to nature must begin at a tender age, perhaps with a lesson as simple as teaching a toddler the importance of allowing that ant to carry its burden undeterred. Later in life the youngster can learn that we call having such generosity of spirit a "reverence for life."

Those summer days seemed especially built for ring-a-levio (alle, alle in free!), stickball and a slew of creative adventures, from castle-building to a game of "Stanley and Livingston" (for which we would mount an expedition and beat the woods above the Flushing Meadow in search of the missing missionary). We certainly had to bring a fresh supply of imagination with us to play each day; we may have lacked fancy toys, but then we didn't become dependent upon them either. We did have some toys that were violence-oriented, and occasionally, we would hear a parent worrying aloud about the water guns or cap pistols we carried. I suppose we could have done without them, but they were certainly less harmful and more lighthearted than today's advanced toys of destruction, such as the excessively violent—and expensive—laser-gun tag game now on the market.

We simply aimed our cap pistols and said, "Bang, bang. Gotcha!"

"You did not! Missed completely. What a lousy shot!"

"I am not. I hit you in the shoulder, right where I aimed."

"Lousy shot. Missed completely."

"Oh yea!"

"Hold it! No hitting. Only shooting."

It was a negotiation of sorts. With laser tag, there are no negotiations; everyone knows you're "dead" from the weird light that goes on over your heart when you've been shot.

We lived in a simpler world. There was no crime in my neighborhood and we played safely on carefree streets. After supper (people ate earlier in those days), we would sit on the curb playing sedentary and often intellectually stimulating games. The leader of those curb games was Moo Moo Murphy, a.k.a. Muriel Murphy, a teenager with red, red hair and freckles all over. I loved her. She was a natural teacher, able to manipulate ten or fifteen noisy, independent kids with the skill of a circus lion tamer. Except she did it without a whip.

If the rains were falling we would take cover and bring out the playing cards for a game of "Go Fish." The card deck had long since been discarded by grown-up bridge players, and it was a disgrace. The cards were bent and torn and soiled. Each card was recognizable by its affliction. The tear in the corner was the king of diamonds, the strawberry jam stain was the six of clubs. When I was in the Marine Corps and found myself in shower-room poker games, I longed for that deck of cards.

The Flushing Meadow swamp which, in 1939, became the World's Fair grounds, was a fantasy playground par excellence for all the children in the neighborhood. In those days it was all rushes and little streams filled with wonderful wildlife, all of it destroyed when the World's Fair was built. But before then, the swamp was a primeval wonderland. Our vivid imaginations conjured bogs of quicksand and Indians lurking behind the tall grass.

In summer and winter we played outside, driven in only by dark, rain or cold. Although our parents sometimes disapproved of our strange activities or scolded us gently for staying out too late, we gadded about free and unsupervised.

We had some lively and raucous times. One of our favorite activities occurred in early January when we formed rival gangs to collect discarded Christmas trees. People would put their trees out on the sidewalk; but they wouldn't last three minutes because we had organized patrols. We'd bundle the trees and drag them to a secret place until we had seventy, eighty, maybe a hundred trees in all. Then we'd raid other storehouses and add yet more trees to our stockpile. The object was to see who would have the biggest and best bonfire on an appointed night.

On the edge of the neighborhood, between Forest Hills and Corona, were tomato and potato farms. The outfielder prayed for divine protection when a heavy hitter put a ball in the cultivated rows beyond the outfield. If God was good, it meant the farmer was in another field and we could retrieve our ball. If not, well, such are the ways of Providence, we learned at an early age.

My childhood games were ones of cooperation, reflecting a gentler, more genteel, less competitive world. The educator Brian Sutton-Smith, who gave us good counsel as an early advisor to the "Captain Kangaroo" staff, has written about the games children play and described them as preparation for the society in which they live. The highly competitive individualistic games, such as King of the Hill, for example, were rarely played by my companions. Our games prepared us to work together, to accommodate to each other, to help each other.

School reinforced those values. At P.S. 3 we learned about "brotherhood" and the importance of resolving conflict peaceably. Mr. Dunphy taught me to play basketball in the paved schoolyard. Well, not really. In 1934, at seven years of age I could hardly get the ball *to* the basket, much less *in* the basket. But it was a fun game, and that was Mr. Dunphy's lesson. He also taught me to feel confident about myself. "I think I can, I think I can," said the Little Engine That Could many years later on "Captain Kangaroo." But Mr. Dunphy taught me to say that to myself years before, and I came to believe it and to prove it to myself. When you build self-esteem and confidence in a child, you build a well-adjusted and happy person.

In the third grade I switched to Our Lady Queen of Martyrs School, almost a mile away and on *the other side* of Queens Boulevard. It wasn't a difficult street to cross compared to the adventure it comprises today. The two outer lanes were for autos and, in 1935, drivers were quite civilized in their attitude about running down small children. We calculated the odds to be favorable—in daylight. The center of the boulevard, however, held the terror of the trolley cars. They came fast, swaying from side to side, and with bells ringing, perhaps in warning, perhaps in anger. Lewis Carroll's Jabberwocky could hold no greater terror for innocents wending their way to our humble school.

I loved school and I loved learning—not surprising, considering I was a happy child, constantly encouraged and praised by my mother. The teachers liked me because there was little in the world that did not interest me.

Sometimes, my constant curiosity got me into trouble. My two older brothers had "things" in their rooms which were fascinating to me— and strictly off limits. By the age of fifteen, Bill had a most impressive classical record collection and a phonograph which was, by far, the most *verboten* thing in the house. I loved the fabulous music which would magically, it seemed to me, emerge from the speakers. My lifelong love for classical music started from an early age, with Bill's collection. I loved to watch him as he would remove the 78-rpm disk tenderly from its jacket, place it on the turntable and carefully, oh so carefully, lower the needle into the first groove. Automatic turntables and all the other paraphernalia which make such an operation so foolproof and simple today were still far in the future. In the mid-thirties this was strictly a manual procedure requiring great delicacy.

It was not an operation for the clumsy hands of an eight-year-old, yet I decided to try it one day in Bill's absence. Ten records and numerous scratches later, I left Bill's room gleeful, but a bit frightened that he would discover my transgression. Needless to say, he didn't appreciate my curiosity. But I will always be grateful to him for not making me feel too terrible about my mistake. Nor did my mother, who painstakingly explained why I mustn't touch Bill's "toys."

If I had been beaten for my misbehavior, either by Bill or my mother, I do not believe I would have given much thought to the seriousness of my actions. I would have been filled with resentment and perhaps a desire for revenge. A rational explanation made me come to terms with my wrongdoing, made me *think* about it, and solved the problem for all time. Hitting a child is always an admission of defeat. It may bring conformity and immediate obedience, but it does not address the underlying causes of the misbehavior. It is a shortcut, pure and simple, and though it may bring temporary results, it leads to more serious damage to the child. Parenting was not meant to be quick and easy; it requires patience and intelligent handling of misbehavior. Hitting a child in anger is especially dangerous. The physical and emotional damage to the child can be long lasting. Many people, including me, call it child abuse.

I can't say that my mother never hit me. She did, but not often, and not in anger, and not hard. Most important, she never tried to crush my spirit. As a result, I never became fearful of exploring the world, secure as I was in the knowledge that she loved me.

To paraphrase the milk commercial, "You never outgrow your need for love." Love is the critical ingredient which makes children grow and grow and grow. Spend large amounts of time with a child and she will *know* that you love her. There is no need even to tell her; if you invest the time, she will *know.* The same approach works with your spouse, right? Try coming home from a bad day at work some evening and telling your spouse, "Honey, I'm busy, go watch television." Just don't forget to duck.

·   ·   ·

We never know when we have it so good. Without television to tell me how the rest of the world lived, I had no way to know that my childhood was idyllic. I realized that later, of course, and I knew then that my great early years had prepared me well for the less than idyllic times which followed. Boy, was I lucky!

Chapter 2
A Father's Dream

Nearly a century divides my father's birth in nineteenth-century Ireland and my first grandson's birth in the New World in 1981. The years from the end of the last century to nearly the end of this one have been years of profound and rapid technological, social and cultural changes.

My father grew up as a subject of Victoria, ruler of the British Empire, which included all of Ireland. But the Empire was a distant place. The soil my father and his family tilled in Roscrea, County Tipperary, in the 1890s was farmed by horse and hoe and hand. There were, of course, no telephones, radio or television, and his life was an insular one. Families stayed in one place from birth to death, as rooted to the land as the hedgerows marking out the fields. They experienced the joys and irritations of contiguous multigenerational existence.

In the 1980s my three grown children live hundreds of miles from their parents and from each other, communicating frequently via telephone signals bouncing off satellites in geosynchronous orbit around the earth. Immense technological changes, especially those of the last thirty years, have caused similarly immense changes in family life and structure, particularly where children are concerned. In the past, when the roles of men and women were clearly defined, most fathers did not have the time or the inclination to participate fully in raising their children. They missed out and so did their children.

Fifty years ago the "typical" American family—father at work, mother at home with the kids—was a pattern for over eighty percent of American families, including mine. Today that pattern can be found in only ten percent of our families. Two thirds of mothers are working outside the home and almost a quarter of our children live in single-parent households, almost always with a female parent who works outside the home. Thanks to fast cars and fast jets, we often find ourselves, as my children did, going to faraway places to school, to marry, to settle. This means that the old-fashioned extended family, from grandparents to aunts, uncles and cousins, is not handy for baby-sitting, visiting, and advice, exactly the type of support and warm hand-holding most needed by busy and beleaguered parents.

In most two-parent families, mothers contribute significantly to balancing the family budget, and fathers, as well as holding down a job, share household chores and the rearing of children. Many American families are under pressure, struggling with fatigue, inadequate and expensive child care, and the constant effort of balancing careers with quality parenting. (My mother would not understand the rather new concept of "quality parenting;" to her, parenting was parenting, and there was only one way to do it.)

Although I grew up in the middle of the Depression, my father's livelihood and our family life were relatively untouched by its pernicious effects. Mother was mother, at home all day to see to our needs, and father was father, the provider, a remote figure and a virtual stranger to me for the first thirteen years of my life.

I remember him as a stern and serious man, hardworking and purposeful, as most immigrants are. He had come to the United States from an Edwardian Ireland, where the establishment of the Republic was still twenty years away. Political strife, religious persecution and economic hardship had bred the dream of emigration in young Irish hearts. Yet my father arrived in an America where the tag line in newspaper employment advertisements often read, "No Irish Need Apply." I came upon this line with great shock as a twenty-year-old doing research in a library. When I confronted my dad and asked him why he had never told me of this added hardship, he commented, in his still thick brogue, "Ach, it didn't matter. We made our own way."

Made their own way they did. Irish looked after Irish in the immigrant community, and my father managed to get a job as a delivery boy with Daniel Reeves, an Irish-American grocery store chain.

The Daniel Reeves stores of the 1930s were typical of the presupermarket grocery stores. Each store was like a modest "mom and pop" shop of today. Over the years my dad was promoted first to clerk, then to store manager and executive, eventually having jurisdiction over the many stores on Long Island, a territory of one hundred and twenty miles, west to east. I truly believed he visited hundreds of small stores every day. Why else was he never home?

Without exception, Dad left the house prior to daylight, before my eyes had opened on a new day, and he returned, exhausted, after my eyes had closed under sweet-smelling sheets. At the time, there seemed nothing strange about this life-style, which must have been devastatingly hard on both my parents. Most heartbreaking in hindsight, however, was the lack of a relationship between my father and his four children. I could never easily approach him to talk about something that was bothering me. I am certain that his inaccessibility was related primarily to his work schedule, but I also believe it was cultural; fathers, in those days, did not do women's work, and that included the rearing of children. Until television and fast highways wiped them out, this nation had cultural pockets, areas such as Appalachia, where men did not bother with a male child until he was old enough to hold a gun and learn to hunt, and with a female child until it was time to negotiate her dowry. The lines between the work of women and the work of men have only recently blurred.

We know that young children learn from the earliest age, the latest research indicating that the womb itself is a learning environment where the human learning process starts. We also know that we learn much of what we will learn by the time we are seven years of age. Yet parents and other adults often view young children as creatures incapable of learning, too incomplete to bother with. Young children are not all that different from the adults they will become. They lack the experience, and thus the learning acquired, from living as long as adults, but they have the intelligence to learn, and are constantly experiencing emotional events that will set patterns for life. The old saying, "As the twig is bent, so grows the tree," displays a deep folk wisdom.

It is important to relate to children in a serious way from birth. Paying attention to a child sends signals that you care for that child. Keep in mind that a child has not lived those many years in which experiences contribute to an adult's fund of knowledge. A child's knowledge of a particular subject should not be assumed. It is usually necessary to search for other reference points within her experience, so that the child can understand the conversation. Most important, the child knows, by your attention, that you care. Do this on a regular basis, and you will acquire bonus points for frequent caring, worth more than any you can earn from an airline for frequent flying.

Part of letting children know you care involves complimenting them and building their self-esteem. A testimonial to the importance of praise is my still strong memory of one incident that happened more than fifty years ago. It was one of the few occasions when my father openly articulated his pride in my childhood achievements.

My father loved his garden; it was a legacy of his roots in the soil. One warm spring Sunday, when I was about six years old, I was at my father's feet watching admiringly as he dug around a scrawny bush and pulled at its stubborn roots, determined to clear a patch for some dahlias, his favorite flowers. He dug and dug, pulled and pulled, and then stopped to talk for a moment to a neighbor over the garden fence. While they were talking, I went over and grabbed hold of that bush, which was probably as big as I was, and started to tug.

My father turned to look at me and watched as I pulled the shrub out of the ground. Never mind that it was his work that had gotten most of the roots up—I felt triumphant. I pulled the bush up and put it down, breathless, and, to my delight, heard my father whispering, just out of earshot, "Strong as a bull that boy. He's wonderful."

I never let my father know that I had heard and he never let me know how he felt about my childhood achievements. Admiration had to be expressed discreetly, and if I had caught him out, he'd have been embarrassed. Too bad. I could have used some confidence-building from time to time. Never withhold a compliment from a child. Every young person needs a locker full of confidence.

When I was older, Dad enjoyed showing me off more openly to friends and neighbors who would come to visit on a Sunday. The thirties were the Golden Age of radio and, to put it mildly, I was a radio buff. My mind was stuffed to overflowing with the trivia of radio and my ability to remember the most minute details made my father proud.

"Go on, Bobby, tell them about Gangbusters and Mister District Attorney, tell them about Patsy Kelly, tell them who sponsors Fred Allen, tell them what was in Fibber McGee's closet this week, go on, tell them," he would say.

Like a circus sideshow freak my mouth would spill the contents of my trivia bank. Stars, producers, advertisers, the complete Sunday through Saturday schedules of the NBC Red Network, the NBC Blue Network and the Columbia Broadcasting System.

My father's pride made me feel loved, and I rose easily to the challenge of his expectations: that I should do well in school, be kind to people—especially those less fortunate than myself—and be tolerant of the differences between them. My father was a fair man who, despite his own experiences of discrimination when he first arrived in America, displayed no such attitudes himself. Yet racial and ethnic slurs were common in the America of the thirties. It was socially acceptable to express prejudicial views quite openly. The media, particularly the film industry, often reflected this American societal trait. The fact that such views today are usually expressed secretively, whispered in the corners of locker rooms or in private offices, offers some hope. Openly expressed, in the home particularly, pernicious views easily reach the ears and minds of the young. Perhaps not completely understood, they are a message received nonetheless, not so much because of content, but because the holder of such views is a parent, the ultimate authority on any subject and a hero in any child's life.

Even conversation between parents not intended for young ears, but overheard, can have a great and long-lasting effect. "Can you believe it, they promoted Julio today. That Spic can hardly speak English but they moved him ahead of me. It's that government quota thing!" Click, click. The words are overheard, and the child gets the general idea.

It may be generations before a Belfast child can look upon someone of the opposite religion with an open mind. Years of bloodshed and kitchen conversation about the Papists and the Prods have made that prospect dim, if not impossible. We mold the views of our children from their earliest days in many ways, some open, some subtle. Long after they are gone from home these views remain with them, some as haunting as a demon.

In 1940 my father's world, his hopes and dreams of permanent financial security for his family, collapsed when the Daniel Reeves stores were sold to Safeway, a California company which was moving into the New York market with a new approach to food merchandising called the supermarket. As new top management was brought in, the buzzword was "modernization," and my father, one of the old-timers, was laid off.

Dad could not understand what had happened to him. For people who grew up in the last thirty years, his bewilderment may be difficult to fathom. Today, people take a job and give their loyalty to a company, but when a better offer comes along, few hesitate to move on and better their position. This is normal and makes good sense. In my father's day, however, men stayed with a company for twenty, thirty, forty years, and the very *thought* of going to work for the competition was considered an act of disloyalty. In return, most companies, like Daniel Reeves, returned that loyalty and stood by an employee in bad times, if at all possible. So, when Dad found that senior management would be replaced, he had a real problem comprehending how this could have happened to him after the loyalty he had given the company for over thirty years.

When he lost his job, he came home, sat in a chair, and hardly emerged into daylight for months. My mother would say, "Your father's ill," but, as a thirteen-year-old, I had difficulty understanding the nature of his illness, which seemed to be both mental and physical.

My world was in turmoil. Suddenly this remote man, almost a stranger, was home all day and we were packing boxes and preparing to move to our "other," much smaller house on nearby Booth Street, the one my father had bought as an investment at the end of the Roaring Twenties. Now it was to be our home, and my childhood castle, sand patch, musty basement, summer porch and all, was to be sold.

Americans are more mobile today than in my childhood. It is not unusual for a family to pick up and move on every few years. But moving is an emotional, as well as physical, disturbance for a child. Adults are better prepared to release friends, and secure enough to make new ones. Adults understand the need for a move which may involve a better job or some other positive reason. These reasons are meaningless to a young child, however, who may have a tendency to resent the move.

Young children are small machines in search of security. Important to their assurance are Mother, Dad, other relatives and friends, as well as the physical comforts of home, their room, particular objects, a toy bear, a blanket—all the familiar sights, sounds and smells of their restricted world. A move cannot be avoided, but it can be handled with sensitivity to the disruption it causes a young child. The result will be comforting and assure minimal trauma. Especially distressing to a child is the thought of losing touch with precious friends. Young friendship often seems "cute" and even humorous, but to the child, such friendships are very serious and a critical factor in healthy development. At the moment when you may not be taking such a friendship seriously, a stern look from the child seems to say, "Don't tread on this." Remember that when next you uproot a child from a close friendship.

My daughter, Laurie, came home one day from her first grade class in tears, sobbing almost uncontrollably. After calming her down and, in fear of her answer, we asked Laurie what had caused these gushing tears. "My very best friend, Julie, is moving, and I'll never see her again," she replied. "She's my very best friend and all year, I've spent all of my time in school with her and I love her and I'll never see her again." Resumption of heavy sobbing.

"Well, honey," we said, "you can keep in touch. You can write to her and exchange letters. What's Julie's last name?" we asked obtusely.

Laurie looked at us incredulously. "How should I know?"

The move was made and I survived. Our new house was close enough for me to wander back to the old neighborhood to see old friends, and I found some new friends in the new neighborhood. My mother, as usual, kept the family going. But the stress took its toll, exacerbating the high blood pressure she had suffered from for many years. Often, I would come home from school to find her lying down with a wet face cloth on her head to ease the headache pain. I can still feel her softness as I would touch her soothingly and take the cloth from her head to refresh it under the cold water faucet.

Stress is an ordeal for a family, and children suffer it too, often less visibly than their parents. Children are self-centered, especially not-quite-socialized teens. I felt resentful, cheated that because of our new financial circumstances I would be unable to follow Jack and Bill to Chaminade, a splendid private preparatory school. But I was beginning to understand my father's pain and disillusionment, and to see the very human being in this stranger of my early childhood. When he finally went back to work after about a year, I really began to appreciate his character.

My father was a small man, under five feet seven, who could not have weighed more than one hundred and thirty pounds. When he found work again, it was with a member of the same Reeves family, Peter, who was starting his own modest chain of grocery stores. Peter did not have room for my dad in a store but he did offer him work in the chain's warehouse. So, my father, this slight man in his mid-fifties, spent ten-hour days moving very heavy cases of canned goods from the distributor's trucks into the warehouse and then loading the company trucks for delivery to the stores. He would come home at night exhausted. He had gone from being an executive to being a physical laborer, and it was a challenge that he felt in his body. This weariness, combined with his still substantial pride, showed every evening in the look upon his face. I'll never admire him enough for that.

Fortunately, it was only a few months until Peter Reeves made him manager of a store in our own Forest Hills, a post he had graduated from at Daniel Reeves a quarter-century before. But my father was thankful for the work and I was relieved. I spent many after-school hours and Saturdays as his delivery boy and sorter of empty soda and beer bottles. Those were pre-aluminum-can days, and I never knew there were so many brands of beer and soda in bottles of different sizes and configurations to be fitted into wooden cases, forty or fifty at a time. It became an intellectual challenge to devise a system for getting the bottles into the cases more efficiently in less time. The cellar was home to a family of rats and the sooner I was out of there, the happier I was.

A few years later, when he witnessed my reluctance to leave my job as an NBC page to work for the new television program, "The Howdy Doody Show," my father said, "Don't be a fool. Never mind how good NBC has been to you. You don't owe them anything. You go and do what you think is right for you and never mind about loyalty to the company."

It was good advice. I took it and my career was given its start. But I'll never forget that the advice, sadly, came out of my father's own disappointment in life. And who knows? If I had disregarded my father's wisdom, remained with NBC, and moved into the management training program, I could now be an NBC executive spending my days, as the great comic Fred Allen once observed, building molehills into mountains.

Chapter 3
Childhood's End

In his novel, *The Power and the Glory,* Graham Greene writes, "There is always one moment when the door opens and lets the future in." Many children are reluctant to see that door open, holding it tightly shut, as against a howling wind, so much do they enjoy childhood. Others cannot wait to cast aside the world in which they live to enter a grown-up world they hope will bring them greater happiness than they have found in childhood. I was certainly not eager to have childhood end, but I knew that halcyon days were behind me. Edna St. Vincent Millay wrote in her poem, "Wine from These Grapes," that "childhood is the kingdom where no one dies." But my childhood ended on March 5, 1943, when my mother died. I was fifteen years old, in my second year of high school, and one day I returned home to find my mother suffering from one of her pressure-related headaches. Then the headache turned into a coronary thrombosis.

She never went to the hospital, which was not unusual in those days. The physician just said, "There's no point to it. There's not much we can do for her except hope the thrombosis dissolves." Only forty years ago medicine was so much more primitive than it is today, that the scientific advances made in those two-score years are awesome. Mother stayed in bed and soon slipped into a coma.

The death of a loved one is stressful, but *watching* a loved one die over a period of days is traumatic. She was lying in bed with her eyes closed. I would sit for hours at the foot of the bed and stare at her, trying desperately to *will* her to life. She would breathe deeply, breath after breath, and then her breathing would stop, for minutes at a time, it seemed. I think my breathing stopped with hers and then, joyously, her breathing resumed. Until, on the fifth day, it ceased. Years after moments of great emotion, we are able to remember the trivial. A light snow was falling just then, and I remember going outside with only a light sweater to shovel the dusting of snow from the walk. As I shoveled, I remember trying to come to terms with this thing called death.

To a child, death is remote and thus all the more difficult to understand. Often, those to whom a child looks for comfort and explanation —such as a parent or sibling—are themselves so involved in grief that they can be of little comfort. Because adults often feel a child lacks the capacity to understand death in a clinical sense, they assume that a child does not grieve. But this is a great error. Usually a child is greatly affected by the death of someone close and is in need of comfort and at least an attempt at explanation.

Such attempts sometimes bring unexpected results from the mind of a child. My grandson, Derek, was very fond of a family pet, a nice dog named Max. When Max died, Derek, who was about five years old, asked his mother, my daughter, Maeve, if Max had gone to heaven. Maeve replied that she thought he had because Max was a very nice dog. Derek thought for a bit and then asked about some other pets and their chances at heaven. Like so many children, Derek is a dinosaur-freak, and when he asked Maeve if the extinct dinosaurs had gone to heaven she thought she had nothing to lose in replying in the affirmative. "Oh, no!" said Derek, "That's awful. The dinosaurs will eat Max!"

The death of a pet can be a major event for a child and the resulting conversation can be jolting to an adult. A friend had two young children and a dog named Patty. One day Patty was hit by an automobile and killed while the children were at preschool. My friend wrung her hands over how to tell the children and then decided that a forthright statement would be best. The children returned from preschool and their mother said, "Children, I have some bad news. Patty was hit by a car and killed." The children said that that was too bad and went out to play. They returned to the house an hour later and began calling, "Patty! Here, Patty, here girl." Their mother said, "Don't you remember? I told you Patty was hit by a car and killed." "Oh," they said through great sobbing, "We thought you said, 'Daddy.'"

Although that story is amusing, children do grieve over the loss of someone or something close to them, and their parents must take it seriously. I greatly admire those people who have a talent for understanding the emotional needs of children, especially their need to grieve. My good friend Fred Rogers of "Mister Rogers' Neighborhood" has done much work in this area, and through that work, I think he has helped many a child through a difficult time. His ministry is directed to the emotional needs of children, and he is very good at reaching the child who is in need of his love and understanding.

I know Fred is embarrassed when I refer to him as "my patron saint," but if I have such a thing, Fred wears the halo! I have heard adults comment that they find it difficult to watch Fred because his manner is so deliberate and unhurried. That may be a comment on our society, in which adults are unable to appreciate the softness and gentleness of Mister Rogers. In any case, Fred is directing his efforts to those young people who are in need of his comfort and he is right on target. Many lives have been affected in a positive way by the work of Fred Rogers, and I am grateful for what he has done.

My own grief process was lengthy. My poor father was in shock, and our relationship lacked the emotional basis needed for him to be of consolation. My brothers, fighting a war and newly married, came home for the funeral, but I'm sure their commanding officers would not have understood my need for comforting in the midst of global conflict. Jack returned to the Army Air Corps and Bill to the Navy. That left me with Dad and the one who missed Mother perhaps most of all, Catherine, my thirteen-year-old sister.

Catherine, our baby, was still very much in need of her mother, and she was cut loose from childhood cruelly and abruptly. We were a rather odd trio, Catherine, my father and me, alone in a mostly silent house. We muddled along, however ineptly. Dad did the shopping, something at which he was expert; I spent more and more time out of the house; and Catherine somehow managed to fend for herself.

According to Elisabeth Kübler-Ross in her book *On Death and Dying,* it is quite common to go through a period of denial after the loss of a loved one. But "denial" is entirely too mild a word to describe my reaction. If the world was flat, I would have leaped off the edge, which, figuratively, is about what I did. I seemed to lose all ambition and didn't care very much about anything. I went from being an optimistic, pleasant kid to someone morose and uninterested in anything to do with the future. Spencer Tracy couldn't have made a greater and quicker transition from Jekyll to Hyde.

My grades in school plummeted. I was little comfort to my father or sister. Grief and loss are wrenching for all of us, but children who suffer the loss of a parent at an early age are particularly affected and need the loving sustenance of caring adults to survive. Catherine and I didn't have much assistance. In addition, adolescence has its own insistent agenda —the search for identity, sexual awakening and separation. If the movement through this developmental phase is disturbed decisively by the loss of a parent, a youngster will usually become confused.

I was confused. Not surprisingly, therefore, I was sinking to the bottom of the pool. Two things kept me from drowning. First, I had been given a pretty good foundation. I had high self-esteem, and my mother's early love and encouragement were still a great supporting force, even in her absence. Second, I had a mentor, a wonderful woman named Gertrude Farley, who was an English teacher and my guidance counselor at Forest Hills High School.

Miss Farley monitored me attentively as I was trying to recover from the trauma of my mother's death. She did not like what she was seeing and knew something had to be done. I don't know how atypical Gertrude Farley was in those days, but she went to great lengths to save me from myself by practicing what I call "holistic education." I believe that we could succeed in saving many of our children from failure if the schools were able to identify those with emotional or personality problems and perform a referral function to address those conditions. My academic deterioration had nothing to do with the quality of teaching or anything else happening in the classroom. I was suffering from an emotional problem that made high scholastic performance impossible. Because Gertrude Farley and other teachers knew this, they were able to intervene and reverse my downward spiral.

We are quick to blame the schools for failing to educate our children to function in an advanced society. We point to incredibly high dropout rates, in many places over fifty percent, and condemn school systems for abysmal failure. There may be much wrong in American education today, but I do not believe teachers should be blamed for failing to teach children who, because of problems unrelated to the classroom, find it difficult or impossible to learn. In this advanced nation, children are our principal underclass; twenty percent of our children, almost fourteen million, live in poverty. Along with poverty comes hunger, poor nourishment, and other health problems. A hungry child doesn't learn. Millions of children are physically or emotionally abused, and such children do not concentrate well in the classroom. If our teachers could be trained to identify a child with a problem and had referral agencies available, we could treat these conditions and work to restore such children to good health and enhance their ability to learn.

To train teachers to perform this holistic function and to provide the services necessary to address a child's problems will cost money, but not nearly as much money as we spend on remedial programs that deal with our failures. Our worst failures end up in jail and cost us over thirty thousand dollars a year. Functional illiterates who end up on public assistance cost more money than the small amount that would have been needed to help them in the second or third grade. If we had been successful in helping them then, they would be earning wages and paying taxes today.

There is a good reason why this holistic approach must be implemented in our schools. In years past, the extended family served as a support system. Today, with a quarter of our children in single-parent homes and so many homes in which both parents work, the family is often not serving as the nurturing place it once did. You can jump up and down and shout for mother to get back in the kitchen and for Dad to stay married to Mom, but that is not going to happen. We must face reality and find other ways to do what once was done, almost always, at home. Is there, then, another universal place where children can be helped? The schools, of course, and every kid has one. A holistic approach in our schools holds great promise for meeting the needs of our young people, and therefore our needs for the future.

Gertrude Farley cast a look at this scrawny sixteen-year-old, the object of her concern, and knew that a frontal attack, a lecture or a pep talk, would be useless. She knew she needed something irresistible to set me back on track. Aware of my interest in radio, she steered me toward the high school production group, and it was there that I was given my first opportunity to transform my fantasies into art through the broadcast medium. Our radio plays and information programming were broadcast over the school's loudspeaker system. The ponderous notes of Dvořák's *New World Symphony* would introduce a science program. A little of Mendelssohn's *Midsummer Night's Dream,* and we began poetry lessons. Our efforts were pretty professional and had the effect of restoring me to life.

Heady with my success in high school radio, I began to think about working in the real thing. I had heard about the NBC page staff and thought that to work at NBC, in Radio City, would be a dream fulfilled. I longed to walk close to the stars, to take messages for the soap opera heros and heroines and their almost-as-famous producers, to watch the decision making of advertising agency representatives, to be part of the world that had filled my head for years.

The NBC page staff had been founded in 1931, a few years after the network was formed. Being a page was considered a prestigious entry-level position at the network, which was continually searching for management potential in its young staff. I wouldn't have stood a chance of getting a job as a page before World War II because it was rumored that, at the very least, the basic academic requirement was a Phi Beta Kappa key. But all the healthy, young, talented men over eighteen were in uniform and NBC was forced to lower its age and academic requirements.

Lucky for me. I was almost seventeen and about to enter my senior year in high school when my application was accepted, and in June of 1944 I donned the dark blue uniform with light blue forages of the NBC page. There was a military-like inspection before each shift and discipline was serious. We had a quartermaster, Mr. Ruthe, who maintained the uniforms with their detachable starched collars, and supplied collar buttons, white gloves and stern advice, much like an urban Mister Chips. NBC certainly was serious about the appearance of its pages. My salary was $13.50 for a forty-hour week on the 5 P.M. to midnight shift. In September I continued going to Forest Hills High, and when the final bell of the day at three-thirty sent most of my friends to the playing fields, I headed for the subway and the F train for a thirty-minute ride to Rockefeller Center. I rarely arrived home before 1 A.M. and did most of my homework and reading to the clickety, clack, clatter, clatter of train wheels. In those days, I found the New York subway system a wonderful learning environment.

All that year at NBC I was tired but extremely happy. Today adolescents are more sophisticated and more knowledgeable about their world than I was as a seventeen-year-old. It was a year of education and maturing as no other was in my young life. I listened, engrossed, as older network employees told enchanting tales from the early days of radio, bloopers of announcers and soap opera actors, stories of great stars and their great lives. Much of this, in retrospect, was apocryphal, but my imagination was captured. I was getting out of my neighborhood, my world was expanding, and I was becoming financially independent. Often, I would save as much as $1.50 from my $13.50 weekly salary, after taxes of $2.50! Along with this great wealth I was acquiring a greater treasure, knowledge of the broadcast industry.

One of my favorite jobs as a page was handling the seating of audiences for radio shows. On a daily basis, I was close to those fabled comedians, actors and musicians of my childhood, such as Fred Allen, Patsy Kelly, and John Barrymore. I would show members of the audience to their seats and then stand quietly in the rear of the studio and enjoy the program with the audience, while learning more each day about this wonderful world of radio.

The NBC Symphony Orchestra was created in 1937, especially for radio. It was led by that giant of the music world, Arturo Toscanini, and rehearsed and performed in a studio built for music, Studio 8H, in Radio City. During rehearsals, pages would be stationed outside the doors with instructions to admit *no one,* and it was made clear that this prohibition included the pages.

On one occasion, I was assigned to the balcony door, on the ninth floor, listening to the tones of Wagner, which were beautiful but muffled. The music moved me, and I had an overwhelming desire to hear it clearly. I knew the door I was guarding was several hundred feet from the podium and figured that I could not possibly be detected if I snuck into the darkened balcony. After all, I wanted to enjoy the full acoustical effect. As soon as I entered, however, Toscanini put down his baton and stood quietly at the podium. The orchestra ceased playing. I stood deep in the shadows, waiting for them to resume and entertain me. But it was not to be. In less than sixty seconds, the balcony door opened behind me, and my supervisor beckoned angrily to me. I had to plead and beg to keep my job and, fortunately for me, neither Toscanini nor the orchestra management insisted on capital punishment. I will never know how Toscanini knew I was there, but he was obviously master of more than the music. He could easily have had me fired, but did not. If it were not for this kindness, my career would have come to an early end and the Captain would never have been born.

The page staff was not the only NBC unit short of employees during wartime. I was offered a job as a message clerk by the Traffic and Communications Department, which ordered the telephone lines linking the network stations, and managed the teletype and telegraph communications between the affiliated stations and the network headquarters. I accepted and spent the next few months during the spring of 1945 in this position. Each evening I would arrange the messages from the stations and carry them to quiet desks in the sales, publicity, engineering and other departments, where they would be acted upon early the next morning. The job was clerical in nature, but it was also an observation post from which I could learn how the network functioned. Since they weren't confidential, I read the messages to the sales department and came to understand how radio programming was sold to advertisers. I learned of promotion and publicity schemes and just how the telephone company was the physical link between stations. It was far from the creative world, but it was the business part of show business.

Many actors and producers do not want to know anything about the business side of television. I can understand their reluctance to become involved in a world which many of them consider foreign to their art and undesirable. However, my underpinnings in the business of radio and television learned in my page days and elsewhere, have been invaluable in securing a long lifespan for the "Captain Kangaroo" program. I may be best known to the public for my creative contributions to children's television, but much of my time is spent in the *business* of show business, keeping the doors to the Treasure House open. My knowledge of sales and advertising, affiliate relations, government relations, promotion and publicity all have contributed mightily to keeping the Captain on television.

We live in an age of increasing specialization in which young people tend to concentrate on smaller and smaller circles of areas that interest them. They discard many academic subjects as not being valuable in their pursuit of a specific career. They ask, how can Shakespeare possibly be of value to someone who wishes to practice medicine? If I want to be an accountant, why should I waste time on modern European history? Parents, and even the schools, often encourage this academic concentration to the detriment of a complete education. When I was a college trustee, parents would often ask how their investment in tuition would help their children get a job and increase their earning power. A well-educated person is, of course, a better job candidate and, statistically, earns more in the course of a lifetime than someone with less education. Furthermore, in this age of specialization, it is the generalist who is better prepared to adapt to changing conditions in the world and in the marketplace. I have always felt that the many broad experiences I enjoyed in my formal education and in my early work experience have enhanced my abilities as an actor and as a producer. I believe that adults should encourage their children to be complete human beings, with broad interests, before concentrating in a specialized area. They will then be prepared to seize a variety of opportunities, and to accept change, inevitable change.

Despite its proven success, a liberal education can be a frustrating process. My daughter, Laurie, returned home from school on one occasion complaining about her trials with Chaucer. Exasperated, she asked my wife, Jeanne, "What possible use can I make of a quote from *Canterbury Tales?*" To which her mother replied, "Someday your daughter will ask you the same question and you can reply,

> ". . . *The droghte of Marche hath perced to the roote,*
> *and bathed every veyne in swich licour . . .*"

My granddaughter, Kaelan, is still a toddler, but I want to be around when *she* asks that question!

That first year at NBC was a good one, and things at home were improving. I came to understand my father and our conversations were frequent and caring. As the old joke says, "I was amazed at how much he had learned since my fifteenth birthday." I guess I had learned a few things about life myself.

Chapter 4
From the Halls of Montezuma

The war years of 1941–45 were times which made young men mature quickly. In more normal periods, young men in their last year of high school think about finding a job, or look forward to college and the promise of the future. They are often days of giddiness, anticipating emancipation from parental restriction. For me, this process was accelerated by the all-pervasive effects of the World War. Over twelve million men and women were in uniform, and many had made the ultimate sacrifice of dying in remote and strange locations worldwide. Every young male cut his sixteenth birthday cake with an eye to his future in uniform.

Young people make different decisions when they know that their future may be shortened. The violence of war places a pall upon the natural joy and optimism of youth. In addition to my personal problems associated with my mother's passing, I developed an almost fatalistic attitude toward the future; academic accomplishment was not a high priority for many of us growing up in the foreground of war.

I often think of this when I am asked about the effect of nuclear threat on contemporary children, which many child professionals believe has a bearing on today's young people and their attitudes toward school, sex, drugs and virtually anything beyond the present. The evidence is far from conclusive, but when I consider how much my attitude and that of my peers was affected by the violence of war, today's threat seems even more cataclysmic. The possibility of a nuclear holocaust is with us all and may have a profound effect on some, if not all, of our children.

Nineteen forty-five was the year I became certain that I was bound for a career in radio at NBC. At that point, television was thought to be years away. However, before I could pursue my goals, there were the Germans and Japanese to be dealt with. It was spring and things in Europe were going well for the Allied Forces. Roosevelt, Churchill and Stalin had met that February in remote Yalta to draw the map for post-war Europe. Hitler was not out, but he was certainly down, and as soon as his demise was final, full attention could be turned upon the fanatical Japanese war machine.

I would turn eighteen at the end of June, 1945, and I knew I would be drafted within months. I was not about to wait for a summoning letter from my Uncle Samuel, however. For if I enlisted, I could assure myself of serving in the uniform of my choice, and I had very definite ideas about the color of that uniform.

During my last year in high school I had met a young man who had served as an officer in the Marine Corps and was now back in civilian life. I was young and impressionable and an idealist, and my new friend had a greater effect upon me than a John Wayne movie. He convinced me that, for a young man who wanted only the best, there was but one choice—the United States Marine Corps.

I wasn't much of a fighter; I might even have been suspected of being quite a peaceable young chap. I was, however, committed to the goals of the allied war effort, as only a man with the pure ideals of youth can be. The war against Japan was an island-hopping affair and the beaches of the Japanese homeland would be fiercely defended by a people committed to an Emperor and a culture difficult for westerners to fathom. The Marines had carried a substantial portion of the Pacific-war effort and, though only five hundred thousand in number, would be assigned a large role in finishing the effort. It would probably take several years to accomplish, and I wanted to play my part in the drama to make the world safe from aggressors. I had a brother in the Army Air Corps, and another in the Navy. With me in the Marines, we would only have to convince my baby sister to join the Coast Guard and we would be a family going for the hat trick.

The Marine Corps, however, didn't want me. The Navy doctors who served the Marines took one look at my terrible teeth and turned me down. But I was determined. Off I went to see a friend of mine whose father was a Public Health physician. "I am of a different opinion," he wrote the powers that be. And so I was invited to become a member of the United States Marine Corps Reserve (serial number 577540) and was shipped out to Parris Island in South Carolina for boot camp.

I don't know precisely how my dad felt about his third son leaving for the Marines. He did not allow me to see too far beneath the surface, but I sensed a sadness, an apprehension about him. In front windows in our neighborhood, as throughout the nation, were hung small gold-fringed banners with stars. There was a blue star for every son or daughter from that household in service, and by 1945 too many of those banners also bore stars of gold signifying a son killed in the war effort. It would have been impossible for my father not to be apprehensive sending a third son off to war. He knew that his sons would be in harm's way for many months and years to come.

Today in the United States, thanks to relatively inexpensive air transportation and a splendid system of roads, most children get to travel the countryside. Many middle-class children have been to Disneyland and Opryland and many places in between. This is good; children learn from these travel experiences, and our regional differences have become less important than our similarities.

When I was six years old, my father had taken us by ocean liner back home to Ireland to see the family farm with its thatched roof cottage, across the rural road from Carrick Hill. I have some fragmentary memories of that trip. A few years after that we rode in the family Buick to view the "Old Man of the Mountain" in his New Hampshire granite splendor. A couple of times Mother and I, on a shopping trip to Manhattan, splurged, spurned the trolley, and took the Long Island Railroad from Forest Hills to Manhattan. Until now that had been the scope of my train and travel experience.

On Flag Day, June 14, 1945, two weeks before my eighteenth birthday, I was sworn into the U.S. Marine Corps Reserve and put on a train from Pennsylvania Station in New York City to South Carolina, passing *en route* such fabled places as Philadelphia, Baltimore, Washington, and Richmond. From behind the soft focus of a dirty train window, I imagined Faulkner novels come to life, full of trains that would pull into sleepy little southern towns early in the morning. I can still feel the early-day heat and sense the drowsiness the train ride induced. Black porters trundled luggage, freight, crates of eggs, and canvas bags of U.S.

mail onto the dirty platform. Everywhere were the signs I had heard of but had never seen, "Colored Men," "Colored Women," "Whites Only." Though bound for boot camp in the deep south, we recruits were all white, not a black among us. President Truman had not yet integrated the Armed Forces, and the war against the racist Hitler was fought by segregated troops.

I was inexperienced but bright enough to know that prejudice was not exclusive to the southern states. I had seen blacks living in northern squalor, not welcome in most society. Years later, I was to read remarks by the North Carolina journalist, Harry Golden, which made a great deal of sense to me and put my first experience of segregation into perspective. Speaking of the south of years gone by, Golden made the point that there was at least one significant difference between the prejudice in the north and that in the south. In those days, the act of being prejudiced was against the law in the north, but protected by law in the south. Back in 1945, to drink from a water fountain marked "Colored Only" would have made me a lawbreaker. Leaving my seventeenth year, I had much to think about.

In the nineteenth century the children of privileged families were sent abroad to finish their education. Such travel does broaden the mind, and perhaps all youngsters should take time off between high school and college (not to go to war, please) to see the world. I certainly benefited from the opportunity to travel at that age. My Marine Corps experience was, in some ways, like Shelley's Italy, but not nearly so polite.

As the train came to a steamy stop in the small South Carolina station, the tranquility of the lazy and hot summer morning was shattered by the piercing shouts of a stereotypically profane Marine sergeant, who greeted us by screaming, "All right you baby-face f—— a——, get your asses off this train and line up! Now!" It was just like in the movies, I thought, only the movies were not nearly so graphic, not nearly so colorful.

It was high summer when we arrived on Parris Island, and the rampant fly, tick and mosquito population, which had been feasting on years of Marine recruits, looked upon us as a fresh meal. Our first battle was against these insects, and it was a battle we lost. But that was the least of my worries. Training was tough, exacting, oppressive and demanding, in both a physical and mental sense, and the discipline was rigid and severe. But I loved it! Perhaps I didn't quite love it at the time, but there was an intense feeling of pride in accomplishing something that was enormously difficult. I even looked the part. You should have seen me in my shorn, skinhead splendor, a far cry from the Captain's Dutch Boy/Beatles hairdo of a decade later.

My Marine Corps training has served me well. It may be difficult to see how it could be of value in the entertainment world of an actor, but it taught me to approach my work in a systematic manner, and to complete tasks, no matter how difficult they were, no matter how discouraged I became. I learned that doing your best meant precisely that, and that failure to do so everyday was costly to me.

Everyone has heard about the pride of the Marines. Through the training process, both physical and psychological, we were given a very positive feeling about our capabilities, a very high self-esteem, something more parents should give to their children. It is cruelty not to expect the best from a child and to allow him or her to "goof off." Such treatment deprives a child of the joy of accomplishment, of never knowing how well he or she can do, which can lead to insecurities and lower self-esteem.

I remember that my son, Michael, would raise his eyes heavenward whenever he felt my "pumping gas lecture" coming on. I wanted to make it clear to Michael and his sisters that we expected the best that they were capable of doing. "If you decide, later in life, that you want to pump gasoline, an honorable but not demanding occupation, you may do so," I told them often. "It's your decision. But right now, you are not in a position to make that decision. So do your best and you will be prepared to do whatever you want to do." Michael did do his best, went to the college of his choice, did his postgraduate work, and is successful. More important, he is happy. I wonder if his sons, Britton and Connor, will be victimized by the "pumping gas lecture"? I don't know, but I do know that their parents expect the best from them and they are happy, well-adjusted children. It is important to expect the best of children. A child is done no favor when an adult sets low standards.

There is a nice game that people play which I call "Where were you when . . ." Where were you when you heard about the German surrender? When you heard about JFK's being shot? When you heard about the A-Bomb? I know where I was on those and many other notable occasions, and I'll never forget how I was introduced to the nuclear age.

I had been in boot camp for over eight weeks when I was introduced to the nuclear age. We had become physically and mentally hardened and ready for those Japanese beaches, or so we all thought. In early August we left the main camp at Parris Island to spend days in the "boondocks." Living in the "boonies" was living the rough life, not that the old Quonset hut back at home base had been luxurious. But now we slept in pup tents, crawled under live machine-gun fire, waded through rivers and streams and, at all times, fed the mosquitoes our blood. We started moving at first light and continued nonstop through early evening. Therefore, when on an August mid-morning, our Drill Instructor, or DI, summoned us to sit in the *shade* of a large tree, we knew something momentous was at hand.

The DI, reading from hand-held notes, said, "The Lootenant told me to tell you a—— that the US of A has dropped a ay-tomic bomb on Japan. I never heard of a ay-tomic bomb, but they tell me that it is like a thousand f—— tons of f—— dynamite and it looks like the f—— Japs have f—— had it. But if you think you a—— are going anywhere you are f—— wrong. So go, go, go!" Thus was I introduced to the nuclear age.

The war and my fighting days were over, but my commitment to the Marine Corps wasn't. The lieutenant commanding our unit called me in to see him.

"Congratulations, Private," he began. "You see these bars on my uniform. Well, in about four months you'll be wearing them. Just sign right here."

"Sir, may the Private ask the Lieutenant what it is the Private is signing, sir?" I asked tentatively.

"Well, son," the lieutenant—two years older than me—said, "right now you are in the USMCR, the Reserves, and to go to Officer Candidate School you will have to sign on in the USMC."

I was not completely ignorant. I knew that as a reservist I could be held no longer than six months after President Truman declared the war over. As a "regular" Marine I would be in four years and for many active reserve years thereafter.

"Under those circumstances, sir," I replied, "the Private respectfully declines."

With the most disgusted look he could summon, the lieutenant dismissed me.

I often think that if I hadn't declined that commission, my life might have turned out entirely differently. I would have been in the Marine Corps until 1949 and been called up for the Korean Conflict in 1950. No college, no television career, no nothing.

I had been offered OCS because I had scored highly on the many tests given in boot camp. Instead of OCS, I became a "closer" of schools. I closed Japanese Language School, closed the Signal School and a few others. With no schools left to close, I was assigned to the Paymaster and, after a short stint in Camp LeJeune, North Carolina, I sailed from San Francisco for my last assignment in Hawaii. On the troopship *Rockbridge Ranger,* I would spend dark nights forward in the fo'c'sle, immediately behind the bow, peering at starlit skies as the ship dipped into each succeeding wave. There was a rhythm to life, I felt at those moments. I didn't know what was going to happen to me when I was discharged, but I would be nineteen and I was convinced that the world would be wonderful.

Chapter 5
A Funny Thing Happened
on My Way to Law School

Whenever the sweet smell of pine is in the air, I am given over to a feeling of optimism, of freshness. The Great Lakes Naval facility is located in woods of pine in northern Illinois, and it was there, in the late summer of 1946, that I was discharged from the Marine Corps. The Marines had been a wonderful maturing experience for me. At Great Lakes they gave me a plastic card to show that Marine serial number 577540 had been honorably discharged from service with the gratitude of the President of the United States. I have difficulty remembering my telephone number but I'll never forget my serial number. I was also given a small gold pin emblazoned with a bird, wings spread, to wear when I bought my new suit. For that purchase, or for anything I wished to do or buy, they handed me three hundred dollars "cash money" and a train ticket home to New York. I was feeling very good and I was not alone.

The entire nation seemed to feel good about itself. An enormous physical and emotional toll had been assessed in order to conclude World War II, but two evil aggressors and their awesome war machines had been trampled, and that created a great spirit of accomplishment and optimism across the land. People lived happily without toasters and new cars and abided food shortages while the wartime economy shifted to gear up for peace. Newly united couples often could not find a place of their own, so many moved in with their in-laws and the domestic peace was put to the test. But everyone knew it was only temporary because a new world had dawned; we had peace in our time and for all time. The United Nations had not celebrated its first birthday, but it was up and running and would surely see that we would never need to tolerate war again. If we were all naive, we will have to be forgiven. The sacrifices of those last few years could never have been made had not the dream of a lasting peace been our goal.

Like almost everyone else, I moved back with the family. My father had remarried, perhaps hoping to create a whole, standard family unit once again. Dad was, I believe, particularly concerned for the welfare of my sister, an adolescent who still missed her mother extremely. My stepmother, Edna, was a kind lady, but she had a completely different philosophy of parenting than my mother had, and Edna felt her way was best. Ours was a strained household, and the one most hurt by the tension was my father, who wanted so badly to do what was best for his children and could not understand his failure.

There are many ways to parent a child successfully; many roads can lead a child to the land of happy and well-adjusted adults. But many parents, including my stepmother Edna, don't realize this and feel that there is only one way to parent a child, and that it is their way. Yet rigidity may be the most inappropriate attitude for parenting. It is critical to recognize that children are unique; no two are alike. Children of the same parents, growing in the same environment, under the same influences, can be radically different from one another. Isn't that wonderful?

That's a good beginning. Having a positive attitude about whatever differences exist between your children adds to the job of parenting and facilitates the design of a flexible program appropriate for each child. My own three children were very different from each other. All are of equal intelligence and yet each had a distinctly different learning style. Michael was eager to please but also easily bored. A comment from one of his early teachers was, "Michael is very social." He certainly *was* social—and bored. He was not being challenged and, with his work complete, he turned into the class' social director, just what every first grade teacher needs. Fortunately, his teacher knew all this and began to load him with challenges and extra work, rather than punishing him for misbehaving and talking too much. Michael loved it and retired from his social director's post to undertake a position more appropriate to the classroom, that of a student.

Laurie didn't need extra assignments, she invented them. "Slow down, Laurie, relax," became a slogan that Jeanne and I said often, right through our daughter's three years at law school. Laurie was her own taskmaster and very demanding. We would scheme to find ways to get her away from her schoolwork. And when she wasn't studying, she was busy playing team sports. She loved field hockey, especially scoring goals. She had to excel. Tennis can be relaxing, but not when Laurie took up the game. She became fiercely competitive from the moment she first wrapped her hand around the handle of the racket. She was a delightful child to parent but she was certainly a different challenge from Michael.

Our youngest, Maeve, went to school to "see my very best friends." She was an open and loving child. While Laurie held back a little until she came to know someone well, Maeve was everyone's closest friend from day one. Maeve could be a good student or a mediocre student, depending on her current mood. When the chips were down, however, and she knew she had to get the grades in order to be admitted to the prep school or college of her choice, Maeve came through.

I am not ashamed to admit that on one occasion we bribed Maeve to do well. She had become enamored of a breed of dog, the Skye terrier, and wanted one badly. It was at a time when she was wrestling, with meager results, with the subject of mathematics. Perhaps it was a matter of genetics; her difficulty with math made her my soul mate. Her mother and I hinted that a significant improvement in math might, just might, result in a cuddly puppy as a companion. The turnaround in her grades was incredible, and the Skye terrier was delivered, as promised. That dog taunted me and bit me for the next decade. In fact, the dog taunted and bit everyone in sight, except dear Maeve, of course. But it was worth every bite for the motivation it instilled.

If rigidity is inappropriate and self-defeating for parents at home, conformity is inappropriate in the classroom. Instead of recognizing the uniqueness of each child and working with the child's strengths and special needs, many schools demand conformity from students. "By graduation, we must all be the same" seems the motto of many schools, both primary and secondary. And for many students, graduation never comes; they are among the alarming number of students who rebel against this motto and stop learning at an early age. The first few grades are critical in motivating a student to learn. Early failure becomes an insurmountable barrier to learning. A student becomes like the football team that is losing twenty-eight to zero in the first quarter; they spend the whole game playing catch-up ball and rarely succeed. The high dropout rate in high school is constantly cited as a great problem in the United States. But I say that kids don't drop out in high school; they drop out in the first grade and merely hang around for ten years before making it official.

For most schools, conformity is a defense mechanism. The classes are too large, the teacher is not a teacher but a police officer and meeting the individual developmental needs of each student is impossible. The community which, for budgetary or whatever reasons, allows such conditions is wasting what money it does spend on education. When my son, Michael, was being overly "social" in that first grade class, the teacher was able to recognize the condition and deal with it. She had few enough students to make individual attention to individual needs possible. Such conditions allow for good teaching, and isn't that why we build and staff schools? Every child is unique and every parent and every teacher must understand this to successfully parent and teach.

Back from service, I returned to NBC to reclaim my page job; the law had provided that it would be waiting for me, since I had been a GI. This time the plan was to work days and use my GI-Bill benefits to go to college at night. This would mean long days and hard work, but hard work had never stood between me and something I wished to do. If an opportunity turned up in the highly competitive radio business, that would be fine, but I was more practical than I had been only eighteen months before, and I knew I needed to prepare myself for a career. My brother Jack had completed his first year of law school before going into the peacetime Army. Now, five years later, he was finishing his education. I had been listening to his views on the law as a profession since childhood, and my admiration for him steered me to the same decision.

The law also fit my criterion as a profession in which I could do something good with my life. My idealism had only been sharpened in the Marine Corps, and I wanted to find ways to be of value to society; the law held that potential. I also figured that if I ever decided on trial work, my acting talents would serve me well. For there is a very thin line between a fine actor and a good trial lawyer. With the G.I. Bill and my NBC page job, my plan was to work my way through school.

For an NBC page, the worst assignment was as the fourth floor receptionist. It was a dark and quiet floor. The reception desk faced elevators whose doors opened only once every five minutes, if that. The dreaded assignment was rotated so that no one would have to serve there more than once a month. It was an assignment that was used as a threat by our supervisors. "Smith, if you don't straighten out, I'll assign you to the fourth floor!" "Oh, no, sir! Not that, please. I'll be good, I promise."

I became the most popular member of the page staff by requesting *permanent* assignment to the fourth floor. I loved it because I was able to study, virtually without interruption, for my prelaw classes at Fordham University. Little did I know that I was soon to be permanently sidetracked from my goal.

Immediately behind my desk was the tiny office of a new arrival to New York radio from Buffalo, named Bob Smith. Not yet thirty years old, he played piano and hosted the early morning "drive time" radio show for WEAF, the flagship station at NBC Radio. He also hosted a Saturday morning radio show for children called "The Triple B Ranch." I knew nothing about Bob Smith or his shows because I was on the D train on my way to work when he was on the air.

One morning Bob's writer, a genial guy named Vic Campbell, approached my desk and asked if I ever listened to Bob's radio show. "Uh-oh," I thought, "A loyalty test." But Vic was above such strategies. He merely wanted to know if I was interested in making a few extra dollars doing research for Bob's show.

"Each day, we have a segment called 'That Wonderful Year.' We take a year, like 1923, and I'll tell Bob what songs were published that year and he'll play them on the piano or roll some records. I'll write a script for him to weave between the music about how much a suit of clothes cost, some historic events, what happened in baseball and so on. Your job will be to go to the library and dig up the information about each year."

In this modest way began my long relationship with Bob Smith. What if Vic Campbell had not offered this small assignment? What if I turned it down? What if? Any life is a mosaic of what ifs. How many times do we say, "What a lucky so and so! He gets all the breaks."

Children, older children particularly, ponder the role of luck in life, and it is important to disabuse them of the notion that luck somehow falls to some and not to others. Luck is properly named "opportunity." I am convinced by my life experience that the difference between "lucky" people and "unlucky" people is the ability to recognize opportunity, to evaluate it and make timely and informed decisions. Afterwards people say, "Gee, you sure are lucky!"

If children regard luck as a mysterious god that only visits some people and not others, they come to feel they have little control over their lives. Children must know that luck *is* opportunity, and that it visits almost all of us regularly. Children must know that they do have control of their lives, that they can prepare themselves to recognize opportunity and to act on it. A child who knows early in life that there is a causal relationship between his or her actions and the results of those actions will understand the importance of working to succeed. Some children will have to labor harder than others, but all can succeed. Too strong a belief in luck can lead to a paralyzing and deadly fatalism. But if we can motivate children to work to succeed even in adverse circumstances, we will make significant improvements in society.

I seized opportunity that day on the quiet fourth floor of NBC. I accepted Vic Campbell's offer and made my way to the newspaper microfilm files in the stately library on Fifth Avenue. I loved doing the research, and I was thrilled when my first contributions were made a part of "Wonderful Year, 1923," performed by Bob Smith. Bob played, "Yes, We Have No Bananas," on the piano before telling his audience that in 1923 Washington was blowing its lid over the Teapot Dome scandal and that a single American dollar would buy you four million German marks. It was a subway World Series and the New York Yankees beat the New York Giants. The segment ended with a few strains on the piano and Bob segued to a recording of Gershwin's *Rhapsody in Blue*.

Bob also needed a "Boy Friday" for his children's quiz show on Saturday mornings. So guess who was elected? I seated the children, handed out prizes, and generally helped out. For the first time it occurred to me that my future might be before a microphone, not a jury. As modest as my contribution was, I was now in big-time show business.

Chapter 6
Confessions of a Visionary

Today, in question-and-answer sessions that follow my speeches, lectures and quiet chats, someone will almost invariably comment, "To know in 1947 that television was about to explode! What a visionary you were." I smile and reply that it wasn't exactly that way, but . . .

If I were to be completely candid, I would say that very few people had the foggiest notion that radio, as we knew it then, was about to be swept away by the greatest media revolution of our times. The visionaries were David Sarnoff and William Paley, who pushed back frontiers we ordinary souls didn't know existed.

Because television has always been a part of their lives, it is difficult for people under forty to understand what a significant difference it has made in the American home. On a daily basis, from the earliest age, television exposes us to the world—its farthest corners, its intrigue, its violence, its beauty. Through commercials, advertisers appeal to our basest instincts and our noblest dreams. Consumer America has been built upon this hype, and we are living life to the world's highest economic standards, largely because of television. It would not be too much of an overstatement to say that, through television, modern America has been shaped.

Before the 1939 World's Fair in Flushing Meadow, New York, however, hardly anyone even knew what television was. At the Fair, we were fascinated by the panorama through which General Motors predicted round-shaped autos, so different from the square ones on our rough roads, which would travel on "superhighways" and carry ordinary families many miles each day. Incredible! We saw the future according to Dupont, "Better things for better living," and the vision of General Electric. How bold we thought it to predict that one day all homes would be "electric" at a time when President Roosevelt was just bringing electricity to the American farm. We picked up our pickle-shaped pin at the H. J. Heinz exhibit before making our way to ponder what was perhaps the most unimaginable prediction for the future—television. The RCA exhibit showed the tiny and fuzzy picture, while Americans stood gaping at the new wonder. Surely, we thought, this could not be in our future. Buck Rogers was more believable.

Eight years and a World War later, I was sitting at my fourth-floor page desk, handing tour guides small slips of paper providing them with information about the radio soap operas on their tour route. It was a time when "One Man's Family" and "Ma Perkins" kept American ears glued to radio. I would leave home early each morning in 1947, stop at the Radio City coffee shop for a cup of tea and an English muffin. "Burn a Churchill," the counterman would shout. Then, after a day of paging, I rode the subway to an evening of classes, finally landing at home and in bed by 1 A.M. On Saturdays I would be in the studios to help with Bob Smith's "Triple B Ranch" radio show and then rush off to the library to do Vic Campbell's "Wonderful Year" research for the week. There were also laboratory classes at Rose Hill and a Saturday evening classical music program on the college radio station to host. Who had time for visions?

Bob Smith would tip me a few dollars for helping with the Saturday morning children's radio show, and Vic also paid me for my research. With these sums added to my page salary and my GI Bill benefits, I was managing quite well. It helped that a subway ride was a nickel and a good hot meal could be bought for under a dollar, a sandwich for a quarter. My father's financial circumstances were poor, and I helped with what was left over. I was what would be called today an "emancipated student," responsible for his own tuition and expenses.

Financial responsibility is, many believe, something children learn at ten or twelve years of age, a time when they can count well and understand the need for accountability. But I believe financial responsibility begins much earlier in life. More than mere accounting talents, financial responsibility is, in my mind, a matter of attitude. In many modern families a child's allowance is regarded as a birthright, bearing no relationship to his actions or habits. I believe a child should learn, early on, that quarters, dimes and dollars do not flow like water from a tap.

I did not receive an allowance as a child, although I'm not against allowances in general. I knew that if I wanted money for some purpose I needed to earn it. There was, therefore, a very direct relationship between the Hardy Boys novels that I bought and the work that made that purchase possible. My childhood neighbor and friend for life, Roberta Ranney, had a nice dog, and when Bobbie and her family went on summer vacations, I fed and walked the dog for pay. The dear Ranney family kept me in reading material for several summers.

There is nothing wrong with being generous with children, as long as they can appreciate the value of generosity and not assume that gifts are part of their birthright or the natural order of things. We tried to make our children understand this, and each has been fiscally responsible from an early age. In turn, they are passing on these same lessons to my grandchildren, who work for what they receive. The results of these lessons are evident whenever I visit a toy store with either of my grandsons, the cousins Britton and Derek. A trying experience, to say the least. Although only seven, they already exercise consumer talents and incredible expertise. They take their time, examining each toy carefully, turning the box over and around. Then it's back to aisle four to reexamine that other toy. Then back to the first one. Then, they discuss each toy's relative value, sometimes going on to examine yet another one. I'd rather be watching the baseball game, but I admire their decision making process, even if it takes an hour or two or three. I never rush them, for they are learning to spend *their* money. Their younger brothers, Connor and Alex, still have a tendency to grab everything in sight and toss it in the shopping cart, like normal three-year-olds. Their time as smart consumers will come, I'm sure. My granddaughter Kaelen will soon also be taking me with her to choose a doll. Or will it be a basketball? Whatever it is, I know that I'm destined to miss my share of ball games for many years to come.

By late 1947 I had given up the Hardy Boys and was spending my allowance on Plato and Aquinas. At the same time, the Radio Corporation of America was converting factories to turn out televisions and needed to create a market to sell what it hoped would be millions of sets. Most people thought RCA a bit daffy, figuring it would never wean America from the movies and radio. After all, Gable was back and

Garson had him, and Jack Benny had Mary, Phil, Dennis and Rochester, and we were all splitting our sides over them. America still filled movie theaters; it would not be until late 1948 that Milton Berle would empty movie theaters on Tuesday nights—and deliver a jolt to the movie industry—with his hilarious show, filled with slapstick, pies, and corny jokes.

If you were foolish enough to buy a television in 1947, there was not much to see, except perhaps the nine o'clock showing of "Skiing in Switzerland," with more snow on the screen than on the mountains. Chicago could not see what New York was seeing. There was no cable to link them as yet, and the poor people in between saw nothing, because they didn't even have a television station to transmit the wobbly and snowy pictures. RCA, people said, had a long way to go, and just about everybody agreed that television was many years in our future.

The executives at RCA also knew they had a long road to travel but they had their subsidiary, NBC, shorten that road by developing the programs that would create the demand for television sets. NBC thought that children's programming could sell sets and other things, an axiom proved early on in the new medium.

To this end, NBC invited Frank Paris, the brilliant puppeteer, to bring his marionettes from the stage to the small screen for a new show, "Puppet Playhouse." Bob Smith was to be the host, and Elmer, that fellow who was always saying, "Well, howdy doody, kids," was also brought along.

Although Bob was to play host and "carry" a few segments of his own, Frank Paris was supposed to be the star and to retain control over the program.

One of Bob Smith's segments involved games, quizzes, and stunts for children, and Bob needed someone to carry props and prizes on set. The successful and well-paid radio actors scoffed at the notion of such work for little or no pay, and so once again, Bob found the answer to his problems at the front door to his office, in the form of an amiable page —me—always ready to serve.

The first "Puppet Playhouse" was scheduled for Saturday afternoon, December 27, 1947 at 5 P.M. The big day came, and so did the Blizzard of '47. New York came to a virtual standstill, and I never made it to the studio.

Bob was understanding, since I was not the only one snowbound that day. The show did make it to the airwaves, and my guess is that the snowstorm probably helped build its audience, and quite a few people saw it. There were less than one hundred thousand sets in the nation at that time; however, most were in the Northeast. New York and Philadelphia formed the extent of the network, but history, in retrospect, had been made; a classic program and several careers had been launched.

I have appeared on television about fifteen thousand times, and I am still counting, but my first appearance took place, one week late, on January 3, 1948. I remember being quite self-conscious; at twenty I had almost no performing experience, unless you count high school and college radio. I wore a sport jacket and carried prizes to reward the bright children who had correctly answered questions about Grant's Tomb and a bridge in Brooklyn. I don't think I dared once to look directly into the camera—what courage that would take—but I do remember figuring out that the camera with the shining red light was the "on-air camera." I also remember the studio lights, so bright and hot! The folks working in tiny Studio 3H would bring thermometers to work to prove their workplace was hotter than Dante's Inferno.

The original "Puppet Playhouse" was not particularly innovative, nor did it try to be. It recreated for television the tried-and-true puppet show, some drama, some song and dance and not-a-little Punch and Judy. Bob Smith's sidekick, Elmer, had been created by Frank Paris. In the same family as Charlie McCarthy's sidekick, Mortimer Snerd, Elmer was almost ugly enough to be cute. The children, in what was soon to become the Peanut Gallery, loved him, especially when Bob, in his rich basso voice, would have him say, "Well, howdy doody, kids."

Bob Smith was not a ventriloquist, and when Elmer, and later Howdy Doody, spoke, Bob was never in the picture, but off to the side with a microphone boom above him to pick up the puppet's words. Then the director could cut to a "two" shot showing the puppet and Bob, and Smith would say, "I think that's great, Elmer."

Then the director cut back to the puppet alone and, as the puppeteer moved the puppet's lips, Bob would say, "Gee Mr. Smeeyath, I think so, too!" Perhaps the most critical person in this "mix" was the microphone boom operator. Often a new boom operator would be caught "swinging" the mike from Bob to the puppet when Elmer was speaking. Despite the mechanics, Bob's performance was very convincing, and I never remember a child in the studio noticing that Bob spoke for the puppet.

The show was a great success and was soon extended to three, and then five afternoons a week. The program had started out as Frank Paris' "Puppet Playhouse," but the talents of Bob Smith, his writers and staff soon made Bob's portion of the program the most popular, and the tail was wagging the dog. Elmer had metamorphosed into Howdy Doody, and the name of the show was changed. All this had Frank Paris shaking, and the inevitable contract dispute followed. Frank thought he could achieve quick results by absconding with the Elmer puppet. No Howdy-Elmer-Doody, no show. But he hadn't counted on the ingenuity of Bob and his writers.

These events took place in the spring of 1948 when the scrappy Harry Truman, having spent almost four years in the White House after the death of Franklin Roosevelt, was seeking election in his own right. Few people gave him much chance; after all, Tom Dewey just *looked* presidential. Politics was in the air.

It is generally believed that the presidential television age began with John Kennedy and Richard Nixon in 1960. I disagree. The first effective use of television by a presidential candidate was made in 1948 by Howdy Doody. When Frank Paris disappeared with the puppet, so did Howdy from the show. We all worried. Where was he? Was he safe? Yet he assured his audience through notes and telephone calls, show after show, that he was safe and they would soon be told the reason for his disappearance.

Through weeks of convoluted script turns, the suspense built. "Where is Howdy Doody?" a nation asked. If the truth were known, Howdy was with a woman, Velma Dawson of the Disney Studios in Hollywood. She had been engaged to redesign the puppet after the trouble with Frank Paris. Redesigned and built he was and, after weeks of anticipation, he reappeared on television, totally transformed into a handsome puppet—and a presidential candidate. He explained that he had decided to run for President to represent the kids of America, on the young and young-at-heart platform, an ice-cream cone in every hand. But he felt he needed more charisma to satisfy the demands of the television camera. So he had taken off for a face-lift and now returned, exclaiming, "Here I am. Howdy Doody for President!" Although we didn't know it then, Howdy was a dozen years ahead of his time.

NBC executives had thought they had a big hit on their hands, but now they were sure of it. A "giveaway" was suggested. Children could write in and get a "Howdy Doody for President" campaign pin. A young executive who had just joined the company visited the office one evening after a show and asked how many buttons he should order for the giveaway. After discussion, the number five thousand was settled upon. But in three weeks there were eighty thousand requests. Eyes at NBC popped! Television had arrived as a marketing tool and Howdy Doody was in front of the parade. The young executive agreed. His name was Robert Sarnoff and not too many years later when he was chairman of the company, it was his parade.

The new Howdy Doody soon appeared both as a doll and a puppet, and on lunch boxes, hats, shirts, and bed sheets. He inspired "look-alike" contests and uncounted fan letters. His was the face that launched a television generation. It was a nice face, freckles and all.

Soon to be contributing to the enormous popularity of Howdy and Bob Smith would be the shy kid in a sport jacket with the armful of prizes. Unbeknownst to me, I was about to be transformed into a figure in a zebra-striped canvas suit, armed with a horn and a bottle of seltzer. Clarabell, dear Clarabell.

Chapter 7
A Little Honk Here,
A Little Squirt There

I continued to wear a sport jacket and a bewildered expression for the next two months as I wandered around the set handing prizes to the children and setting props for the next dramatic event. I was really an on-camera stagehand, but not nearly so well paid. After each show the producer, the director, writers and cast would return to Bob Smith's small office for a crowded "postmortem," a critique of what had worked and what had not. In the final act of the evening, as he locked the office door on his way home, Bob would reach into his pocket and pull out a five-dollar bill, which he handed me, with thanks.

Still, I didn't feel very much a part of a show. Dressed in street clothes, I felt that I was performing a utilitarian role, not that of an actor. I was too young and without experience. I had never really performed for anyone, much less for one of the most difficult audiences, children. I was also confused about the show, and in that I was not alone. All of us were bewildered by working in the new world of television. All, that is, except Bob Smith. His presence was strong and professional from the beginning.

In addition to working on the set, I also wrote cue cards, fetched coffee and did whatever else was needed. One day, Bob was to be fitted for the new Wild West costume which had been made by Brookes, the costume house. Bob asked me to get the address and stand by with a cab right after his radio show, so that he could have his fitting and be back to the studios quickly. I looked up the address in the phone book, we took the cab to Madison Avenue and walked into Brooks Brothers, the famous, and then exclusive, men's clothiers. "Hi," I said to the stuffy salesman playing doorman, "I'm here with Buffalo Bob to fit the cowboy suit." The salesman sniffed and Bob knew sooner than I of my error. It seems that I had overlooked the distinction between Brooks Brothers and Brookes Costume House.

I was flustered, but all Bob said was, "Oh, for . . . Come on, Bobby, get me a cab. . . ." We finally did end up at the correct Brookes, and Bob, who had now evolved into Buffalo Bob, was fitted for his Wild West costume. Bill Cody never owned a finer suit of clothes.

I try not to make mistakes but I make them, nonetheless. Perhaps this is because I take chances and travel roads that are far from risk-free. Overall this has been a good strategy, and I have done some pretty interesting things in television and elsewhere because I have been willing to depart from the safe and certain and take chances.

Young people should understand that making mistakes is acceptable. They should understand that avoiding mistakes is desirable, but that each of us does make mistakes with some regularity. When an adult comes down hard on a child for making a mistake and does it often, a lesson is learned: "don't take chances." This leads to a pattern of "safe" behavior where little is accomplished. Obviously, I am not talking about risk taking in the physical sense, such as riding a bicycle off a tree limb or skating on thin ice. I am talking about exploring the unknown, and, to a young child, the unknown is a broad expanse.

A good teacher knows that a child must be taught to think, a process necessary to exploration. Mere memorization will not produce a scholar or a well-functioning adult. An adult who is able to perform well on a daily basis, handling the many small and large decisions we make each day, is a person who learned early in life that taking chances is okay, even if a mistake occasionally results.

The indecisive, insecure adult may have been punished for early mistakes and has retreated to a position of making only certain or safe decisions. That's a hard way to go through life. Children should be taught that taking chances, exploring, and thinking independently are desirable, even if, as a result, they sometimes end up with a blooper.

Consider, for example, this story about eleven-year-old Mark, who mistakenly and innocently left a leaky pen on the living room sofa. His mother was very upset and shouted to him, "How could you be so *clumsy?* How could you be so *stupid?*" Silently, Mark left the room. Mom's harsh words made him feel horrible. It was, after all, an accident, and he hadn't *meant* to damage the sofa. But still, he kept thinking to himself, he must have been careless to let it happen, even stupid.

Criticism can either sting and leave a lasting hurt or be to the point and constructive. According to the experts, there are three basic rules to observe: Don't attack personality attributes. Don't criticize character traits. Deal with the situation at hand.

I recovered from my mistake that day at Brooks Brothers with thanks to Bob Smith. He had every right to be blowing steam from his ears. I appreciated his calm—his very quiet calm!

With Buffalo Bob in his splendid Wild West outfit, I was the only unadorned, plainclothes character in the house. The whole show was becoming a strange mixture of Wild West show, Alice-in-Wonderland surrealistic fantasy, Punch and Judy, and vaudeville slapstick. Producer Roger Muir had been unhappy with my appearance from the beginning. So he did what a producer is supposed to do—he made a decision, and this time sent *me* to Brookes Costume with orders to come back with a custom-made clown costume for myself.

By now I knew the address, but when I arrived I was told that Roger had added to his instructions, "Make it inexpensive," always a familiar line from a producer's mouth. Brookes had some material left over from a previous order, a bizarre bright green zebra-stripe bolt of canvas. Surely, no one had been clothed in this material; perhaps it had been designed as wall covering for a less-than-reputable night club. It was on sale, and they were dying to get rid of it. Measurements were taken, a clown suit made, a yellow ruff added around the neck, and part of a clown was born. But this silly suit still framed a youthful and bewildered-looking Irish face. Enter Dick Smith, make-up artist of extraordinary talents.

Dick Smith was to go on to Hollywood to become one of the most famous make-up artists. He was a genius in working with latex to fashion masks, facial features and, in my case, a bald pate to crown the head of my clown. He commenced making molds, and as he plopped spatula after spatula of plaster on my face, I muttered, "I want to get out of show business."

"Relax, you're not in it yet," reminded Dick.

As the plaster cast became warmer and warmer, I began to panic.

"Patience, please, only another half hour," the master assured me.

From that cast came a bald pate fringed in red hair, with a puff of red hair at the very crown and a bulbous nose. Dick taught me to use grease liners to draw huge purple-and-white eyebrows high on my forehead. The same liners were used to make my lips disappear, replacing them with a gigantic smile which covered most of my chin and cheeks.

Like a patient removing the bandages after plastic surgery, I tentatively looked in the mirror and knew my life had changed. Not only did I look different, but I felt different. I was emerging as a character. Like a king knighting a subject, our writer Eddie Kean dubbed me "Clarabell the Clown," and began to write me into the show.

I was soon a resident of that zany universe, Doodyville. I would peer straight into the camera and smile, a very warm smile, I hoped. I flopped around in my huge shoes and squirted a seltzer bottle right at Buffalo Bob, to the delight of the children in the Peanut Gallery. A box was belted around my zebra stripes and a horn was attached to the box. I honked "yes" and I honked "no," but never said a word.

There has been much speculation about why Clarabell did not speak. It is said that the producers would have had to pay me more if the character spoke, in compliance with union rules, but that's incorrect. We did not have a union for television actors in those days. The "four A's," the unions representing actors in the movies, on stage, in radio and in variety halls, could not decide who had jurisdiction over the fledgling medium. Soon, they would form a Television Authority while making a decision. I was instrumental in working with George Heller, the executive director of the Authority, in codifying rules regarding working conditions and standards. One of the rules that came straight from Clarabell was the stipulation that a character was not to be designated a minor character or a "walk-on" because he had few or no speaking lines. Clarabell, and other silent principal characters since, have been paid as principal performers.

Clarabell did not speak because a "classic" clown has always been a pantomime character. No sooner had the latex dried on my bald pate, than I was back at my natural haunt, the library, to research the subject of clowns. Clarabell was to number among his ancestors the clowns of Greece, Rome, and Europe of the Middle Ages. Harlequin, who carried a "slapstick" to paddle his peers, along with Pierrot, Pickelherring, Grimaldi's "Joey" and Grock were all ancestors to Clarabell and all spoke nary a word. This clown was to be a classic, a pantomime, and a jester to the Buffalo King and his court.

I had no training as an actor, no experience in show business, no musical talents. But luckily, it turned out that I was pretty good at comedy pantomime. Clarabell would not have been half the lovable character had he spoken. I think the children liked him that way also. I felt sorry for the thousands of children who met fake, talking Clarabells, crudely made-up, on the many merchandising gigs at shopping malls and shoe stores put together by Bob's brother, Buffalo Vic, and Bob's manager, Martin Stone. I told Roger Muir, our producer, of my unhappiness with these events, but he was helpless to do anything; his authority went no further than the television show. I never talked to Bob about it, however. In his eyes, I was a worker, pure and simple, and although some of my ideas for comedy might be incorporated into the show from time to time, Bob Smith made it clear to us all that he was the boss of the show and *the* authority on children.

Bob was the final word on any subject. But Bob was also *every* word; he did not welcome suggestions. There was no question in my mind that the show belonged to Bob, including my character, Clarabell. I had been trained that any undertaking is best approached with a collegial attitude. I felt that there must be a leader, a final decision maker, but that all members of the crew should be heard and allowed to contribute ideas. When "Captain Kangaroo" finally came along, I was that final decision maker, but I also listened to many very talented producers, writers and actors. They were being paid to contribute, and they could not contribute if they were not heard. There were times when I made unpopular decisions and times when, I am certain, I made wrong decisions. The "Captain" was, nonetheless, a team effort by many bright and very creative people.

Teaching young people to work in cooperation with others is critical in a society where virtually every activity is a joint undertaking. John Donne's statement that "No man is an island, entire of itself" has greater meaning in today's highly interdependent society than it did in Donne's world, three hundred and fifty years ago. Yet we often teach children to be highly competitive, to be loners, to disdain cooperation. Many high school athletic coaches say that one of their greatest needs is to teach kids to be "team players." A batter comes to the plate and swings to hit a home run when, with a man on first, nobody out, and one run down, a sacrifice bunt is more appropriate. Some children are victims of a psychological problem which makes cooperation impossible, and professional help should be sought as soon as such a condition is suspected. Most children are merely victims of a society which teaches the need to win and the need to be a winner, at any cost. The refining of a child's talents and the development of his or her intellect is important, but the need for cooperation is a lesson to be taught early on.

Very young children are naturally self-centered, and only time and growth will change that. When they were very young, my daughters shared a bedroom, until Jeanne decided that having a guest room was not as important as giving each child a place of her own. While they were sharing a room, cooperation was important. Laurie proposed that they divide the room in half, and ran a string down the middle of the room to do so. It was only after she agreed to this arrangement that younger Maeve discovered that the door was in Laurie's half and, thus, Laurie had effectively kept Maeve out of her own room. At summer camp Laurie was the one who got the letters from home because Maeve was too young to read. Laurie was supposed to read them to Maeve, but refused to. Resourcefully, however, Maeve outwitted her older sister by having her counselor place a weekly phone call for her, so she could catch up on the home front. Today things have changed, and these young women are on the phone several times a week, helping each other with nurturing tips. They are mothers to each other's children, the essence of cooperation. All it took was some growing up.

While Bob Smith didn't welcome suggestions, by observing him I learned many facets of my craft. Professionals who have worked with me, particularly on live performances, will often comment that I have a "clock in my head." I have an ability to time material and to perform within stringent time requirements. This talent was very important in the "live" days, when we performed eleven hours of live television weekly. That "clock in my head" is a gift from the master, Bob Smith.

Although we are radically different in our philosophy, Bob Smith fathered me in television, and like a good father, he taught me much.

I have heard that on the last scheduled "Howdy Doody" television program in 1960, the camera cut to a shot of Clarabell, who, with a tear in his eye, spoke for the first time, saying, "Goodbye, kids." When I first heard this story, I could not believe it, but apparently it happened. To have the last act of a classic character be an act of disillusionment is unfathomable to me and very sad.

Staying in character was important to me and at times most difficult. I would often accompany Buffalo Bob on personal appearances. Howdy and the other puppets were full-screen characters on television, but on a stage they were too small to be seen by the audience. But Clarabell was bigger than life and, with his broad comedy, the perfect companion for Bob before large audiences.

In 1949, Howdy Doody, the former presidential candidate, and his friend and mentor, Buffalo Bob, were invited to the nation's capital to assist in the "I Am An American Day" festivities on the steps of the Capitol. Clarabell was also invited, and on the big day I found myself on the Capitol steps in zebra stripes, bald pate, big smile and horn, seated incongruously between Attorney General Tom Clark and the Vice President of the United States, Alben W. Barkley. I would not have spoken in that company if I were the most loquacious clown on this earth. The ice was broken, however, by the Vice President, on my right, who leaned over to me and spoke loud enough for the Attorney General, on my left, to overhear.

"Clarabell," said the Vice President, "Tom Clark here is a much bigger clown than you are and he doesn't need all that makeup!"

The Attorney General guffawed as Alben Barkley chuckled contentedly at this joke.

Clarabell looked the Vice President right in the eye and gave him a big, warm smile. But he didn't speak!

Chapter 8
Wedding Bells

In July of 1950 an attractive redhead came onto the set of "Howdy Doody" and introduced herself to me as Annie Laurie, a friend of my sister, Catherine. After some small conversation, I became bold enough to suggest we have dinner. She laughed because, as I learned later, my sister had told her that if nothing else, I was good for a dinner.

Although Anne Laurie was her real name, most of her friends from high school and college called her Laurie. I was old-fashioned enough not to address a woman by her last name, and so I called her Jeanne, her middle name. It was easy to see why she preferred being called anything other than "Annie Laurie," which was also the title of an old song. And by the time she became a teen it was worse. Jeanne's father was a funeral director. So when a boy called her phone number he would hear the answer, "Laurie Funeral Home." More often than not, the young man would conclude he had been the victim of a joke. Jeanne has a great sense of humor, but she didn't laugh much at Annie Laurie jokes.

Jeanne was a very secure child and probably because of a happy childhood, was able to weather what teasing was directed her way. But many children, especially those who are less than secure, have a miserable time with teasing. Good-natured teasing with a secure child can be a healthy, enjoyable part of childhood. Teasing with a nasty edge or teasing aimed squarely at a child's weakness, say, poor academic performance, can be cruel and unsettling to a child, even contributing to emotional problems.

Children themselves can be very cruel to their peers. Many adults view teasing as harmless when, in fact, it can be a crushing experience.

If a bully attacks a child physically in the schoolyard, we tend to be outraged at the cruelty of the act. A verbal attack may be of greater consequence, resulting in greater damage, though it will be psychological, not physical, and not as evident.

"Sticks and stones may break my bones but words will never hurt me" may be the most fallacious saying of childhood. A bloody nose will heal far faster than a bruised psyche. Adults should take seriously the cruel banter of childhood; it is a cowardly act, often taking place out of the earshot of adults. The results of this cruelty may be displayed as unusual quiet or withdrawal in a child. An attempt to elicit information may reveal the underlying reason. "Johnny said I was ugly and that's why nobody likes me." It seems so trivial and silly, but it is of great seriousness to a child and must be addressed. It is interesting how perceptive children may be when they verbally attack another child. They seem to sense that a child is insecure and concerned that she or he is not liked by other children. Armed with this intuitive knowledge a child may say, "You're ugly and that's why nobody likes you." That is all the confirmation an insecure child needs. Sticks, stones and words are all in the arsenal of childhood cruelty.

Anne Jeanne Laurie graduated from the College of New Rochelle in the spring of 1950. She had the splendid liberal arts education for which the Ursulines are noted and was trained as a speech therapist. They were not hiring many therapists that spring, however, and she decided to pursue her true love, broadcasting. She took an entry level job as a receptionist in the office of William Noble, president of ABC Broadcasting. ABC was then owned by the Life Savers candy people but had only recently been spun off, by government decree, from the parent network, NBC. Therefore, her office was in the same building as my studio at Rockefeller Center.

Jeanne's family had only recently acquired a television set and she was a bit old for "Howdy Doody," so I don't think it was an interest in Clarabell that first brought her to meet me. She may have been completely unfamiliar with the show. Despite its enormous popularity nationally, there were millions of Americans who still thought howdy doody was a friendly greeting and Clarabell was a cow. Maybe it was the prospect of a free dinner that had lured her my way.

We met for dinner and then we met again. I was living at home and still juggling what had become a career in television with college classes. Despite the success of "Howdy Doody" and the growth of television, I was still planning to enter law school. I was making very good money as an actor; television had, by then, been organized by the actors' union and the minimum payment for five half hours weekly was over four hundred dollars—1950 dollars, that is. Along with some personal-appearance income, I was doing well at twenty-three years of age. I now had the tuition money for school, but did I have time to go to class? Not really. And now, only a month or so after meeting this young woman, I was talking marriage. We set the date, five months hence, for December 30, 1950.

In those days, men and women married young and hardly thought twice about starting a family. Children were considered a natural part of life, and not something separate that you sat around for years making decisions about. It was not really very different for us than it had been for my parents when they married thirty-five years before, in 1916, because in 1950 it was still assumed that, when a woman married, she would stop working and stay at home to raise a family.

The careful and often agonizing thought that many parents of today give to having children is, I believe, on the whole, good for the children who eventually result. In my younger days, couples often had children with little regard to the nurturing circumstances they were able to provide. I am careful not to generalize, because many of these couples were the most loving and generous of parents, providing a warm, secure home where the children were the focus of family life. Other couples, however, found themselves unable to cope, emotionally or financially, with the need to nurture children. Careful planning for such adults might have avoided these circumstances until such time as they were prepared to parent successfully. Nurturing children is no easy task at best, despite its great joys; good planning, as in any human endeavor, usually produces good results.

Jeanne is a funny woman. Maybe when your father is a funeral director you are compelled to develop a defense mechanism; perhaps her sense of humor came from this need. Her father, Henry Laurie, was himself the son of a funeral director and was not noted for his joviality. I am sure that with his close friends he had his laughs, but I had to work very hard to earn anything close to a smile. "Does he like me?" I would ask Jeanne that summer. "He thinks you're terrific," she'd reply. "You could fool me!" He was, in many ways, the stereotypical undertaker; his nickname was "Digger."

Her father's ancestors were Irish and Scottish, hence the family name. Her mother, Anna Schmitt, a diminutive and kind woman, was the daughter of German immigrants. Her family was large and close-knit. One never asked Aunt Kate how she felt without risking a ten-minute compendium of her medical history. Uncle Andy was never assigned critical tasks; he was the one that brought the garbage to the picnic and dropped the lunch down the incinerator chute.

Jeanne was an only child, but there were cousins on both the Laurie and Schmitt sides, and a maiden aunt, Betty Laurie, who doted on her niece. It was the sort of family that was so typical in those days, but which is not as common today. Everyone lived within minutes of each other in the Bronx, except for the Jersey cousins, the Mahers, whom they saw often at the end of a Sunday auto trip. Surrounded as she was by aunts and uncles, there was no need to look for a sitter for Baby Jeanne. If Johnny was busy, Paul or Otto or Mae or Kate or Betty was available. She often had a roomful of relatives attending her every need.

The extended family met a great nurturing need. The wonders of modern technology, for which we are so thankful, have had an effect on the family unit. My daughter, Laurie, went to distant St. Louis to attend law school. In my generation she would have come home only at Christmas and in the summer, on the train. With the availability of jet airplanes, however, she often came home just to have her hair done. She married a classmate, John L. Sullivan, from central Illinois. This bringing together of two people from distant places is commonplace today and possible because of modern roads and modern jets. But it has taken Laurie and millions of other new-generation families away from their parents, aunts, uncles, and cousins who make up the extended family.

Relatives from the extended family are often not available to sit for children, to be companions, to be co-nurturers with parents. The television set is a more commonplace sitter than relatives, and a child does not derive the same benefits from the television as Jeanne did from playing a game of Chinese checkers with Aunt Kate and Uncle Andy. Andy was color-blind and would invariably move one of Kate's marbles, at which point she would slap Andy's hand and the board and marbles would tumble to the ground. Jeanne is really expert at picking up marbles, a talent honed in childhood. She fondly remembers the closeness of her uncle-niece relationship, only one of many such relationships that are often missing from modern family life.

Now, in 1951, Jeanne and I discussed whether she wanted to pursue a career in broadcasting or as a speech therapist. It was not our automatic assumption that she would remain at home to raise children, but it was her ultimate choice. When the children were gone from home and launched in their own families, Jeanne returned to school and earned her master's degree, this time in the relatively new field of gerontology. She is a bright woman with much to offer people in our aging population. Despite all this, she has often pointed to her role as a mother as being the most satisfying undertaking of her life. Anyone who knows our children will agree that she is a great mother; her children would be at the head of that rooting group.

Although women have clearly gained tremendous freedom of choice and control over their lives during the past few decades, they often are anxious about their decision to become mothers, worrying, appropriately, about how leaving work might damage the course of their careers. Other women who choose motherhood over a career often question their own decision. These are times of anxiety and I would hope that society would be supportive of women. Public policy should recognize that there are a variety of family structures in today's America and, for the sake of the children, we should be supportive of the family, regardless of the form it takes.

Jeanne and I both love children, and each of us came from a culture where children were valued. We each had a happy childhood, which made it easier to anticipate the joy of beginning a family. Valuing children is probably the most essential quality in a society if a successful nurturing system is to be built. In America we often talk about children, Mom and apple pie in the same sentence. Yet sometimes this is simply rhetoric, because the proof of our words is not there when it comes to public policy to care for children and families. The future will bear the price of our failures because of shortsightedness.

Three weeks before our big day, the wedding train seemed headed for a derailment. Jeanne and I had visited friends, and on the way home, I became violently ill. I pulled the car off the road, got out, and Jeanne came to my side. A truck driver pulled over behind us and asked Jeanne, "Want any help with the drunk, lady?"

Jeanne took over the driving and at ten that night we arrived at her family's doctor in the Bronx, who diagnosed the condition as acute appendicitis. "Ridiculous," I exclaimed and insisted on my own physician.

So Jeanne drove me back to Queens, where, after midnight, we awakened my good friend and physician, Lenny Vigderman. He said, "Acute appendicitis."

In great pain, I said, "He's right!" And Jeanne rushed me to the hospital.

I underwent an emergency appendectomy and spent the next ten days absent from the show, while recuperating from my surgery. Jeanne's great concern was for our wedding day. She stopped doctors, interns, and nurses to ask her vital question, "Can you get married three weeks after an appendectomy?"

The answers were many and often humorous. To this day, Jeanne will not repeat all the advice that was given her. But I know most of the answers were not much comfort to the bride-to-be.

The wedding took place on schedule, in St. Barnabas Church in Woodlawn, with relatives and the show's cast present. When word got around that Clarabell was getting married, the neighborhood kids took up watch in great numbers outside the church. The wedding party, including the bride and groom, left the church, elbowing their way through the crowd. The kids hardly noticed us; their eyes were peeled for the horn-honking clown. As we pulled away in our wedding limousine, the thought occurred to me that the disappointed crowd might storm the church, like the Bastille, and search beneath every pew for the missing zebra-striped clown. Clarabell, dear Clarabell.

Chapter 9
No More Clowning Around

"Howdy Doody" made television history in its first year on the air. Along with "Uncle Miltie," "Howdy Doody" was moving television out of the barroom and into the living room. Television sets were selling by the millions, as fast as factories could turn the tiny things out, and audiences were expanding exponentially. In 1949, the Hooperatings, the rating system then in use, ranked "The Howdy Doody Show" as the sixth most popular program on television, just above "The Chevrolet Tele-Theater" and just below "Ted Mack and the Original Amateur Hour." Considering that these other shows were designed to appeal to a much larger potential audience of adults, Howdy was enjoying great popularity.

We were generally a happy cast on "Howdy Doody." We had our small grievances from time to time, and Bob Smith was not the easiest person to work for because he was often inconsistent. But it was clear that it was his show and that he was the heart of it. His musical talent was major and he had a good feeling for comedy. I was learning from him and grateful that he had given me the opportunity.

Rhoda Mann, the young woman puppeteer who operated Howdy and other puppets, had been working with puppets for some time, but this was her first major performance. Bill Le Cornec, a veteran actor, was enjoying his various roles on Howdy Doody. Bill was a gentle, quiet and nonassertive man. He performed and was cordial and polite to all.

Then came Dayton Allen.

Dayton Allen was a successful radio actor who also did voices for animated cartoons at Terrytoons and other animation houses. He was a performer of gigantic talents. His ability to create characters using dialects, various voices, and incredible imitations of famous people seemed limitless. I knew Dayton from my page days. I had taken many messages from his agent and others telling him where next to go with his bag of voices. I suggested to writer Eddie Kean and producer Roger Muir that Dayton would add many characters to the show. They agreed and introduced him to Bob Smith, who guffawed at his many "fast-delivered" lines and jokes.

It was my impression that Dayton had never operated a marionette prior to this time. The marionettes—more complicated than hand puppets—were dolls with many strings: one for each leg and arm, one for lips, one in the back for posture control, one for each eye, perhaps one for each eyebrow, and more. It requires considerable talent to operate such a doll while speaking lines and listening to others. Dayton learned quickly and was soon the creator and voice of Phineas T. Bluster, one mean character.

Dayton ultimately added many characters, including the popular Flub-a-Dub. Eddie Kean enjoyed writing convoluted plots using Dayton's characters, and he was soon a major force on the program. Unlike the rest of the supporting cast, Dayton was accustomed to center stage and he took it. During rehearsals he was outrageous, often obscene, totally spontaneous, a brilliant comedian. He would get laughs from cast and crew, from writers and producers. If a vote had been taken on who was the most talented person in the studio, Dayton would have won in a landslide, providing it was a secret vote. No one dared risk Bob's ire with public praise of Dayton, but we could not control our laughter.

Dayton's popularity collided head-on with the ego of Bob Smith. I believe Bob's ego was an important part of his bag of talent; a solid ego was needed to project the personality in his character. The problem arose when the cameras were turned off and Bob's ego was still turned on.

I was not as secure in my craft as Dayton Allen. He needed no assurance that he was performing well; years of laughter and applause had confirmed that for him. I was new, young and insecure, and an occasional "Good job, Bobby" would have carried me for miles. But it was not in Bob to compliment us. Interestingly, I have never received a single comment from Bob Smith on my work as Captain Kangaroo. It is as though more than eight thousand "Captain Kangaroo" broadcasts have not taken place.

My name is Robert and my friends call me Bob. But from the time I began working with Bob Smith, I gave up my name and began responding to his use of the childhood diminutive "Bobby." I was not alone. Directors "Bobby" Rippon and "Bobby" Hultgren joined the "Bobby bunch." There was only one *Bob* in Doodyville and his name was Smith, or as Howdy Doody so often said, "Mister Smeeyath!"

The birth of my son, Michael Derek Keeshan, in October, 1951, influenced my thinking about television and its potential for helping children to develop. In the preceding few years, I had given no serious thought to how television was affecting children, nor to its possible use in nurturing young people. I was merely a very young student who was swept away in the rapid growth of the new medium.

With Michael's birth, I had come far, from a college student uninterested in the needs of young children, to a young parent concerned about the influences in my child's life and the influences upon his peers. Many parents today, having grown up with television, accept it as an inevitable presence, an effective sitter for their children, and give little thought to the influence upon their children of the programs and commercials viewed.

When an adult sees a television program or commercial, it is with a full "experience bank," knowledge gained from life, which enables him or her to make judgments about advertising claims or to view program material critically. A child has very limited experience to draw upon and therefore accepts more readily what is presented in such an effective manner.

When I watch "Joe Isuzu," that car salesman on television, making claims that his auto comes equipped with a washer/dryer, I know that the claim is ludicrous and intended as humor. Less obvious exaggerations are more difficult for me to assess, and impossible for an inexperienced child. Many bold claims were once routinely made in commercials on children's programming—a plastic rocket was presented and its action portrayed by film footage of a *real* rocket launched into space. How many children were disappointed when the tiny plastic toy did not perform as shown on television? "Don't be the last kid on your block to have . . ." and "Get this toy and you will be the most popular kid . . ." was the language of early television commercials directed at children. In response to public pressure, the broadcast industry cleaned up its act with the Television Code for Children's Commercials. (The code was struck down by the courts, which held that it violated antitrust legislation prohibiting companies from acting in concert; even angelic intention can run afoul of the law. Though the code is not binding on stations and advertisers, however, most unilaterally adhere to its suggested guidelines.)

When a young child views a soap opera, a game show or a situation comedy, she or he is unable to make judgments based on life experience. The child sees a world being revealed for the first time. When a character is depicted as a sex object or as using sex to accomplish goals, when Dad is made to be a ninny, when greed is rewarded with huge prizes before a wildly cheering audience, the child tends to accept these as true to life portrayals of the world. The child's "value bank" is being stuffed with ideas which are, very likely, quite opposed to those ideas of which most adults would approve. Television is competing very effectively with family values.

There are programs which, I believe, can be of great benefit to a child. "The Bill Cosby Show" is an outstanding example. Cosby portrays family situations in an entertaining, realistic and positive way. Children can benefit from such a program.

Although my mother would have liked Bill Cosby, she would have certainly hated television. In a very different world, insulated from media influence, she had me to herself, to shape as she saw fit. Radio was not in much competition with her ideas, and its use was easily limited. The insular world of my childhood does not exist in today's United States. Today, parents have little hope of isolating a child from the influences of television. American parents have a difficult task; they face stiff competition in setting values.

Early television had its production roots in radio, the stage and movies. Little recognition was given to the intimacy of the medium, its entry into the home and its availability to all family members. Production techniques peculiar to television were slowly emerging and questions about program content were just beginning to be raised by critics.

. . .

Howdy Doody was an entertaining show in a wholesome way; yet little attempt was made to educate or inform. Bob Smith, in current interviews, does point out that he would occasionally sing a jingle such as, "You don't cross the street with your feet, you cross the street with your eyes. . . ." Such material was useful, but it was hardly a structured curriculum or organized educational material such as is found on "Sesame Street," "Mister Rogers' Neighborhood," or "Captain Kangaroo." But Bob's formula was one that worked and there was little reason to tamper with it.

A critical questioning of the television fare for children began as soon as the novelty of it began to wear off. That didn't take too long. As early as 1949, Jack Gould wrote an article for the *New York Times Magazine* entitled "Family Life (After Television)," in which he posed some serious concerns about the effects of television viewing on the American family, and suggested ways in which television could be used for purposes besides entertainment. Gould was one of the first, and many followed. (Bob Smith did not care for the views of Gould, putting down his criticism to "jealousy." Gould's proposal that television be used to teach foreign languages brought a guffaw from Smith. "Who's going to tie kids down with rope to watch such a show?" Both were right, of course. Television could not be educational unless it was also entertaining, but it could be educational *as well as* entertaining. That debate has continued for forty years.)

Meanwhile, the struggle between good and evil continued in Doodyville, with the nasty Phineas T. Bluster duping the gullible Dilly Dally to do his evil work, while Howdy, aided by his good friend, Buffalo Bob, tottered on disaster's edge until the last moment, usually about three minutes before the hour, when a solution would save another day for the good guys. Clarabell was in the middle, never really taking sides. One time he would help Bluster, another Howdy, sometimes both, in the same plot on the same show. Most of all, Clarabell liked to sneak up on Buffalo Bob, with the Peanut Gallery screaming in gleeful warning, and let go with a full charge of seltzer.

I played slapstick comedy with an enthusiasm that sometimes got me into trouble. The most popular program on television was the "Texaco Star Theater," starring Milton Berle with his old jokes, his antics, and his slapstick. The program literally changed Tuesday-night America. Sports schedules were rearranged, P.T.A. meetings were moved to Wednesday night, excuses were made when a host was foolish enough to toss a party on Tuesday evening. Milton Berle was king on Tuesdays and television was his throne.

Buffalo Bob and Clarabell were guests of Uncle Milty one evening, and the major sketch was a birthday party given by Buffalo Bob for "Little Boy Miltie," a selfish and mean little kid. When, at the conclusion of the scene, Clarabell brought on the birthday cake, "Little Boy Miltie" would not share with the other kids, insisting, "I want the whole thing!" Three times he said it until Buffalo Bob said, "You heard him, Clarabell, give him the whole thing!" I reached back with the cream cake and let Berle have it square in the face. Blackout. Applause. Curtain.

Berle instructed me in rehearsal not to be gentle, but to give him the cake full force in order to achieve the greatest comedic effect. Unknown to all, a stagehand had failed to remove the metal pan beneath the cream cake. When I hit Milton Berle full in the face, the pan hit the bridge of his nose. As the curtain closed, he chased after me shouting, "You broke my nose, you son of a. . . ." Though it was hardly my fault that the plate was left beneath the cake, Milton was powerful enough to have caused me trouble. He was nice enough not to do so, and I was very grateful to him for that. Years later, when Milton appeared on "Captain Kangaroo" several times, I was tempted to remind him of the incident. I didn't. I was afraid his nose might still hurt.

For all his pathos and comedy, my Clarabell did not have the quality that Bob Smith considered the essence of talent. If you could not play at least one instrument really well and read music—all talents he possessed in abundance—you had no talent, period. Over the years, the producers and writers had tried to teach me the fundamentals of music. I remember an instructor they hired to teach me to play the drums. He was required, much to his dismay, to give me morning lessons, since the show was in rehearsal afternoons. Often he was too hung over from the previous night's gig to care much about my rather novel beat. They bought me a marimba, a xylophone, a triangle and a slide whistle. Even the average seven-year-old can do something interesting with a slide whistle, but not I. Since those "Howdy Doody" days, some of the finest musical talents in the country have tried to teach me song-and-dance routines for "Captain Kangaroo" and numerous evening television specials. Like their predecessors on "Howdy Doody," they all failed. It was no accident that I was replaced as Clarabell by Bobby Nicholson, another "Bobby" and a Buffalo buddy of Smith's. Bobby was a fine musician who played trumpet duets with Buffalo Bob, smiling in delight, at the piano.

I have particularly unpleasant memories of my departure from "Howdy Doody." It was an unintended, unplanned and abrupt exit. The manner in which I was informed was nothing short of tacky. If the staging of the exit had not been engineered by Bob, it was certainly done with his knowledge and approval. Nothing happened on that show without Bob's knowledge and approval. It all began with an agent.

Bob Coe was an agent, and like most agents, the second thing he always said after telling you his name, was "I can get you work." He had been hanging around the show and saying this to Rhoda, Bill, Dayton and me. We never thought of ourselves as a package, but each of us found the notion of other acting roles appealing. Since my marriage, I had given up on the idea of the law and had become committed to acting as a career. An agent seemed like a good idea to me.

Bob Smith's manager, Martin Stone, a television entrepreneur and the de facto manager of "The Howdy Doody Show" found out about Bob Coe, and he didn't like the idea. He found the concept of one agent representing four of the actors threatening.

I could understand that, and I explained to Marty that Bob Coe had been specifically instructed not to deal with anything having to do with "Howdy Doody" and would, in fact, not collect commissions on any monies we earned from the show. His only role was to find us other acting parts. But Stone was adamant. (One dictionary defines the word adamant as "a very hard stone.")

"Fire Bob Coe or the four of you will be fired," Stone warned. Years earlier, I had been active in suggesting working standards to the newly formed Television Authority, and now, Martin Stone was accusing me of forming another union. But we had no intention of discharging our agent, and management had no intention of letting us get away with what it deemed an impertinent insurrection, as we found out on December 22, 1952.

Bob had asked several of us to help him with a Christmas show for Navy families aboard an aircraft carrier at the Brooklyn Navy Yard. I rode to Brooklyn in a limousine with Bob, and he was friendly, warm, even jovial. He was happy with the Navy Yard show, and we arrived back at the NBC studio around 1 P.M. to rehearse for the live "Howdy" program of that afternoon.

It had been a pleasant morning, and the holiday season heightened our good feelings. I was especially looking forward to this Christmas because my firstborn, Michael, was a toddler, able to enjoy the festivities, and Jeanne was pregnant with our second child. It would be the nicest Christmas yet.

In the studio, Bob tossed some friendly remarks my way and we all settled down for rehearsal. As the cameramen positioned themselves and put on their "cans," producer Roger Muir came to the floor and asked everyone—cast, technicians, stagehands—to listen to an announcement he had.

"There has been a disagreement between the show and four cast members," Muir began.

There was a hushed silence in the high-ceilinged studio, a cough of embarrassment from a stagehand on the catwalk above. The stage and technical people knew this was inappropriate; it was none of their concern. They did not appreciate being forced to witness a public hanging, especially when friends and colleagues were in the hay wagon.

Muir continued, "Dayton, Rhoda, Bobby and Bill have refused to resolve this disagreement and, therefore, their services will no longer be required. They are excused from rehearsal."

Stunned, I looked, past a crowd of sad and embarrassed faces, for Bob Smith. I caught his eye and he turned away. Replacements for each of us were on the outside of the circle and now moved in to take our parts and begin rehearsal. It had been planned days before, but left unexecuted until we had performed the Navy Yard benefit. Bob, with all his cheeriness and banter in the limousine, had been acting a role. The deed had been done. It would not be the best Christmas yet, after all.

Almost four years later, shortly after "Captain Kangaroo" went on the air, I had lunch with Roger Muir and was persuaded to stop by the "Howdy" studio during rehearsal. Bob was not overly friendly and feigned being very busy rehearsing a musical number. And there was not a word about the Captain, who had already been praised by *Life* and

Look and numerous other publications. I was sad because I wanted to acknowledge my debt to Bob.

I talked to Bob Smith on one other occasion. A few years later, my director, Peter Birch, called me on the studio announce during rehearsal to tell me Bob Smith was on the phone. Heartened that at last he was proposing lunch or dinner, I hurried into the control room to take the call.

"Hello, Bobby," said Bob Smith. "Listen, you know it's near Christmas and I know you probably give liquor to your crew and, as you know, my brother, Buffalo Vic, owns a liquor store in New Rochelle and I thought we could help you with your order."

"Thank you, Bob, I'll think about it," I said and hung up. Thought about it I have, with sadness, for a very long time.

Chapter 10
100 Percent Unemployed

Most people have become accustomed to hearing the monthly government statistics on unemployment, which are usually under ten percent. But, as newsman Harry Reasoner once said, "When you're out of work, the unemployment rate is 100 percent."

After being fired by Bob Smith, I was 100 percent unemployed for more than eight months. My last check was waiting for me on that December twenty-second; there was no severance pay, only the amount I had earned up to December twenty-first. I had been married less than two years, had bought a house, a car and furniture. Jeanne had given birth to Michael and was pregnant with our second child. I was not financially prepared for an extended period of unemployment. They were very stressful times.

For someone who has never been unemployed, the worry and frustration of being out of work may be difficult to understand. It is often said that the unemployed are lazy. "Anyone who really wants to can find work." Many unemployed do find work at minimum or almost minimum wages. If you are supporting a family, this places you below the poverty line in the government's statistics. In America, where we breathe the promises of opportunity, one in every five of our children lives in poverty. That often means malnutrition, if not hunger, insufficient clothing, and a lack of proper medical and dental care. It often means child abuse, as well.

The physical and emotional abuse of children takes place at every social and economic level in our society, but economic stress in a family is, without question, a breeder of it. When a parent is "at wits' end" in trying to provide for family needs, when banks and other creditors are pestering and threatening, when television is showing the good life and a family is living the low life, raw emotion often takes over. The crying, whimpering or pleading of a child can cause a distressed parent to lash out.

The National Committee for the Prevention of Child Abuse, of which I am a director, tries, through media campaigns, to reach parents in distress to let them know that help is available through counseling and other referral services. Education of adults is the key to preventing abuse of children, but the development of public policies to eradicate the economic conditions that lead to it are also very important. Trying to correct the results of child abuse costs taxpayers big money; the social cost is incalculable.

My education had stopped short of law school; there was no other profession that interested me. At twenty-five, I was a veteran television actor, with five years' experience, just about the age of television. I made the rounds, as so many actors before and after me have done, seeking acting work. But no one was in the market for clowns at that time and, though my acting talent for commercials and other roles was impressive, the television business had become competitive. All those radio actors who had looked with disdain upon the medium five years ago now recognized that the blue-lighted screen was in the American living room to stay, and they wanted to take an active part in it. Every time I met with a casting director or producer, I was given the impression that I was in competition with half of the people in the United States, which was probably not far from wrong.

We had told Martin Stone that, in hiring an agent, we had had no intention of threatening "The Howdy Doody Show," but we had also no intention of being fired. Now that that had happened, we instructed our agent, Bob Coe, to determine if anyone was interested in using the talents of this awesome foursome—Dayton Allen, Bob Keeshan, Rhoda Mann and Bill Le Cornec—in the building of a new children's program. Soon, word came back. There was interest, at CBS!

Not one of us had any writing experience, but we collaborated on the creation of a show which featured marionettes. The hero, after whom the show was named, was "Billy Buttons," a nice young boy who was always being challenged by an elderly villain. There were some other puppets and a clown. Does this sound vaguely familiar? It was a shameful rip-off of Howdy Doody, but not nearly so cleverly written, nor so well produced. CBS had given us everything we asked for in the way of sets and costumes and production facilities. Yet we failed to come up with an original show, well done. Some years later, when I was at CBS doing "Captain Kangaroo," I located a kinescope of the show and showed it to my associates. It was embarrassing and it was easy to see why CBS had passed on "Billy Buttons." They wisely wanted no part of it.

In my "Howdy Doody" days at NBC, although I was known by reputation, I had not met very many program executives at other networks or stations. This made it more difficult for me to see those people who could help me restart my career. ABC had recently been acquired by Paramount and new money and promises were being pumped into the company. I met with the program director of the local station, WABC-TV, Ardien Rodner. He was sympathetic and, although he could not help me at the time, he turned out to be the person who brought me back to television—and to life.

Jeanne borrowed money from her father, who could not understand my stubbornness in insisting on my dream to return to the small screen. In his world, men did what they had to do to support their families; they got a job. He had a point, of course, and by the spring of 1953, my hopes were fading.

I was concerned that the stress of these times would affect Jeanne, now in her last few months of pregnancy. Michael was eighteen months old and toddled through it all with little visible effect on his cheery good nature. We made it a point to shield him from our anxiety as much as possible, and this strategy seemed to work. However, it was not possible to shield the baby Jeanne was carrying, of course. There were times when she would be upset, understandably so, and I am sure this stress affected the baby.

Many people believe that children are inert when they are young, that they're not really affected by their environment. Of course, this is not so. If children were unaware of what was happening around them, they would never learn. Children are alert and attentive to everything around them from the moment of birth. In fact, according to research by Dr. Jerome Bruner at Harvard, even a fetus in the womb is affected, both positively and negatively, by its environment.

Recently, in France, obstetricians, by using a hydrophone, demonstrated that a soon-to-be-born baby could hear the sounds of the doctor and the mother and could even hear the music being played in the delivery suite, in this case, Beethoven's *Fifth Symphony.*

If an unborn child can hear music, the different tones and pitches of male and female voices, and the rhythms of language, then what effect might this experience have? Can a baby distinguish between a relaxed conversation and an argumentative one? Does a baby still inside the womb "know" when its mother is upset?

Only a few years ago it was believed that a newborn infant "saw" and "heard" very little of the world surrounding her. But research indicates that, at three months, babies are able to distinguish between colors, and that babies can react to hearing their own names as soon as two weeks after birth. Even the complex rhythms of language are absorbed and processed by a tiny child's mind. As Professor Patricia K. Kuhl of the University of Washington's Department of Speech and Hearing Sciences says, a six-month-old baby is capable of detecting changes in the spoken word and grasping small units of language.

It's only logical that if humans learn from their environment, if they are open to its influence, they will be aware of negative influences too. Every family has good days and bad days and experiences crises of various proportions throughout life. Though it is virtually impossible for parents to insulate children from all the pressures those parents may feel, an awareness of the effects of such pressures on their children is vital. Children are sensitive to changes in parental moods and this sensitivity ought to be appreciated and dealt with before emotional damage occurs.

My daughter, Laurie Margaret, the child Jeanne was carrying during all this stress, has always been a driven achiever. A lawyer today, she has always found it hard to relax, even as a child. Jeanne and I have often surmised that perhaps her more highly strung temperament resulted from her life in the womb during those months of insecurity.

Things didn't get better as the time of Laurie's birth approached. In those days, soda bottles were made of glass and were returnable, to be refilled by the bottler. Two to five cents were added to the purchase price of each bottle to encourage consumers to bring them back so the bottler could wash and refill them with a new charge of Coke, Pepsi, or ginger ale. Fortunately, we had been living a busy life that last year of

"Howdy Doody," and the basement was full of such glass bottles. I filled paper bags with them, at two cents each, and some weeks that meant being able to pay for groceries. I was also behind on my house mortgage payments. Unknown to me, my very kind neighbor, George Mintzer, called the bank and explained my situation. The bank manager was sympathetic and George told me, "Don't worry. Just do what you can."

I had no idea how long the bank manager would tolerate my situation and I feared that, despite George's gallant efforts, any day now the sheriff would be at the door with a hammer, nail and foreclosure notice. I wondered if the sheriff would be wearing a handlebar mustache, like the villians in silent movies.

Perhaps humor is a good defense when living through such travails. I often think back to how close I came to disaster when I hear of the foreclosures, the loss of a lifetime of dreams, that take place every day in America. The farmland disasters of the last few years are particularly poignant because they involve people whose life has always been tied to the land, often for many generations. The disruption of so many families must have a great effect on our society in ways difficult to measure. We must never accept such family tragedy as so commonplace that we do not acknowledge the failure of society that it represents. If we lose our compassion, we shall be diminished as a society of hope and promise.

For almost six months I had been seeking a paying job and now, in my wisdom, I decided I would also seek a nonpaying job. I placed my name before the voters of my Long Island school district and sought a place on the board of education. The homes in the community in which I lived were occupied mostly by young people, many back from the war, building young families. We knew our children would add to the burden of what used to be a small school district. We wanted careful planning to provide for the education of those who would later be known as our baby boomers. Many of the old-timers in the community could not believe that such radical growth would occur. (The district, in fact, went from less than five hundred students in 1953 to six thousand students by 1960.) It became a classic battle of the old versus the new. It was just what I needed at this time in my life.

As the day of Laurie's birth drew near, I knew I was in trouble. Our physician, an old family friend, was sympathetic, but the hospital was neither an old family friend nor all that sympathetic. I had no health insurance—it had run out with Clarabell's demise. My father-in-law, other relatives and assorted family friends were standing in line, taking turns in telling me to get my act together.

The big day came. Laurie was born on June 22, 1953 at 6:22 P.M., the same minute at which her brother, Michael, had been born twenty months before. A good omen, I thought. Then I began to think of how I would ransom the newborn child—how could I possibly get Laurie out of the hospital? Finally, from her maternity bed, Jeanne slipped me her engagement ring. I console myself that she has a prettier ring today, but I will never forget the despondency I felt when she handed it to me.

Laurie came home, slept days and spent nights wide awake. And two weeks later, my nonpaying job came through. The voters elected me to the school board by the huge margin of six votes. At a school meeting, a longtime, rather distraught resident of the district ran up the aisle of the crowded auditorium announcing, "My God, look what they've done. They've elected a clown to the school board!"

Chapter 11
Reprise, Bring on the Clown

The summer of 1953 was a pleasant time despite my economic woes. Newborn Laurie was our joy, though it was taxing to discover that the sun put her to sleep and the moon woke her up. As I have said, the differences between children make parenting fascinating. Something that works well with one infant is often useless with another. From the earliest days, infants develop their own individual personalities. Parents have to be flexible and adapt to the needs and demands of each child.

My nonpaying job was going well. As the sole newcomer on a seven-person school board, my life was interesting. I soon learned that people of good will are able to overcome differences—whether they are differences of opinion, age or experience—and can work toward a common goal. My election to the board enabled the "newcomers" to participate in the governing process. But it was the good will of the "old-time" members that made it work.

The five years I spent on the school board brought me some of my most satisfying experiences. The tiny district grew in population, and good planning made it possible to meet the classroom demands in an orderly manner. Four new elementary schools and a new secondary school were opened in that five-year period. More schools have been opened since I left the district. That early planning contributed to making it a fine school system from which many thousands of children have benefited.

I was raised to understand that I was expected to render services to my community. I have served educational institutions from primary grades to the postsecondary level. I have been involved with hospitals, hearing and speech organizations, and athletic leagues, to name but a few. I hope I have made a difference in my community and in the nation, but the greatest benefit of this participation has accrued to me. The pleasure I have derived in these endeavors has been greatly rewarding.

Our nation relies on capable and dedicated volunteers to make function the many organizations that care for our citizens, schools, health care institutions, Scouts, heart associations and thousands of others. Parents do a great service to children when they instill in them, from early on, the notion that people should serve in any way they can to further the work of our community organizations. When America first got to know the Kennedy family, we learned of the obligation bestowed on them to serve the community and the nation. It is true, we do not all come to life with the advantages which bless the Kennedys, but the philosophy is as valid for any one of us. Serving your community yourself is the best way you can teach this behavior to your children. And those children who learn the lesson will be an asset to the future and to themselves.

As well as I was doing on my unpaid job, I was about to give up on my dream. I began to give very serious thought to something other than television. It was August, eight months since I had been fired from "Howdy Doody," and I thought about a career in insurance, in banking, and in real estate. Just about every real estate broker I knew had worked in something else before turning to that profession. It seemed to be the perfect "second career," regardless of a person's background. Then the telephone rang. Was I happy I had been able to pay my phone bill!

Adrien Rodner, the program manager of WABC-TV, the ABC flagship station in New York, asked me to pay him a visit. The ABC station in Chicago had been successful with a children's program called "Time for Fun," featuring a clown character, and Rodner wanted to replicate the show in New York on WABC-TV. Today, the Chicago program would be taped and the tape sent to New York. But these were the pretape days of live programs, however, and to replicate the show meant doing it live in New York.

Rodner knew I had done only network television, but would I be at all interested in doing a clown on local television, he asked? Did I leap across the desk and kiss him? No, I did not, but I came close. I played it cool, responded in the affirmative, and my career had new life.

As the shining star on my résumé, Clarabell got me the job, but the clown I was to play on "Time for Fun," Corny the Clown, was different. Clarabell had been a slapstick character, but I felt a tenderness for his "softness," his whimsey, the mischievous twinkle in his eye. Clarabell squirted Buffalo Bob with seltzer, oh yes, but he did it for the sheer joy of it; seltzer-squirting was what gave him life. After I left, however, Clarabell had become even more slapstick, and a certain meanness had crept into his character. This new Clarabell squirted Buffalo Bob with a vengeance, as if to hurt him.

In the latter days of my employment on "Howdy Doody," particularly after Mike was born, I'd decided I would like to produce a quieter show for young people, a show that would have some educational, as well as entertainment, value. I did not feel that "Howdy Doody" was detrimental to children, not at all. But "Howdy," like most of television, was a derivative of other media. I was fascinated with the potential of the television medium and wanted to experiment, using its intimacy and its access to an individual child in a home setting to try to develop concepts unique to it. Corny the Clown afforded me the opportunity to experiment with some of my evolving ideas.

When management decided to replicate the Chicago "Time for Fun" in New York, they really meant replicate its success; the content of the show, they told me, need not be derivative of the original. "Let's make Corny a gentle clown," I suggested the first time I met the New York show's producer, Bob Claver. The Chicago program was produced by Jules Power, who has been associated with many fine television programs, such as "Watch Mr. Wizard." But it was his representative in New York, Bob Claver, who was to work with me in designing the show. I was only twenty-six years old, but Bob was even younger, and he had fresh ideas and a willingness to take chances.

Despite my strong feelings that a classic clown should never speak, Corny had to; on a one-man show we had no choice. Besides, the show centered not on a "performance" by Corny, but his backstage life. It was understood that Corny worked in a circus nearby, and every noon just as the show went on the air, he would enter the park, the setting for the show, sit on a bench, unwrap his brown-bagged sandwich, have lunch, and talk quietly to the children at home. I had only the park bench, a water fountain and the painted park scene behind me to work with, but it was wonderful. Our ingenuity was tested and it worked.

I had the brilliantly dumb idea that Pudgy, the Keeshan family cocker spaniel, would be a great addition to this ad-lib, live show. It was a great idea, but it turned out that I would never be able to take the train to work again!

Pudgy was a unique animal. If the American Kennel Club wanted to demonstrate what a cocker spaniel should *not* look like, Pudgy could have been their model. But she had personality like no other dog. When her tail wagged so did the hind third of her body. I would sit on the bench with Pudgy on the grass beside me and tell the children at home that she could do many tricks. "Pudgy, roll over," I would command, "roll over." Pudgy would just sit there and stare at me because Pudgy was far from trained.

Pudgy was a glommer, a forager of anything edible. I would unwrap my brown paper bag and remove my sandwich, placing it beside me on the bench. I would then turn to talk to the camera and Pudgy would jump up on the bench and steal my sandwich.

"See what a smart dog Pudgy is. She knows how important a good lunch is. She loves that tuna fish sandwich, but then Pudgy loves any kind of sandwich. I know you are just as smart as Pudgy and are finishing your lunch. What a trick dog!"

Pudgy could be counted on to repeat this performance daily, and our mail indicated that children at home would giggle in anticipation. I would start to unwrap the paper bag; Pudgy would coil, ready to jump. I would stop unwrapping the bag and go on to something else. It might take ten minutes of anticipation before the sandwich was unwrapped and devoured by Pudgy for the benefit of all the children at home.

There was a water fountain in the park which bubbled with refreshing water constantly—until Corny bent over to drink, that is. Then the water would cease to flow. Corny would stand erect and the water flowed once again; he would bend to drink and the flow would cease. Corny would creep up on the flowing fountain from ground level. As soon as his head came even with the fountain, the water would stop. He would declare that he was not at all thirsty and he was going for a long walk. With a "Shhh" to the audience he would walk away, then sneak up on the fountain. No water. He would try disguises, hats, coats, lampshades—to no avail. The children loved it. The real artist was the stage-

hand who controlled the flow of water to the fountain. He had to anticipate me and stop the flow just as my lips reached the nozzle. Never, in
the two years I played Corny, did he get a drink. It went on and on.

Children love to anticipate, particularly when they know what is
going to happen. They love to hear familiar stories, stories to which they
know the ending. In programming for adults, a repeat broadcast has
diminished value compared to the original broadcast. In programming
for children, however, a repeat program is an advantage; children love to
see a repeat of a favorite program or story again and again. Many children's television specials are in their tenth year, or more, on the air.

Adults would do well to keep this "anticipation factor" in mind.
Some adults will say, "Oh, surely you don't want me to read this book
again. How about something new?" Something new may be fine, but
children love to hear what they heard and loved before, just so they can
anticipate occurrences in the story, and enjoy the security of knowing
what happens. This process gives children a feeling of control which is
very important to them.

Some adults find that changing the familiar events in a story, from
time to time, gives a child an opportunity to correct the adult. "And then
Grandma said to the wolf, 'My, what big toes you have!' " "No! No! Not
toes, big eyes, big teeth." This exercise of power by the child can be fun
for the storyteller and the child.

Corny the Clown would have some interesting conversations with
the children about crossing the street, riding the schoolbus, playing in
safe places. He would place a dozen toy automobiles on the park bench
and announce, "The cars have just had a meeting. They took a vote, and
they agreed that the cars would not drive on the sidewalks if the boys
and girls would agree not to play in the streets."

Corny might be sitting on the bench on an autumn day when a leaf
would float down and land next to him. With great enthusiasm and
reverence he would pick up the leaf and show it in a close camera shot.
"Just look at those designs on this leaf from an oak tree. And look at this
one. It, too, is an oak leaf, but different. Every leaf is different, even
leaves from the same tree. I hope you spend some time looking at leaves,
in the city and in the country, and I hope you spend some time thinking
what a wonderful thing a leaf is." He would then introduce a musical
number which would accompany pictures of leaves and trees, great and
small.

Children take their cue from adults who are important in their lives. If such adults show interest and enthusiasm for nature, then children will assign an importance to nature. If an adult is insensitive, the child is going to follow his cue. Adults have an awesome power over a child.

To give us an opportunity to reset the studio for another segment, the live program was divided into three parts. These parts were separated by old cartoons, which the station provided. The animation was from the twenties and thirties, originally designed for theatrical use, and showed, in a blatant manner, the prejudices accepted in public displays in that era. The station refused to allow me to prescreen these cartoons because it tied up technical personnel and added cost to the program.

Fortunately, Bill Beal, my director, was sensitive to my feelings, and when something offensive occurred in a cartoon, he would fade out of the film to me, live in the studio. I would explain that I did not like that cartoon very much and go on to something else.

Some of the material in these cartoons was very offensive. Blacks were portrayed in the "blackface" tradition saying, "yassah" and "nossah" and generally groveling to all other characters. Jews were depicted by men in long beards and long black coats. A golfer addressing a ball would shout, "Fore!" Then a man with a long beard would jump from a sand trap and shout, "Three ninety-eight!"

I was not very popular with management for treating these cartoons with public contempt. After nine months of unemployment, I suppose I should have learned my lesson and been more compliant. Although I have felt intimidated by authority in my life, particularly when I was a youngster, I have never hesitated to challenge it when I felt deeply that something was morally wrong. I have generally been able to sway a corporate executive's position with the force and persistence of my verbal arguments. Few of us are able to be effective standing alone. In the case of the cartoons on WABC-TV, I had the advantage of having a sympathetic producer and director. The one who showed the most courage, since he was a station employee, was director Bill Beal, who disobeyed management directives.

Finally, after a few weeks, someone in management got the message, and I was allowed to prescreen the cartoons. I spent an hour each day with a very patient Tak Kako, the station's film editor, slicing out the offensive material or eliminating cartoons altogether. Tak, who is an Asian-American, jokingly used to say that I was a pain in the neck for causing the station so much extra work. But he was secretly pleased that I was doing something unusual in those days, when civil rights considerations and sensitivity to other cultures was not common in white America.

In the early days of television, programming ideas were generally directly lifted from another medium—stage, film or radio. The pressure to fill time was the most compelling factor. Industry executives and critics predicted that television would never find enough material to fill an eighteen-hour day for three networks, let alone enough for independent stations. In the rush to fill air time, little thought was devoted to the substance of what was going out.

It would be some years before television became more sophisticated, reflecting changing mores and issues in the nation. Some argue that television, as a reflective medium, will always feature programming several years behind the changes taking place in society. Others argue that television does not reflect society but, through programming and commercials, sets new trends, creates fashion and sometimes displays moral standards at variance with those standards generally accepted by society. It was evident to me that we could not wait for television to mature; programming for children had to be thoughtful and caring now, for we owed that much to our young audience.

The history of cartoons on television has been a troubled one. In the early years of the industry, most children's programming featured live people. Many adults fondly recall the programs of their youth—"Howdy Doody," "Rootie Kazootie," "Lucky Pup," "The Small Fry Club," "Hopalong Cassidy," "Ding Dong School," "Mister I-Magination" and many local programs. These productions were live or on film. Then the networks found that animation was a cheaper way to produce programs for young people. The cartoons of the late fifties and sixties were hard slapstick comedy and, increasingly, horror and violent programming. They had great appeal, were repeatable and relatively inexpensive.

Such programming all but eliminated real people from Saturday morning network children's programming. "Captain Kangaroo," for example, was one of the last Saturday programs featuring real people, including jugglers, acrobats and the beloved Banana Man. Eventually,

even the Captain was dropped on Saturdays with the logic that animation appealed to an older child and the older child controls the television set. Many of these Saturday programs continue to be produced to
attract an adult and preadolescent audience. This makes them more
attractive to advertisers who are not interested, generally, in very young
children.

During the early animation days competition seemed to arise among
programmers to see who could present the most violent programming.
Monsters, goons, misfits, extraterrestrial bad guys and plain old-fashioned gangsters wreaked mayhem across Saturday morning television
screens. Finally, there was a reaction. America underwent one of its
occasional soul-searching periods. The violence of the Vietnam War had
been seen in every living room. Three great leaders had been assassi-
nated—John Kennedy, Martin Luther King and Bobby Kennedy. I remember sitting in a restaurant lunching with a network executive the
day after Bobby's death. He wept, as he took personal responsibility for
a violent generation; his programming had had its worst effects. It was
an overreaction, of course, but I was relieved to see someone in power
recognize the link between violence on television and aggressive and
antisocial behavior, a link that many scientific studies, including one
from the Surgeon General, had already shown. I went to Bobby's funeral, in St. Patrick's Cathedral, and thought that perhaps some good
could come from this terrible violence. I was naive; the use of violence
in the pursuit of profits continues on television more than two decades
later.

However, there was a reaction to violence in juvenile programming.
The Federal Communications Commission, in the days before deregulation, was raising an eyebrow, and broadcasters were becoming uncomfortable; perhaps even they thought they had gone too far and were
placing their license to make money in jeopardy. The late sixties and
early seventies saw a "sanitization" of animated programming.

If one offense is corrected, can another offense be far behind? This
seems to be the history of broadcasting. If we can't maximize profits one
way, let's find another. And find another way, the industry did. The
overcommercialization of children's television, Saturday morning in particular, has been of concern to thinking parents and consumer advocates. The development, in the last few years, of what I call toy-shelf
programs, shows derived from a toy product, has been particularly

Bob Keeshan created the original horn-honking Clarabell the
Clown on "Howdy Doody."   (NBC)

Captain Kangaroo in 1955, playing a game of "Crossing the Street" with his audience.
(CBS, Bob Stahman)

"Tinker's Workshop," the immediate predecessor of "Captain Kangaroo," ran on WABC-TV from November 1954 to August 1955.
(ABC)

Hugh "Lumpy" Brannum as Mr. Green Jeans in 1955, doing what he does best, making things grow. *(CBS, Jerry Saltsberg)*

Music has always been an important aspect of the Captain's show. *(CBS, Emil Romano)*

Mr. Bainter the Painter, one of Lumpy Brannum's principal characters. *(CBS, Mario Ruiz)*

Captain Kangaroo speaks to Grandfather Clock.   (CBS, Bill Warnecke)

Bob Keeshan in mufti in 1960—at this time the Captain Kangaroo makeup aged him thirty years! *(CBS Photography)*

The Keeshan kids—Michael, Laurie, Maeve—in 1957.

Pudgy, the Keeshan family cocker spaniel, got his start in television when he played opposite Corny the Clown, Bob's character in the noon show "Time for Fun."   (ABC)

alarming. Toy manufacturers underwrite the development and production costs of these programs and, thus, the profits are greater for the broadcaster.

Many parents regard this as a blatant exploitation of their children. These programs have been labeled nothing more than "feature-length commercials" by the child advocacy group, Action for Children's Television. ACT was formed in the sixties by a small number of Massachusetts women who objected when a Boston television station cut "Captain Kangaroo" in half in order to air a local and more profitable program. At first the station all but ignored these amateurs and their pleas. Then the women picketed the station, drew media attention and, in a couple of weeks, the station relented, recognized the power of the women and restored the "Captain" to his full length. The women went on to organize ACT and have, over the past two decades, been outstanding advocates for American children.

In a climate of deregulation, the work of ACT and other consumer groups has been made much more difficult, but they have not given up. They have brought an action in which the court directed the Federal Communications Commission to review its directives relative to children's television. They have lobbied the Congress along with other groups. Last year both the House and the Senate overwhelmingly passed legislation which would limit commercials in children's television and require stations to provide a minimum of quality programming for America's young people. But President Reagan vetoed the bill as "an infringement on the free speech rights of broadcasters." And because the Congress had adjourned for the election process, there was no opportunity to override the veto. Almost unquestionably, similar legislation will be introduced during the next session of Congress.

A nation that does not shelter its children, including protecting them from exploitation, will pay dearly in the future. Public policy and broadcasters' self-regulation ought to place a higher price on the future than on the bottom line.

But it is parents who have the basic responsibility for their children. They have a right to demand high standards and fairness from advertisers and broadcasters, but they cannot expect the education of their children to be the prime responsibility of others. Teaching children about the purpose of advertising is a parental function. Some schools have courses in which marketing and advertising practices are studied to encourage young people to be smart consumers. Even very young children can be taught to be skeptical and to recognize a commercial for what it is. A parent who is even mildly successful in teaching consumer skills will find a trip to the supermarket in the company of young children to be a more pleasant experience.

I've occasionally had my struggles with advertisers on my programs. Even when television was young, hucksterism pervaded the medium. Television is designed as an advertising medium. The rules by which advertisers had to abide were few in the early days. Until the 1970s when the Television Code for Children's Commercials was fashioned, it was considered fitting for a show host and other characters to do commercials to plug a product. Buffalo Bob did it, and so did I.

At the time, on "Captain Kangaroo," I didn't see this as a bad thing. I saw myself as a buffer between the advertiser and my special audience. Often, the maker of a fine product wanted to sponsor "Captain Kangaroo," but the company had no commercials to use, or had only commercials which had been made for an older audience and were inappropriate for our audience. I would offer to assist in writing the commercial, one that would fit the tone of the show and consider the special needs of our young audience.

At one time, a vitamin company wanted to advertise on "Captain Kangaroo." It was early in the show's life, when few advertisers were interested in the program. The show was losing money, and almost any sane producer would have welcomed one and all from the advertising community. But I could not, in good conscience, allow pills to be sold directly to preschool children. The sales department was furious, for it was a sizeable buy. The matter went up the ladder in the executive suite, finally reaching the desk of Frank Stanton, the president of CBS. Frank looked at the issues and said, "Bob is right. He has a special audience that must be carefully safeguarded." Frank Stanton's decision set the stage for standards which were applied on the "Captain" and affected other CBS children's programs, as well.

Corny the Clown was a reprise for the clown, a new beginning. He regenerated my career, gave me an opportunity to try new approaches to children's television and started me thinking about another character, another program which would lead directly to the doors of Captain Kangaroo's Treasure House.

Corny was seen only in the New York area. He was very popular and in demand for personal appearances. One day, I was making an appearance as Corny at a Long Island shopping mall. Parents and their children filed past to greet me and shake hands. It was a rainy day, and some parents and children had stood in line for more than an hour outside the enclosed area where Corny was seated. At almost the end of the line, I looked up to see familiar faces. There, before me, was my wife, Jeanne, rather wet, with my son Michael in tow.

"Hi, Michael!" said Corny.

Dumfounded, three-year-old Michael said, "How did you know my name, Corny?"

"Just a lucky guess, young man. Just a lucky guess."

Chapter 12
To Grandfather's House We Go

"Time for Fun" was a transitional show for me. Corny had direct links to Clarabell, but he was also a very different character. He spoke, yes, but the essential differences were not so obvious. Corny was a gentle soul who loved children and showed concern for their well-being. He had the spunkiness of Clarabell, particularly when trying to drink from the recalcitrant water fountain, but valued quiet times to appreciate nature and to show love for others.

Perhaps one of the most significant changes in which modern television has taken part is the introduction of the hyperbolic life. On television there is little time to move slowly. In real life, we teach our children to move fast, to compete, to challenge, to exaggerate. Indeed, modern life, in itself, seems to be an exaggeration. Retiring executives, in their farewell remarks, speak of "taking time to smell the flowers." It is a sad comment on our society that a person often waits more than half a century before contemplating the beauty of a rose.

Ironically, while television has been the principal disseminator of this frenetic life style, the medium does have the power to foster contemplation, to engender a more placid, thoughtful life. In those early developmental days, this is how I felt television should be used for young people. Because of its intimacy, it has the power to reach a child in a very personal way. If a relationship could be built between the child and the character, then the entertaining material of the program could be designed to build self-esteem, to make the child aware of her or his uniqueness, and to build self-confidence.

This approach has been inherent in the characters I have portrayed. The program content surrounding those characters has been designed to develop the child emotionally and intellectually. There are other ways to do this and other ways to use television. "Sesame Street" is an example of another approach, using the power of television to sell and hype a product, in this case the alphabet or numbers. "Sesame Street's" product is also useful in the development of the child.

Corny the Clown convinced me that a gentle, intimate approach to children could succeed. Now I was ready to leave clown characters behind and find myself a role more common in everyday life. I had been impressed with the warmth of the grandparent-grandchild relationship. My father, now a relaxed man, would come to visit and enjoy his grandchildren. In 1954, Michael was almost three years of age, and loved these visits from "Poppa Joe." I was surprised to see how quickly Dad had built a relationship with this toddler of mine. He had been too busy to play with me in my youth, and now he had changed. He was great. He seemed to know, almost intuitively, what would please Michael. I remember a Christmas when there were wonderful toys of all sorts beneath the Christmas tree, including some nice gifts from Poppa Joe. When, through all the bustle of a Christmas morning, my dad reached into his pocket and pulled out a few balloons, all other activity ceased. Fancy toys were abandoned for the simple fun of blowing up and batting about red, yellow and orange balloons. Part of the fun had been made by the balloons, but the best fun was from Poppa Joe.

I began to think about a grandfather character and what I, at age twenty-seven, could do inside such a part. I had another crazy idea, an idea for a morning program for children. It hardly seems unusual today, but in 1954 there were few television stations broadcasting much before midmorning. NBC had startled the television world when it introduced the revolutionary "Today Show" two years before. Dave Garroway and a chimp named J. Fred Muggs proved that people would turn on the television set while drinking their orange juice. CBS followed shortly with its own morning entry, featuring Jack Parr. The ABC network was not programming much in the daytime at all. They were too busy trying to play catch-up during prime time. Independent stations, where they existed, slept late.

My idea was for a morning program to help busy families during corn-flakes-and-coffee time. I felt that my family was typical, and in our house mornings were a frantic time. Jeanne was busy with an infant, I was tossing the semblance of a breakfast together, toddler Michael was moving with a full head of steam. Wouldn't it be great if the Michaels of this world, preschool and early school children, could be given their own program at this early morning hour, to engage them and to stimulate their intellectual and emotional growth? The program would not be inane, like so much of children's television, but intelligent, because it would regard its young audience as intelligent themselves. It would be so easygoing that a parent would not mind pouring a second cup of coffee and relaxing with his or her child in front of the set.

Young children are very active in the morning. They are well rested and alert. This often causes a problem for a parent or parents, who are also very active in the morning. When I was raising my children, this early morning time was the busiest of the day. This is even more true in contemporary family households, where breakfast time is also time for *everyone* to get ready to leave the house, for work or school or child care.

Because children are so alert at this hour, they are often more demanding. They remember questions they want to ask, comments they wish to make, and express a need for this, a need for that. Parents may think, "This isn't the time for all this nonsense. Can't these demands wait until we're more relaxed, later in the day?"

Children don't work that way. Young children are unable to shift their demands to a more "appropriate" time. Most demands are likely to surface when they're well rested and they can't be ignored or deferred. A child's concept of "later" is vastly different from the orderly place "later" holds for an adult.

Parenting is not intended to be simple and easy. An adult would be wise to allow extra time in the busy morning schedule for breakfast and dressing, and time to answer questions and satisfy the demands of children. This extra time may mean a small loss of sleep but it will also mean a big gain in the parent-child relationship with substantial dividends paid in the future.

All of my notions about a morning television program for children were germinating while I was playing Corny. I proposed the idea to local program manager Ardien Rodner, but, at least at first, I think he may have feared that I was spending too much time with my dog, Pudgy. It was a nutty notion.

When I have an idea that I believe has merit, I am persistent. I badgered Rodner to a fault. But it paid off. WABC-TV had been airing a modest variety program in the morning. Rodner called me into his office on an early November day in 1954 and said, "You've been pestering me about this notion for an early morning kids' show. Now you may have your chance. We've had a contract dispute with our morning variety show and they've walked out on me. Today is Thursday. If you can be on the air Monday morning, the hour is yours."

Ridiculous! True, I had thought much about this show, but to create the character, write the outline around which I would ad-lib, find film, props, costumes, design and build a set, rehearse cameras and stage-hands, all in only ninety hours?

"I'll do it!" I said to Rodner as I raced out of his office to begin the impossible. Bob Claver had left my noontime show and a new producer, Jack Miller, had been sent in from Chicago. When he heard of what I was attempting, he thought it was insanity. But he offered to help.

We worked through the next nights and the days, taking time out only for the Friday Corny broadcast. Everyone helped out. Set designers sketched out a rough design from our incomplete instructions. "The main character—who are we kidding—the only character, will be a grandfather, a toymaker, remember Geppetto? Yes, like Geppetto. He will putter about, tinker. We'll call him Tinker." People worked as we talked. "He will live in a toy shop. Tinker the Toymaker in Tinker's Workshop." The set designer worked his pencil on a sketch pad. "He wears an apron and a flowing silk shirt and those funny shoes that elves wear." A costume designer drew and made notes on a pad. "There will be toys, dolls, trains and cars on the shelves." A set decorator wrote furiously. "His hair will be gray. We need a wig." We learned there was not enough time to make a wig of the right design and, besides, we didn't have the budget for it. We had almost no budget. "I'll go to the drugstore and get a spray can of gray dye that ladies use on their hair." The director circled the group, shaking his head in disbelief. Soon, too soon, we ran out of time.

But the work had been done. Monday morning at 8 A.M. a new program for children appeared, "Tinker's Workshop," with Tinker the Toymaker. He was warm and welcoming, a grandfather who finds joy in talking to young people, passing on his wisdom, exploring the world with them. Grandparents take their time with children and have a very special relationship with them. Tinker took his time in everything.

The program, unlike the half-hour noontime program, was an hour in length. There were a few cartoons, prescreened, interspersed in the show, but it was basically an hour of ad-libbing, five days a week, no holidays or vacations. This meant that between Corny and Tinker, I was ad-libbing seven and a half hours a week. It was great on-the-job training.

Tinker, like Captain Kangaroo later, was designed to be a quiet, civilized, respectful beginning to each weekday. He would talk about his toys, giving them character. "This doll is named Suzie and she is oh, so nice. She is inclined to be a bit unfriendly to the other dolls, though. But as she grows and learns that she needs to make good friends, that will change.

"This fire engine is named Freddie. He's young and new on the job. He has much to learn. He is often in such a rush to get things done that he does them in a sloppy manner. Just yesterday he was so anxious to get to a fire that he ran three blocks past the burning building. He's learning though, learning from his mistakes. Don't we all. I know I do.

"This doll, dressed as a police officer, thinks himself to be very important. So important that he is rude to the other dolls. Now, they avoid him and he doesn't like that. I guess he'll just have to learn that rudeness doesn't pay."

It snowed one day, and my stage hands went out the rear door of the studio and shoveled enough snow off Sixty-sixth Street and *into* the studio for Tinker to build a real snowman on the set. It melted before the hour was finished, but there was something to learn from that, also.

I talked about how each of us was like a snowflake, no two alike. Each of us and each snowflake is special, one of a kind. A musical number followed—snow music, illustrated by enlarged pictures of individual snowflakes.

Several turntables would revolve, in close shots, carrying figures from the *Nutcracker*. The music of Tchaikovsky would be played as we dissolved, in rhythm, from turntable to turntable. At the conclusion Tinker would comment, "Oh, that Mouse King! I tell you, sometimes, here in the workshop, in the middle of the night . . . what goings-on!"

It was a fantasyland and the children were invited to make believe with us. Or was it real? There was no line drawn between fantasy and reality, for such a line did not exist for me during that enchanted hour.

But the day was not filled with enchanted hours, and in the real world there lived my own Mouse King, the station manager. When Ardien Rodner, the program manager, gave me the green light to produce Tinker, he was taking a chance. His superior, the station manager, was not likely to approve of such a gentle children's show. When he first saw the program on that Monday morning, his reaction was said to be something less than approving. His orders were to "get that thing off my station. Now!"

Rodner, kind man that he was, did not have the heart to tell me to pack my toys and can of silver hair spray and move on. Not yet. He explained to his superior that I had been guaranteed four weeks and then I could be given notice. The cancellation notice was typed and Ardien Rodner placed it beneath the blotter on his desk where it remained for four weeks—until the first ratings were published for "Tinker's Workshop."

Oh, what a difference a rating can make! The first rating showed Tinker beating Jack Parr on CBS and not far behind the "Today" show. Tinker was seen in New York only, so the networks weren't shaking, but Ardien Rodner was rejoicing.

"Do you still want me to cancel Tinker?" he asked the station manager.

"Cancel? Who said anything about cancel? It's a great show, great! That what's-his-name kid, plays the grandfather is okay. Let's build him a little bit. Not too much. Don't want him looking for more money. Good show!"

Oh, what a difference a rating can make.

Chapter 13
Captain 'Roo

At one time, motorists in New York State were given a new license plate each year, which could be attached to the auto anytime between January first and thirty-first. I have always considered the paper hats, horns, and vociferous celebration of New Year's Eve to be strained and artificial. Every year, my celebration consisted of the ritual of removing my old plates and attaching the new ones. So, in 1955, as in other years, I was on my knees in front of my automobile bumper at midnight, celebrating my way.

I had to admit, though, that this year was different. I felt very optimistic. My two shows on WABC-TV were capturing large audiences and, in the case of "Tinker," critical attention and acclaim. Columnists, such as John Crosby, respected television editor for the *New York Herald Tribune,* were giving "Tinker" very favorable reviews for its intelligent, quiet and innovative approach to children.

Although station management was being a bit kinder now that I had put them in a respectable ratings position, I still had a problem, now and then. I arrived in the studio one morning to find a row of storm windows and doors lined up on my set, in front of the toy shelves in fantasyland. The sales department had arranged for a series of storm window commercials, obviously of little interest to six-year-olds, to be done on the set of "Tinker's Workshop." With some persuasion, I convinced the nattily dressed salesman that he would have to move his paraphernalia from the toy shop and do his commercial in front of the cyclorama, a neutral curtain. The pitch was, as expected, noisy and insistent. Because we had such a large audience, and an audience that had come to expect quiet, intelligent programming, the telephones rang with complaints about the insensitivity of the management. In a few days, the salesman, his screens, doors and windows were gone from our studio. In a way, we missed him. Dozing stagehands and technical crew had come to rely on his loud commercials as an alarm clock, something impossible to sleep through.

Insensitivity is precisely what causes such incongruous programming. It continues today, particularly on the local level. One of my pet peeves is the scheduling of an advertisement for a violent motion picture in the middle of a children's program. After "Tinker's Workshop," when I moved on to "Captain Kangaroo," this type of commercial continued to create problems, and we received viewer mail berating us for showing such scenes of horror. Of course, it was not we who were providing the horror, but the local station's sales department. Parents have a right to expect that commercials in a quality children's program be appropriate; after all, they are entrusting their children to the station during a good program, and they should be protected from such commercials during that time. Luckily, after we informed the CBS stations of the parents' reaction, they made an effort to avoid violent advertisements during "Captain Kangaroo."

Youth was a good companion during those frantic "Tinker's Workshop," "Time for Fun" days. I would roll out of bed in Long Island before 4 A.M. each day, shower, place a sleepy cocker spaniel in the car and make my way to Manhattan, arriving before six to get ready for that day's "Tinker." After an hour of ad-libbing, I would wash that grey right out of my hair, removing forty years. Then I would walk Pudgy in Central Park and return to prepare for Corny the Clown. After that show, during which Pudgy would steal my sandwich, I would meet with Jack Miller to plan future production for both shows. If I was lucky, I would be on my way by 4 P.M. and arrive home after five to spend some time with Michael and Laurie. Jeanne was now carrying our third child, due any day now, in late January. Youth was a good companion, indeed; energy was vital then, as it is in any performance.

We associate energy with youth. Rarely do we suspect that a lack of energy may account for poor academic performance by a child. We Americans like to think of our nation as among the healthiest in the world. But that's not so. Infant mortality is shamefully high, and poor nutrition is far more common than many of us would suspect. And both are due to the high poverty rate among our children. This poverty can be found in all ethnic groups; the tragedy of privation knows no color or cultural barriers. When a nation so resourceful as ours allows one in every five children to live in indigence, we must expect to pay a high price. One scenario is simple. A child who is hungry or malnourished is unable to concentrate in class, and is therefore incapable of learning. She fails, and fails again next year. She is soon a dropout. As a functional illiterate, she cannot find a job. She turns to crime or to the assistance of government. All of us, taxpayers and citizens, pay a large economic and social price in losing this human being. Poverty is a terrible thing; poverty among children is dreadful and costly. You would think we Americans would be smarter, if not more compassionate.

My third child, Maeve Jeanne, was born at the end of the third week in January, right on time. She has been pretty much an on-time child ever since. Our children were spaced less than two years apart and, though it made for a frantic few years in our household, in many ways it made nurturing them easier. They have always been emotionally close as children and, as adults, those ties have become even stronger. If only we had been given a share of telephone company stock for each call made among our households, we would now be the principal owners of the company.

When she was a young child, few people could get Maeve's name right. Teachers and children would call her May, Mary, Mabel and anything but Maeve. It is an unusual name, Gaelic in origin, and now she has finally come to love it. But there was a time, as a preteen, when she was not so sure. Her brother, Michael, took a high school trip to Ireland, where he asked the tour bus driver if he had ever heard that particular name.

"Ach, sure," he replied. "There's good Queen Maeve, but best of all, Maeve is the name of the world's largest steam locomotive!"

Michael returned home with this information and a series of taunting, "Toot, toots," annoying his sister to distraction.

When parents name a child, it is usually with some pride; the name has been carefully chosen to honor a parent or other relative, or it has special appeal to Mother and Father. Then, at a certain age, the child may decide to adopt a nickname. She insists that everyone use her new name, even those family members who have called her by her birth name all these years. Her defense of what to others may seem trivial can be a source for friction in the household.

A name is, after all, the phonetic symbol of a particular human being, one who may have decided that this name does not match her personality. Perhaps the name is quite formal and she perceives herself as a free spirit in need of a more suitable symbol. Parents and others would do well to indulge and support her strong feelings. This stage may be transitory and she will be very grateful for recognition of a matter of great importance to her. If she is a teenager, such support on the part of parents is essential.

During the early part of 1955, "Tinker's Workshop" was gathering steam. Unknown to me, NBC and CBS had been watching this modest local children's program with interest. Tinker was now capturing a larger New York audience than both Jack Parr and the "Today" Show. However, the program did not affect the ratings of the other two shows because Tinker's was an almost totally *new* audience. Tinker had attracted children and families who had not been turning on the television set at orange-juice time before. In Cincinnati, unknown to me, Al Lewis had gone on the air the year before with an early morning program, "The Uncle Al Show." The show was very different from Tinker in philosophy and tone. Uncle Al, in striped jacket, played the banjo, sang, danced, told jokes and moved frenetically from one thing to another, leaving the children breathless. "Uncle Al" was garnering huge audiences. A gallery of children appeared on the show every morning and the waiting list for tickets had grown from weeks to months to years. Cincinnati newborns were placed on Uncle Al's waiting list before they left the hospital!

At CBS television, in New York, there was a researcher named Oscar Katz. Oscar would soon move into the program department, eventually becoming the vice-president of programming for the CBS Television Network. This smart researcher had one eye on Tinker in New York and another on Uncle Al in Cincinnati. He gave sage advice to the program department, "If Jack Parr becomes any unhappier getting up early, think children. Big numbers!"

Jack Miller was still working for the Chicago producer of "Time for Fun," but he was also helping me with "Tinker's Workshop" on a daily basis. Jack introduced me to an agent who worked for Mitch Hamilberg, a partner of the cowboy Gene Autry. Boy, was I impressed—this was the big time! We signed what I thought was an agency contract with this fellow, agreeing that if he sold "Tinker" he would get a commission. Jack and I had decided to forgo legal representation in order to save the expense. As a result, we had missed the fact that it was a *partnership* agreement. The lawyer who drew up the agreement for the other side, Marvin Josephson, had recently left CBS to strike out on his own. Marvin would come to rue that agreement when he became my manager, then my agent, and still later my partner.

Then the telephone rang, once again. It was CBS, who wanted us to make a pilot for an early morning children's program. Nothing was assured, because we learned that four other producers, including my old nemesis, Martin Stone, had been asked to make pilots. It was a pleasure to be working with a staff of professionals, this time with enough of a budget to create some pretty decent material.

We filmed our pilot of "Captain Kangaroo" in July of 1955 and went home to wait. It was only a few weeks, but it seemed like forever. CBS reviewed all its children's pilots, including one made by the fledgling television performer, Merv Griffin, and offered us the hour. The air date was scheduled for October 3, 1955.

There was only one problem; I was not available. My old Mouse King, the WABC-TV station manager, said, "No way am I going to allow him to go to CBS. He has a contract to do "Tinker's Workshop" and that is what he is going to continue doing." But this wasn't exactly true. I had been *offered* a contract which I had rejected, and we were still negotiating. No doubt, though, it could be construed that I had been "operating" under this contract.

Marvin Josephson, now my manager, went to the Mouse King, and they had a pleasant chat. They agreed that talent was the *least* important element in a program. The unsigned contract bound me, Marvin admitted, but it also recognized me as the owner of "Tinker's Workshop." "What if—" surmised Marvin to the Mouse King, "what if I could persuade Bob to assign WABC all rights to 'Tinker' in exchange for his personal release?"

The manager was almost across his desk. "Do you really think he'd fall for that?"

"It's worth a try," said Marvin.

"I'd be very, very grateful to you if you could pull it off," said the Mouse King.

A few days later I gladly assigned the station my rights to Tinker and was given my personal release. A new actor was brought in to play Tinker and it continued on for another eight months. I was free to become another grandfather, Captain Kangaroo.

Every so often, I watch a kinescope of that first "Captain Kangaroo" show and I am always struck by how little the show has changed in philosophy over the years. Today we have the glitz of modern technology, much of which we helped to develop on the program. We have had six different sets, four theme songs, some costume changes and much more in production values, such as high-quality special effects. And yet, as it did that first day, the show today adheres to its principles, that children are intelligent and of potentially good taste. The show's aim has always been to help develop that intelligence and good taste, to make that one child at home know he or she is unique, special, and valued. It all came down to nurturing a child's self-esteem through the intimate medium of television.

As a father working long and irregular hours and, later, traveling on concert tours and other appearances, I knew it was important to take time to be with each of my children and to give each of them, individually, my focused attention. This is a way to make a child feel special, worthy, loved.

In the fifties and early sixties, Captain Kangaroo performed with symphony orchestras across the country, as he does today. But in those days, I would do as many as twenty concerts each year, on weekends. It became my custom to take each of my children, individually, on a concert trip every few months. Mike might accompany me to Toronto, while Laurie would make the Houston trip. At one point, Maeve, then about four years of age, was to accompany me to Baltimore by overnight train. The bags were packed and we were saying our goodbyes to the rest of the family, when Maeve burst into tears and ran to her mother. There was some whispering, and Jeanne explained the source of Maeve's discomfort. She would be with me on the train all alone, and I would help her into her "jammies." But Maeve didn't want me to see her in her slip. Six-year-old Laurie was elected to act as chaperone; she packed a bag and off we went. The fact that I often put Maeve in her "jammies" at home made little difference. She would have no part of a man, albeit her father, helping her into her "jammies" in so public a place as a private train compartment.

"Children are highly sensitive to the degree of focused attention they receive," says Dorothy Corkille Briggs in her masterpiece, *Your Child's Self-Esteem.* "Focused attention-direct involvement-'all-hereness'; it is a quality that gets love across. It nourishes self-respect at the root because it says, 'I care.' "

Although I hadn't read Dorothy Briggs' book in 1955 (it wasn't even published until 1975), I had an instinct about undistracted focused attention and its connection to a child's development. On "Captain Kangaroo" I wanted to try to use the camera in such a way that the child would get the message, "I think you are important. You are my sole concern right now."

I remembered my "Howdy Doody" days, chasing Bob Smith across the set with a seltzer bottle while the Peanut Gallery of children screamed in delight. Occasionally, I would catch a glimpse of the television monitor to see a shot of those laughing children. "What about the real audience," I thought, "the children at home? What must they be thinking, watching all those laughing children? 'What are they laughing at? What am I missing?' " I did not want a Peanut Gallery or anyone else to interrupt the relationship between the show's characters and the child at home.

"I want to be talking to one child at home," I told our director, Peter Birch, as we were preparing the pilot. "I want the relationship to be uninterrupted, and I want things to be visually presented from the child's point of view. The children should never be excluded from what I am doing and should never have the feeling of being part of an 'audience.' "

Peter, who came to television from a stage career as a dancer and choreographer, understood and was ready to experiment. He had an intuitive understanding of how to move a camera gracefully and unobtrusively as I ad-libbed my way around a crowded set. If I invited the children to play a game of follow-the-leader, he'd follow me around in a medium or close shot, rather than stay wide on a long shot, which distances the viewer from the action. It wasn't easy for the cameramen, because in those early days there was no such thing as a hand-held camera, and the cameras they did have were absolutely enormous.

Many of the technical developments which have taken place over the last third of the century were used early on during the "Captain." Peter, with an unusual talent for a dancer and choreographer, had a thorough understanding of the technical aspects of television. The engineers would come to us and say, "We have this device that slows the action down or speeds it up. Can you put it to any use? Show us how it can be used and it will help us with our research and development work." We used it for "comedy chases" and for "old-time movies." On the "Captain" we used live production and film; later, we used videotape, music, drama, almost anything that could be found on television. We were a perfect testing ground for the R&D (Research and Development) people.

Peter Birch's great musical knowledge was also invaluable in designing productions, whether live, on film, with puppets or in a "limbo" area, such as the turntables upon which my *Nutcracker* dolls twirled for the "Tinker" show. The music on "Captain Kangaroo" has introduced several generations of young Americans to opera, classical, and contemporary music.

That first morning, on October 3, 1955, the camera showed some doors, made to look like a jigsaw puzzle, with "Captain Kangaroo" written across the front. The sonorous tones of an announcer said, "Boys and girls, CBS Television presents 'Captain Kangaroo.'" The now-familiar theme played as the doors parted to reveal the Captain, in baggy blue jacket with huge pockets, dancing to his desk to hang up the keys to the Treasure House. In future shows I would hang up the keys to stop the music, pick them up to start it again, hang them up, pick them up, all to the delight of the child at home.

I explained to the children that I was a Captain, and I had the big badge to prove it. As far as being Captain Kangaroo, I had the big pouch-like pockets on my jacket to prove *that*. (The name for the show had come serendipitously, as an afterthought. After I saw the marvelous jacket that had been designed for me, the enormous pockets called out "kangaroo." We were looking for a name that alliterated, and so Captain

Kangaroo was born.) From those huge pockets would come almost anything from a ball of string to a teapot or a flip-flop toy dog.

I made a rabbit out of napkins and showed the child at home how to play boat by using two chairs ("Ask your mother or father first") and three pieces of cloth, two for sails and one for our flag. We ran a safety film on traffic lights, and a lemur and a kinkajou ran about the set. The kinkajou, or honey bear, ate grapes when it wasn't grasping things, including my arm, with its prehensile tail. I also did something I still do on almost every program today: I read a book, *The Happy Lion.* All of these activities were familiar to me as a parent of young children, and many of them brought me back to the sort of imaginative activities I had enjoyed as a child in my Forest Hills backyard.

My associates were delighted at creating something new, stretching the medium to new and natural uses. They all hoped we would get past the first thirteen weeks and be renewed for an additional run of twenty-six weeks. I had a better feeling about the "Captain." I did not dare to express it, of course, but I felt we had a crack at a year or more.

The critics noticed immediately that "Captain Kangaroo" was different. "Not only does it (the show) keep the little ones occupied by providing civilized and absorbing fun," wrote J. Shanley in the *New York Times,* "but it also does so without being noisy."

Still, if I had said at that time, "Why, this thing could go on for more than a third of a century . . . ," they would have said, "Lock him up. He's completely nuts!"

Chapter 14
Years of Growth

Like an infant, a television show needs protection in its early life. It needs time to mature, to grow into its world. But few new television programs today get the opportunity for such an incubation period. There is always economic pressure on a program to succeed, to build a large audience, from broadcast number one. While it's true that some defunct television programs were a mistake from the start and would never have improved, others might have succeeded if only they had been given time for all the elements—writing, production, acting—to come together.

In years gone by, television programs were allowed that leeway. The "Dick Van Dyke Show" and "All in the Family" are two programs, not immediate audience favorites, which were given time to grow and went on to be huge successes. Both of these shows might have a difficult time making it under today's rules. Judgments on whether to continue today's programs are not made by creative programmers, but by businesspeople.

Fortunately for the "Captain," the world was different in 1955. We were an early audience success, but the forces that supported television programming, advertisers, did not know what to make of such a unique show. We went without a single advertiser for months and then sold only twenty percent of our advertising time for the first few years we were on the air. We were losing money for CBS, despite our very large audience.

CBS assured us that the program would continue, however, and that gave us a chance to mature. We had brought together some very young and talented people. A viewer identifies with the actors he or she can see on a television program and rarely appreciates the talent behind those visible people, namely the writers, a director, producers, technical and stage personnel. Mister Green Jeans, Bunny and Captain Kangaroo—the characters known best to our audience from the beginning—had some very good people behind them.

My old "Time for Fun" producer, Bob Claver, had rejoined us as associate producer and ran the studio operation. A very gifted young man, Bob Colleary, joined us to hold cue cards and went on to become our head writer, developing some of the finest characters and material on "Captain Kangaroo." Bob Colleary stayed with us for more than two decades before moving to Los Angeles to become a very successful creator and writer of situation comedies. I have said that our alumni populate show business from Sesame Street to Hollywood Boulevard. We developed tremendous talents in production and writing but, while they were with us, their contributions to the success and quality of "Captain Kangaroo" were great, indeed. I am happy that so many creative people were given the opportunity to develop through "Captain Kangaroo," but I am also grateful for their contributions to the program.

The feeling of not having enough advertisers to support the budget was terrible. It was akin to my feeling today when I am unable to find enough underwriters to support new programming for the "Captain" on public television. A producer of a quality program should be spending time on creative matters. Unfortunately, we spend too much time looking for advertisers or underwriters.

The CBS sales department must have felt that I had a death wish. Here I was, with a program in need of advertiser support, saying, "No, we can't put that advertiser on our show." It was a balancing act between our need for revenues to support the program and my convictions about how to sell what to young children. I am a strong believer in the American system of advertising. Our high standard of living is due to our ability to market products and services successfully, and advertising is the cornerstone of that successful marketing. We Americans would be living a very different life if we did not have our system of advertising. I also believe that advertisers and their agencies have a responsibility to the public and especially to young audiences who are immature and uninformed consumers. Exploitation of such an audience in search of profits is unconscionable.

Eventually, many fine advertisers, with good products and a sensitivity to the needs of our special audience, did bring the Captain to American families for many years, and we became a very successful program, commercially.

However, it was not that way in the beginning. On more than one occasion, a toy manufacturer would appear in my office and suggest subtly that, if I would feature his toys on the program, I would be generously rewarded. My partner, Jack Miller, was more openly offered a bribe of several hundred thousand dollars from another toy company shortly after "Captain Kangaroo" went on the air. He was stunned and came into my office in shock. We were both young and, although far from naive, found it difficult to grasp what was happening.

"Please, Jack, just politely show him the door," I said. I've been saying it ever since.

These were "afternoon problems," for the time spent on the business part of show business. The mornings were given over to the show. It was an ambitious schedule. CBS demonstrated its great faith in us in January 1956, when its executives scheduled "Captain Kangaroo" for an additional hour on Saturday morning.

Weekdays, I would arrive in the studio just before 6 A.M. for the dress rehearsal of the show that had been rehearsed the previous day. After that, there was just enough time for notes and makeup before air time at 8 A.M. Few people were aware of it, but each Monday through Friday we performed one show at 8 A.M., Eastern Standard Time, and then, in the forty seconds between 8:59:20 and 9:00:00, we reset the studio and started all over again, doing a complete second program for the Midwest, from Chicago to St. Louis, Dallas to New Orleans, Natchez to Saint Jo.

Because we arrived in the studio so early every morning, there were breakfast snacks, coffee, juice, danish and rolls waiting for us—or at least the crew. The crew arrived a half hour before I did, which turned out to be a critical half hour. Often, by the time I arrived at six, the cupboard was bare. We had a stagehand, Yudi, who was venerable; it was rumored that Yudi had been backstage the evening Lincoln was shot. Yudi would save me a roll or danish each morning, taking it from the table and putting it in his locker. One day, his locker accidentally fell over and, as it was righted, the door sprung open and out fell danish and rolls in great numbers, some of them hard enough to be used in the World Series. The count was rumored to surpass a hundred. Besides collecting rolls and danish, Yudi also liked to open new savings accounts at local banks to collect a toaster as a premium. It was said there were a few toasters in Yudi's locker, as well.

After a couple of years of watching me turn down unsuitable products or commercials, Jack Miller was convinced the show was doomed, that it was only a matter of time. In 1958 we dissolved our partnership and parted ways. I didn't share Jack's pessimism but it soon looked as though he had been right. A month after our parting, CBS put the weekday show on hiatus for the summer of '58. Now, until September, we had but one program a week. Perhaps I should have bent a bit and been more reasonable. But I felt confident that if I stood by my principles, the show would survive, and if it didn't survive, at least we could be secure knowing we had done our best. Luckily, I was right. By the sixties, advertisers were attracted to "Captain Kangaroo" *because* of our principles; we had credibility and it was very good business to be associated with the Captain.

It is difficult for a parent to buck the tantalizing appeal of products dangled in front of children through television commercials. But it is critical that children learn that love and success and well-being are not for sale and do not come brightly wrapped under a Christmas tree or alongside a birthday cake and candles.

Psychologists recognize the seduction behind many media messages to buy; the seduction of believing that material possessions are equated with love or being loved. A child's approach is usually simplistic: "If you love me, you'll buy it for me." That's really putting it on the line, and children do it every day.

Parents and grandparents derive enjoyment from a child's pleasure —further inducement to comply with a child's insistent wishes. And yet, for some parents, this is a trap; they will go into debt to prove a love for their children. In today's easy credit card culture, it is relatively simple for a family to buy beyond its means. This makes the parent-child relationship strained and, ironically, under these circumstances, a parent is less able to give a child that needed security and a feeling of truly being loved, making the whole effort counterproductive.

To teach children that there are limitations on a person's desires is very important. My wife, Jeanne, would tell the children about the many things that she would like but could not have. They would be impressed as she would make decisions: "I would really like this and I would also like that, but I cannot have both, so I will have to make a choice. Come on, kids, help me choose." It was a revelation that someone as powerful as their mother could not have everything that she wanted and had to limit herself. In helping Jeanne make choices, they learned to apply the process to themselves.

Children have to learn self-discipline, the kind of restraint that comes from within. A parent can control a child, but the child will grow and leave home and be expected to function as an adult. What good will the outside discipline of a parent be then? *Self*-discipline serves each of us throughout life. Without the ability to moderate desires, a person will have a difficult time functioning each and every day. Sometimes self-discipline is needed to decide between what is right and what is merely pleasurable.

It is a common misconception, often fostered by television marketing practices, that if you have lots of "things" you will be happy. So how come so many millionaires are miserable and occasionally one commits suicide? Teaching children that there exists a consequence for actions helps. If children learn from overly generous parents that they have only to want and it will be given, they will never learn responsibility and accountability. They will be living in fantasyland and, when they grow up, they will be trapped by their dreams. Having never learned how to make those dreams come true, they will wallow in their unhappiness in search of fulfillment.

The bottom line is that giving a child everything results in dependency, not love. Teach children that the currency of love is not material, that love is something between human beings consisting of caring based on experiences, and you will have laid the foundation for a happy adult life. These are not lessons children are likely to learn from television, or from their peers, for that matter.

To teach such lessons, a parent must live them. Never buy off a child to absolve guilt. Spend lots of good time talking *and* listening to a child. Plan things to do together and follow up by doing them. It is such experiences, both planned and spontaneous, that convert to love between parent and child.

If you are really too busy to spend much time with a child, talk about it with the child. Explain what circumstances, hopefully in pursuit of the family well-being, make spending more time together difficult. A child is remarkably resilient and capable of great understanding. Your explanation, if sincere, will be a message of love, and the child will receive it as such. Don't try to con a child, however. Children are *very* perceptive.

In the Keeshan house we had a wishbook, in which the children could "wish" for something they really wanted. When we first placed the wishbook on the front hall table, we imagined that some outlandish desires would be expressed. We were wrong. Except for the occasional doll, train or plane, most wishes were for nonmaterial requests. It proved to be an exercise to which the children gave much thought, sometimes too much. A wish of Laurie's was simple; she wanted to spend "a week with the Pueblo Indians, in their houses on the hill, in Pueblo, which is a place in Colorado, which is in the U.S.A." Well, you don't get everything you wish for.

Many gifts we give our children don't treat them very well. A toy, for example, should have what's called "play value." If a child cannot bring imagination to the toy, it will soon be set aside. Play value can be found by children in the most astounding places. In 1958 we moved to a new house, a mile from our old one. The movers had boxed almost everything and when they departed, late in the evening, they left empty boxes in their wake. The next morning, my three children were in those boxes, on top of them, under them, around them. The boxes became cars, buses, trains and planes; they were houses, boats, stores, gas stations, the post office, a country estate, the Empire State Building. For weeks those simple boxes combined with their complex imaginations to bring play and happiness and growth.

One of the most recent photographs of my granddaughter, Kaelan, shows her next to a lovely toy, which was a birthday gift. Next to the toy, but *in* the big box in which the toy came, Kaelan can be seen, smiling happily.

Some things never change.

Chapter 15
The Farmer in the Jeans

Gus and Lumpy. Lumpy and Gus. Three of us, together. Some very good people have played regular characters on "Captain Kangaroo" over the years, including Debby Weems and Jimmy Wall, Carolyn Mignini and Kevin Clash. But it was the original trio, Gus, Lumpy and I, who anchored the program for over thirty years, until death did us part. When Lumpy died, in the spring of 1987, something died in each of us.

Hugh (Lumpy) Brannum was Mister Green Jeans, friend to millions of children. Once, when an immigration official on a trip to Costa Rica called out "Hugh Brannum," we had to nudge him to answer. He was accustomed to responding to "Lumpy," a nickname from adolescence. He never told us how the name came to be, and I suspect there was something unseemly in its origin. But he did answer to Mister Green Jeans, and the answer was often hilarious.

Lumpy and I shared the view that humor can be a lubricant in life, smoothing the way in social and business situations. He had the power to find humor in almost everything. Strange, because his early years would seem to have predicted anything but a life of good humor.

Hugh Brannum was born the son of a man he described as a stern Methodist minister in the farmland Bible belt of Champaign, Illinois. He would tell of a rebellious youth and of the disapproval at home of his penchant for that music called jazz. This rang true with me, because I can remember, as a boy of ten or twelve, hearing friends of my parents equate jazz with loose morals, sin and the "work of the devil." It made me tingle to think of it.

Lumpy was a born musician, and by high school he was in the marching band, straining under the weight of a metal sousaphone. He once said he next took up the bass violin because it was "lighter than that heavy tuba!" The logic of this escaped me at the time, but I am certain it made great good sense to Lumpy. Perhaps that bass *was* light to Lumpy; years later, as "The Old Folk Singer" on "Captain Kangaroo," he would casually swing the huge instrument up on his lap, playing it like a guitar, as he sang "new old folk songs," to the delight of audiences.

He went to Redlands, California, for some college education and then spent the next few years roaming the West Coast, playing bass in various jazz groups. The War found him preceding me, by a few years, into the Marine Corps, where he made music on the parade field and in dance halls. It does seem strange that two of the gentlest characters on children's television spent important years in the tough service of the Marine Corps. We talked about it often, celebrated November tenth, the Marine birthday, every year and agreed that it had been a "character building" experience. Neither of us was quite certain what was meant by that.

A decade after the war, Lumpy was playing bass in the great band, Fred Waring and His Pennsylvanians. That meant traveling from Shawnee, Pennsylvania, on a bus for weeks, sometimes months, at a time. He wrote special material for Waring, including a series of delightful children's stories, "Uncle Lumpy and Little Orley." At one point, for thirteen weeks, he had a show on WABC-TV in New York called "Uncle Lumpy's Cabin." That was right after I was fired from "Howdy Doody," and I asked him for a job. There was no budget for another character, so our partnership had to be put off a few years, but I knew his work and I loved it.

It was his gentleness coupled with strength that I found so attractive. Before "Captain Kangaroo" first went on the air, we showed the pilot program to critics and to groups interested in children. After one screening, I was approached by a woman from an organization representing university women, who criticized the program for being so gentle. "We live in a violent society," she said, "and television ought to be preparing our children for such a world."

I assured this woman that she should have no such fears. As we stood in that screening room, I told her, dozens of producers were preparing crime shows, cowboy shows, space shows, all of a violent nature. Children in need of an education about violence would find ample tutoring from other television programs. But I disagreed that our everyday life is violent. It remains a world of cooperation and accommodation, a society where, by custom and by law, Americans consider the needs and desires of others in their actions. Manners are important, and that is what we were trying to teach on "Captain Kangaroo." We were demonstrating that it takes strength to be gentle and to solve problems through thoughtfulness and kindness. If our society was to survive, we needed more of the gentle strengths, better manners, kindness and consideration of each other.

Many parents teach their children to assert themselves, to "insist upon their rights." This is certainly an important lesson, but it is an incomplete one. Most children are never taught that rights are accompanied by responsibilities; if we have a right, we also have an obligation to act in accommodation to others. Many children, asserting their rights, grow up to be rude in their actions at best, criminal at worst.

Almost daily during my childhood, at home and in school, I heard the Golden Rule: "Do unto others, as you would have them do unto you." It is an ancient rule. Confucius, in the East, said, "What you do not want done to yourself, do not do to others." The Greeks, the Romans, virtually every advanced civilization, promulgated a Golden Rule. Yet it is one rarely heard in our contemporary civilization. It is a keystone of ethics, but too many adults teach their children that ethics are for "losers."

What parents do more than anything else in nurturing children is to give them values. True, they provide food for a healthy body and teach fundamentals for physical safety, but more than any of these things, their greatest and longest lasting effect upon their children is in the values they impart. Parents teach these values in informal oral lessons but, most of all, they teach values by example. A parent who, in the presence of a child, admits to the store clerk, "You gave me a dollar too much in change," is teaching values. A parent, speeding down the freeway with an eye in the rearview mirror looking for the highway patrol, is teaching values to his child in the back seat. A parent who cheats on his income tax and brags about it at a neighborhood barbecue is telling his child that ethics are for losers.

Children should be taught the basic lesson that, in a free society, we have an obligation to accommodate others, even to care for others—the true Golden Rule. On a New Year's Day, Fred Rogers of "Mister Rogers'

Neighborhood" called me at home with his annual New Year's greeting. I apologized for my delay in getting to the phone and explained that I was out feeding the birds.

"Oh, Robert," said Fred, "you're always taking care of someone or something."

I had never thought of it that way, but Fred's observation was kind and made me feel pretty good. Taking care of others is something I enjoy and I don't think that makes me a "loser"; caring for others makes one a "winner." Children should know that.

Lumpy Brannum had the gentleness and strength to take care of people, animals and growing things, and so I asked him if he would like to get off the Fred Waring bus and take a ride with us. Lumpy thought this might provide him with a few weeks of vacation and that he could then return to the Waring tour. It turned out to be a vacation of three decades' duration.

In designing "Captain Kangaroo," it was our notion that Lumpy would be the "Mister Outside" to my "Mister Inside." Lumpy's avocation was farming, and he liked animals, which were to be an important part of the show. Little did we know that we were choosing the most natural man ever chosen for a role.

Lumpy was not much of an actor, but that is intended as a compliment. The character of Mister Green Jeans was Lumpy himself. The grouchy character, Mister Bainter the Painter, whom he also played, was also himself, the curmudgeon-in-residence beneath the warm smile. When he put on a wig or costume to play a character in a fairy tale, he would reach into himself to find the hilarious personality perfectly suited for the role. He was as natural at wearing a lady's hat and getting a laugh as Babe Ruth was at swinging a bat and getting a home run. He couldn't act, but he could be himself and that was quite good enough.

Often, early in the morning, during a break in rehearsal, Gus or I would find Lumpy in a corner of the studio, head in the morning paper, grumbling and grousing.

"What is it?" one of us would ask.

"Dirty so-and-sos. Bastards!"

The newspaper told of an uprising, somewhere far away, resulting in death to a few children.

"Sons of bitches!"

Lumpy felt personally affronted by the death of those children. He felt he had not done enough in his life to prevent such tragedy. He felt responsible.

Lumpy also had a knowledge and a curiosity about agriculture but, in practice, his science had its rough edges. It often seemed to me that he grew tomato plants just to be able to grumble about them. "Damned bugs," he would complain. "Damned bugs have eaten every tomato on every plant in every row. Damned bugs!"

Everyone, including technicians and stagehands, dreaded meeting Lumpy on summer Monday mornings because he'd just come up from his home in Shawnee, Pennsylvania, and Monday was the time for him to grouse about his garden. The birds had eaten his corn, cleaning every cob, after finding holes in the protective netting. Some digging animal had dug and enjoyed his carrots and someone else had stolen his eggplants. "I was going to make ratatouille, damn it!" Some people visiting his neighbors drove up on his well-tended lawn and parked their cars. For all his sweetness and gentle manner, Lumpy could work himself into a lather over lawn and garden.

Still, he taught millions of young Americans about growing things; children who lived on concrete and asphalt discovered a green world foreign and mysterious to them and children of suburb and farm learned something extra and lovely about the green world around them. He would combine his love of music and gardening to sing a lovely song about the "feeling you get when you plant something and watch it grow." He would caution patience: "Let it sleep and then one morning, there is a sliver of green, saying, 'I'm here! I've broken through.' " He would tell the children that they have been "part of a kind of miracle. You feel good, and you should!"

The great comedians, Bob and Ray, once did a radio skit about "Captain Kangaroo." Bob explained that he had discovered this wonderful new program "on CBS, early in the morning, an allegory. It's called 'Captain Kangaroo.' "

Ray interrupted to explain that "Captain Kangaroo" was a children's show.

Undaunted, Bob continued on. "It's an allegory about our world. There is this Mister Green Jeans, who represents all that is good with nature, and a bunny rabbit, who represents all that is mischievous in the animal world."

Ray continued to explain that what he was watching was a children's show.

"And ruling above all," said Bob, "was this kind Captain, like a god on Mount Olympus. . . . I just wonder why CBS put it on so early in the morning?"

Perhaps Bob was right; in many ways "Captain Kangaroo" is allegorical. Lumpy assigned a worth to the world of nature that few people were giving in those days. He carried these views into his own life and aided people and groups fighting to preserve the earth from exploitation. Don't exploit children and nature or we will have a bleak future. That was his message when such messages were often very unpopular.

It is only recently that children have been taught to understand that we are interdependent with nature. For centuries the message was, and in some parts of the world continues to be, "You dominate the earth. You are the masters. Alter it as you will to meet your needs or desires." This has resulted in destruction and irreparable damage to our earth. We have wounded our environment. There are strip mines and denuded forests, dirty rivers and lakes, oceans with dying fish. Siberian tigers and orangutans and gorillas and countless other species are endangered because their habitat has been usurped by man, "master of the earth."

It was this attitude that Lumpy Brannum fought by instilling a respect for nature in young people. A child's respect for the ant and green shoot is the parent of the nature-respectful adult. Lumpy knew this and in subtle and creative ways fostered a love for the things of the earth in small children daily.

Children have a natural affinity for growing things. They have a lot in common. Like children, plants grow and change before our eyes. These changes, in children especially, are a demonstration of the miracle of life. Change is a concern to children as well as a daily experience. For them, there is reassurance to be found in the growing things of nature.

Many adults find planting seeds and other "growing" projects to be a source of family fun. It can be a windowsill herb garden, flower bulbs on pebbles in water, a sweet potato suspended by toothpicks in a glass of water, or quick-growing outdoor vegetables—radishes, lettuce or spinach. A child is fascinated by growth and learns patience and responsibility.

My children found their interest in flora as I did—parent to child—and their children are receiving the same gift. Maeve, as a toddler, followed so closely in my garden steps that I always warned her before I stopped walking. Laurie earned a distinction in biology at Dartmouth for her handbook on *Total Sustenance Farming*. They all helped me tend my vegetable garden, but never forgave me for growing Brussels sprouts.

As toddlers, our children each assisted in the planting of a spruce, a Christmas tree of his or her own. They tended those trees for a generation. Last year, someone cut down Michael's tree, a heinous act. Jeanne's pain was great when she found her thirty-seven-year-old son returning from the sight with tears welling in his eyes.

When he was an adolescent, Michael was in charge of watering the terrace plants. On watering day, Mike would look to the sky in search of rain clouds. He would wait from morning to afternoon to evening, putting off the watering in hopes of rain to save him the labor. It was not uncommon to find Michael at 11 P.M., hose in one hand, flashlight in other hand, watering the plants.

On the other hand, give my grandson Derek a hose and tell him to water the terrace plants and he will be happy all day long, and summer days are long. After the first watering experience, however, we found that putting a bathing suit on Derek was smart; Derek watered Derek more than he watered the plants.

From flora to fauna was an easy move for Lumpy and one that he made daily on "Captain Kangaroo." How many animals were introduced on the "Captain"? Over two thousand, without even counting all the various breeds of dogs and domestic cats. Lumpy could be found feeding baby raccoons from a bottle while he told of their habits. A bright cockatoo would sit on the perch of his arm as he cooed to it. He would be saturated by a trunkful of water from an elephant, he would lose a straw hat to a hungry camel; a defensive llama would spit at him, a macaque would bite him, a lion cub would fall asleep in his arms.

He would spend hours with Ruth Manecke, our resident zoologist, studying each animal, learning its habits, being cautioned about its quirks. To point to an animal with its prehensile tail grasping his arm was to him a peculiar joy, and his respect for a wide variety of animals was transmitted to his audience.

After Lumpy's death, our director and executive producer, Jimmy Hirschfeld, put together a tribute to Lumpy Brannum on tape. It was mostly music and comedy and animals from thirty years of shows. At the end of that tape is a song we shot at Lumpy's home in Pennsylvania. Mister Green Jeans, in a rowboat, on a haze-shrouded river, is singing about his journey through life.

> *Down the river in my boat*
> *All my life I want to float*
> *Watching people on the land*
> *Ev'rybody, lend a hand*
> *Come down the river in my boat*

He rowed the boat further down river, becoming smaller to our view.

> *Sing my love song to the sun*
> *Never bother anyone*

The boat moved toward a bend in the gentle flowing river.

> *I want to go where life is free*
> *Across the sky and the deep blue sea*

The boat, now far away, disappears into the mist.

> *Down the river in my boat.*

He sailed the river all his life and always took time to wave to us upon the shore.

Chapter 16
Shooting Up on Violence

In the 1950s CBS Television felt that the future of programming would be enhanced only if well-qualified people were trained in the business. The company looked for men and women with a good liberal arts background, and if a candidate had postgraduate credits in theater or film, so much the better. These people were hired for entry level jobs, not as senior producers; they were to be clerk-typists, script assistants, production assistants, cue-card holders, "go-fers."

For many years, friends, acquaintances, sometimes complete strangers would ask me to interview a soon-to-be graduate looking for employment. Usually, these young people would be receiving a degree after completing work in an undergraduate program in "communications" from any one of hundreds of postsecondary institutions that offer such courses. I do not have the highest regard for most such programs, because usually they do not prepare a person adequately for a job in television, and often the studies are at the expense of more important classes, such as core courses in the arts and sciences which develop the human being.

On many college campuses, including the campuses of some of our most respected institutions, there is an internal competition for students among the various departments and areas of study. Courses in communications, journalism, computer science and others are "marketed" to students. Because young people can usually concentrate in only one major field of study, the competition can be intense. Occasionally, this tug of war is topped off with exaggerated claims, perhaps an assurance of employment at a high level within a field. This ultimately leads to postgraduate disappointment.

Often, I would interview a bright and enthusiastic graduate who would tell me of his or her great qualifications earned in the college-level study of communications. Upon investigation, it would develop that few, if any, course instructors had been on anything but the home side of a television set. The production facilities may have been crude, at best, and the students were afforded little opportunity for "hands-on" production experience, not even an internship at a local television station.

There are many fine communications courses offered at American institutions, however, particularly at the *post*graduate level. I remember touring the studios at the University of Texas, where my host told me that one of the greatest problems facing their graduates was getting accustomed to the comparatively limited facilities at commercial production centers. It was true—the facilities at Austin were beyond what can be found at most commercial stations.

Whether a student has been adequately prepared or not, the largest problem is that of expectations. They have often been lured to believe that their studies will make them sought after and qualified for a high-level position. Not once, but many times, a recent graduate has sat in my office and told me that he would consider the post of producer on my show. When such people find that even an entry level post may not be available to them, great disappointment and some disillusionment results. It is not ethical for teachers to raise expectations beyond a reasonable level. As with any other product, teachers and guidance counselors ought to be subject to limitations on the claims they can make for their programs.

At one time, my office received several calls from a "Professor Smith" who wished to speak to me but refused to tell my associates the reason for the call. Then, the niece of an employee, a college student, asked her uncle if I knew a "Professor Smith." She was being recruited by him for a course he was giving in writing for children's television, and he had promised that if she took the course he would arrange for an interview with Bob Keeshan. She returned to the professor and told him she had called and found that he was not known to the Captain. Annoyed, the professor said, "How could *you* possibly get through. I've been trying for weeks!"

•   •   •

Parents, as well as teachers, often put unreasonable pressures on children by telling them that they can achieve goals which may be unrealistic. This may be a reflection of the desire, subconscious perhaps, that the child be something that the parent may wished to have been but failed to accomplish. It's good for an adult to expect the best of which a child is capable, but setting unrealistic goals will result in failure. Then the child will lose confidence in her ability to meet any goal and the parent loses credibility with the child. Setting hopes which are too high is counterproductive.

The CBS hiring policy of the fifties was wonderful for us. We produced the program "in association with CBS," and the program production people were CBS employees loaned to our production company to put on the show. David Connell, who was assigned to us as a clerk-typist a few weeks after the first show, was soon hired by our company and within a decade became our Executive Producer, before going on to become one of the founders of Children's Television Workshop and a creator of "Sesame Street." Sam Gibbon, Jon Stone, Tom Whedon, Jeff Moss, Al Hyslop and many others passed through "Captain Kangaroo" on their way to "Sesame Street" and other places. During their tenure with us, their individual and collective creativity brought American families some wonderful and stimulating mornings. Viewers may have learned from and laughed with the Captain, Mister Green Jeans and Mister Moose, but the men and women who wrote and produced the show and who were never seen by the audience were as important as those of us on the set who got the credit.

During those early years, I was especially grateful for the support I was given by my production staff while trying to set higher standards for children's television programming during both the commercials and the show. Dave Connell and others perceive me today as a moral standard-bearer. I am proud of that distinction, but the weight of the banner was borne by them, as well; fighting exploitive network and advertising agency practices was made even more difficult in what is a very insecure business.

Over lunch recently, Connell, now Executive Producer of "Sesame Street," reminisced about an incident with a war toy that I'll call "Jimmy X." It was the late 1950s, before the days when assassination became almost commonplace, before the Vietnam War. War toys were big sellers for toy companies, and "Jimmy X" was a big one, with lots of built-in action, including seven attachments designed to kill. As is usual practice, the toy company went to CBS-TV sales and said they wanted to sponsor the "Captain." What was unusual was the anticipation of my resistance by the sales department and by the toy company.

I viewed the film commercial, and it was terrible. This was before the Children's Television Code days, and the commercial used realistic battlefield footage to show properties that even this violent toy did not possess. I asked if they were serious about presenting such a commercial for such a product in such a nice, gentle, thoughtful program for six-year-olds. They certainly were serious, said the network and the agency —almost in unison.

Dave Connell remembers everyone being very tense. It was suggested that I listen to a psychologist who had been hired to convince me that war toys were good for children because they provided an outlet for aggressive feelings.

I suggested, "Why not give your aggressive six-year-old a twelve-gauge shotgun and tell him to relieve his aggressive feelings in school?"

The psychologist ignored my question and continued with argument after argument demonstrating why he thought this commercial would constitute a "service to the American family." He didn't play "Stars and Stripes Forever," but if I had heard the music creep in behind him, I would not have been surprised.

As he spoke, I was struck by how we had come to accept the idea of violence in our society, an idea which may be a self-fulfilling concept. It can be argued that we are a more violent society than in the past but, for most people, violence is not a casual, everyday part of life. But television has given us the perception that violence is all around us. The dramatic programs provide us and our children with gratuitous violence in search of ratings, and the news brings conflict from every part of our earth into our living rooms. Our vicarious experience with violence *immunizes* Americans to it at a very early age, and we are not shocked by that violence but come to accept it, to tolerate it. Few in the United States today are outraged by it.

When I was a child of eight, in quiet Forest Hills, a man killed his wife with a knife during the course of a domestic argument. I remember to this day how shocked I was, how I wrestled with the enormity of the event. I found it difficult to comprehend that a life had been ended, that another human being had taken that life in a violent way. I was from another age, before television brought murder to our homes on a daily basis. Today, few, if any, eight-year-olds would have difficulty comprehending a murder. If it is not a part of their real life, it is a common vicarious experience.

For some children, violence *is* a part of their real life. Drug wars sometimes take the lives of innocent children. Other children, particularly those living in poverty, may turn to violence and crime as their only viable solution to the problems of life. High ethical standards are not compatible with the miseries of poverty. For more affluent children, the acceptance of violence has cheapened life. When a child grows up placing little or no value on life, violence to another human being comes easily. The acceptance of it may breed more of it.

It is difficult to develop a reverence for life in children by selling them toys of violence. Toys teach. If an alphabet toy teaches the alphabet, violent toys teach violence. Watching television programs where problems are solved with a whack on the head teaches young children that hitting is an appropriate solution to problems. Many five- and six-year-olds have to "unlearn" these lessons when they get to preschool or kindergarten, and they are sometimes confused. They learned the lesson of violence on television, and isn't that where "Sesame Street," "Mister Rogers" and "Captain Kangaroo" teach so many lessons? Television is a socializing medium teaching children and adults through its programming. And children, less experienced and less understanding, accept almost everything they see, including violence, as a great way to solve problems.

It is difficult, in a media-cluttered world, to teach lessons of accommodation, respect for others, and that to be considerate of others requires great strength and character. Some years ago, a neighbor's children were "camping out" in a backyard tent. They asked Dad to furnish them with a rifle to be used if "bears attacked in the night." My neighbor explained that a bear attack was unlikely but, in any event, we share our earth with bears and raccoons and other creatures. His son replied, "I'll share my world but not my tent!" They settled for another necessity of modern life, a portable television.

The advertising agency's psychologist failed to convince us and we rejected "Jimmy X" and its seven attachments designed to kill. An appeal was made to senior management and, once again, we won in that arena. It was the best example of how executives can self-regulate. Not all advertisers were a problem; many were very supportive of our standards. I remember a commercial submitted by the Kellogg Company. It had been designed for an older audience and it, very incidentally, showed a bow and arrows. One telephone call to Battle Creek and the problem was solved. The Kellogg Company was a long-time supporter of "Captain Kangaroo" *because* of the show's high standards. They were very understanding, and because of their support, many fine programs were offered to American families through the sixties, seventies and eighties.

Self-regulation of the broadcast industry would be the ideal goal, if television executives could be depended upon to act in the best interests of children and the rest of the American public. My good friend, Senator Paul Simon of Illinois, has proposed that industry executives be freed from antitrust legislation to set their own standards governing gratuitous violence on television. Opposition has come from the industry—guess why—and from such strange places as the American Civil Liberties Union, which opposes any government action on television programming, even, apparently, action which would allow the industry to regulate itself. They don't seem to object to teaching violence to children in pursuit of profits, a practice which may affect the rights of many of us in the future.

It's hard to find someone who likes violence on television. A reporter was said to have asked bandleader Lawrence Welk what he thought of violence on television, to which he replied, "Oh, I like them very much. I also like trumpets and saxophones and drums!"

A-one and a-two and a-three. . . .

Chapter 17
The Etymologist

Riddle: Who has long ears and antlers, uses every means known to humans and hare to trick a Captain out of carrots, drops thousands and thousands of Ping-Pong balls on that Captain's head, draws like the Leonardo da Vinci he admires, tells true time and recites heavenly poetry, dances like a big-foot Astaire, frazzles Mister Bainter with maddening inquiries and beguiling comments and always has the last word, as a true etymologist?

Answer: Cosmo Allegretti, also known as Bunny Rabbit, Mister Moose, Magic Drawing Board, Dancing Bear, Grandfather Clock, Mister Bainter's apprentice, Dennis, and other aliases too numerous to mention. All of these characters were put down on paper by talented writers and producers, but each was given life by Cosmo "Gus" Allegretti.

I wish I knew for sure what elements mixed together make a successful television program. I know certain things are essential—starting with a good idea, treating that idea to some fine writing, adding the right production facilities—not too little, not too much, just enough to show it to advantage. That takes producers with sound judgment who also know how to choose fine talent. Then, you have to get everyone to work together in a collegial mix.

Occasionally, I will find myself jumping in to help the production along by doing someone else's job. This may mean holding cue cards and getting someone a cup of coffee. Anything that will improve a production, even if it means doing a low-on-the-ladder job, is important to me. Many newcomers and many people who have been in television for years are very conscious of caste and will not do anything that they feel is below their rank. To me, however, television is a cooperative effort.

Rank or caste is so important to people in many walks of life that it can impede almost any activity in which cooperation is really what's needed. Children learn an important lesson when they learn to work together with others to achieve goals and complete tasks. Rank has its place, but not when it gets in the way.

Finally, after all the elements of the show have come together, you simply have to hope for the best. A television show does not usually work in a well-planned way; there are too many accidents, combined with too much luck, good and bad, all in the same pot. When the accidents go your way and the luck is more good than bad, you may have a winner.

Hollywood producers who work with situation comedy formulas have an edge, because they have developed those formulas; but repeating the tried-and-true takes away the possibility of producing new and unique programs. And even those producers will admit that formulas are no guarantee of success. What worked well once can—and often does—flop the next time. That's the way it is with children, also. Parents who do everything right, or so they believe, in nurturing a child, may find that their efforts have led to disappointment. There are too many influences upon a child. A human being is a complex organism and the results of our nurturing efforts are not always predictable. A neighbor of mine would tell her son that she was disappointed in his behavior, to which he would answer, "Well, Mom, that's show business." He may have been more on target than he knew.

In retrospect, we were lucky with "Captain Kangaroo" because a very special mix of elements came together to produce it. Gus Allegretti was one of those special elements and continues to contribute to the success of the "Captain" today.

Cosmo Francis Allegretti grew up in Brooklyn, that fabled borough across the East River from Manhattan. He is a few months older than I am. (Among the original trio, that made me the youngest actor on the show, a point I enjoyed making from time to time.) His parents were immigrants to America from Calabria, Italy. Gus is quintessentially Italian, conceivably the most perfect embodiment of that which is Italian.

His love for his mother and his affection for his father are evident in his most casual conversation. He finds great pride in his heritage, a heritage that pervades his ethics and his philosophy.

While Lumpy and I had been whiling away our time in the Marine Corps, Gus had busied himself as a sergeant in the U.S. Army. Many a fresh recruit must have trembled as he gazed upon this sergeant's stern countenance; surely Gus was born with that wrinkled and weathered face. In fact, the recruits had little to fear; beneath that dreaded visage was a deep well of compassion, a spring he rarely revealed.

After the Army he went to college in Ohio, playing some fair baseball along the way. With but a sprig of added talent on the diamond, he might have had a professional career, and what a great loss for us and for America's children that would have been.

In the summer of 1955 we were assembling talents for the show. Although I had never met Gus, we had worked at NBC together in the early television days; while I had been clowning around with "Howdy Doody," Gus had been the puppeteer for "Rootie Kazootie." That show was now off the air and Gus was working as an artist for J. C. Penney. He walked into that first meeting with all the boldness of Anthony Quinn bluffing his way into the sultan's inner sanctum. He gave me the distinct impression that he really did not care if we hired him or not. I later learned that seeming indifference was his manner.

Years afterward he had admitted that he thought we were a bunch of amateurs. "You asked me if I could bark," he reminded me recently about that audition session. "You asked me if I could do birds. 'Oh birds, yeah sure, I do birds.' " What kind of way was that to interview a puppeteer?

Gus is nothing if not irreverent. Once, in an interview, I heard a reporter ask him to divulge the secret of being a puppeteer. Gus replied, "Well, I guess the first thing is that you have to be Italian."

"Italian? Why?" asked the stunned reporter.

"Because puppeteering is talking with your hands. That's all there is to it."

Gus would occasionally inform me that the Calabrese Italians are often referred to as "hard hats, hard heads." This was his way of telling me that I might have to explain something again. In fact, I rarely had to say something *once*—his intuition was that well developed. Gus, Lumpy, and I came to understand one another in fundamental ways and to anticipate one another's words and actions on stage. In the early years, during live productions, this quality added a quantum degree of value to our work.

One thing we did not enjoy about Gus' celebration of being Italian were the handmade cigars he would smoke in the studio, often early in the morning. These cigars were random in shape, gnarled and twisted, as though they had been rolled by a disgruntled gnome. But even their shape was not a sufficient clue to their noxious, rotten smell. That smell sent all who were not then required to work close to Gus to the farthest points of the studio. I was *always* working close to Gus; oh, what sacrifices I made for my art!

Political arguments often stimulated our early morning rehearsal breaks. I believe that labels are meaningless, but Lumpy and I were more liberal than Gus. He was an early admirer of William F. Buckley Jr., as much for his eloquence as his politics. We soon learned not to assume Gus' position on any issue; he often fooled us by taking the opposite stand. He was thoughtful in stating an argument and demonstrated something quite rare today: a respect for opposing views.

Many parents seem to have instructed their children that every conversation is a debate which must have a winner and a loser. That attitude is detrimental for our society and the future. American children must learn that they live in a pluralistic society in which divergent views are possible and merit respect, if not agreement. That is the essence, the magic, of the American system of government. But I am astounded when some people take the position that disagreement is unpatriotic. Last year Senator George Mitchell of Maine eloquently lectured Colonel Oliver North that it was possible for someone to disagree with the Colonel's position on Contra aid and still be just as good and patriotic an American. Our children must come to appreciate that diversity is the strength of this nation and that our form of government gives shelter and protection to diverse views.

In very few places on this earth can citizens agree to disagree. I am fiercely American, devoted to my country, but I know that many fellow Americans disagree with my position on some subjects. That does not make them less American than I. As school children, we had our favorite patriotic quotations. Right behind Patrick Henry's "Give me liberty or give me death" was Voltaire's "I disapprove of what you say, but I will defend to the death your right to say it." Our children would be well served with another quotation from Voltaire, "Liberty of thought is the life of the soul." As I soon learned from our discussions, we may have had different political views, but Gus and I certainly shared a strong belief in the sayings above.

Gus has yet another wonderful quality which enabled him to develop some incredible children's characters: he understands children and their point of view; he does not talk down to them. Seeing the world from a child's perspective is an essential skill when performing for children and one essential to nurturing children, as well.

I have heard child experts suggest that a parent assume a kneeling position and move about a room à la Jose Ferrer playing that very short French painter, Toulouse-Lautrec. But that's not necessary. Becoming sensitive to your child's special and different perspective is what's really important for the adult who wishes to maintain communication with a child or an adolescent. Often a spouse will say, "If only you could see it my way, dear," and we accept that as reasonable. If our spouse has a different way of seeing things and we accept that as his or her right, why can't a child have a different way of looking at something? And should we not try to see things as a child views them?

Much has been said about the generation gap. If the desire exists, however, communication should not be difficult. But some parents *say* they are communicating with their children, when actually they are doing nothing more than *telling* their children what they want them to know. Too often, parents will scold or cut the child off. They do not listen to the child, nor do they solicit ideas about how the child feels. This is dictation, not communication.

Many a parent-child struggle results from the parent's inability to see the situation from the child's perspective. It is necessary to step outside yourself, to put yourself in the small shoes of the child and *empathize*.

Most child experts believe that a youngster who feels understood will be far more accepting of parental authority. But those who feel misunderstood, criticized and ignored become reluctant to discuss a problem with an adult because they begin to believe that adults don't understand. Instead, they only report on the positive things that have happened to them, those things they think their parents *want* to hear about. When children feel they cannot bring problems to a parent, a crisis is brewing.

It is never too early to establish lines of communication with a child, but unfortunately, it can be too late. At fifteen, Mary's eyes are often glassy and she seems disoriented much of the time. Her parents plead, "Mary, dear, what's happening? Talk to us, Mary, talk to us." Why, thinks Mary. You haven't talked to me for a decade and now, because you think I'm into something, you want me to talk to you. Too late, too late.

Parents must talk to and listen to children, and do it whenever the need arises. Communication is not something that can be scheduled like a trip to the supermarket when we run short on food. Communication is an integral part of your daily, on-going relationship. My wife, Jeanne, was always ready to talk to our children, but she was convinced that they saved their questions and problems until the most inappropriate times. About three hours before Thanksgiving dinner, when Jeanne was whirling from refrigerator to sink to stove, one of them would inevitably saunter into the kitchen and say, "Mom, can we talk?"

Whenever Mister Moose said to me, "Captain, can we talk?" I knew what was coming. It mattered not where the conversation started or its subject, the ending was always thousands of Ping-Pong balls upon my head. Children loved this, and years later adults will ask me, with an unrestrained giggle, "Did those Ping-Pong balls hurt?"

Gus continues to do things within many of his characters that might seem uncharacteristic for him. His stern face conceals a complex and multi-faceted human being. Bunny Rabbit is, in some ways, allegorical, and represents the triumph of children over the authority figure. Children are always delighted when the Captain hands over yet another bunch of carrots. Dennis, Mister Bainter the Painter's apprentice, gives Gus the opportunity to be the curious child, the persistent child who *must* ask question after question to find out about the world. The silliness of Mister Moose, knock-knock jokes, bad puns and Ping-Pong balls spring from a hidden aspect of Gus. But Mister Moose was not only hilarious, he was helpful too.

Recently, at one of my lectures, I met a college student who told me he had been a painfully shy child. George remembered being unable to speak to well-known family friends, of blushing, of having difficulty making friends and, as a small boy, of hiding behind his mother's skirts. He remembered being afraid of making mistakes and, worst of all, remembers his mother constantly referring to him as "shy" and admonishing him for this trait. George told me of watching a "Captain Kangaroo" program, with his mother sitting by his side, enjoying her second cup of coffee. Dr. Joyce Brothers was making one of her frequent visits to the program on this particular morning. She would often visit with Mister Moose, who would reveal some problem he was experiencing or some doubt he had. The moose, of course, was a surrogate for children who might be able to identify with the same problem or doubt.

On this program, Mister Moose was telling Dr. Brothers how he sometimes felt shy, and that others would tease him about it. Dr. Brothers talked to him about feeling confident in himself and about the need to try things even if he was afraid of making a mistake. She also said that parents or friends who label a shy child are contributing greatly to the problem. Labels have a sticky side to them; they may not go away, and a label can become a self-fulfilling prophesy.

George's mother had not realized she had used the label so often, and she also had not understood the source of his shyness until that time. She entered into a program of praising her son for trying, even when he made mistakes; she built his self-confidence and stopped labeling him as a shy child. George, now a self-assured, confident young man, was happy to relate this experience from his youth, and I was very happy to hear of the success of our efforts.

We have all smiled, even laughed, at the antics of Snow White's dwarf friend, Bashful, but life is painful for the Bashfuls of this world. Shyness can be addressed in a successful manner, however. In his book, *A Parent's Guide to the Shy Child,* psychologist Philip Zimbardo firmly states that no one is born shy. He feels that shyness can be traced to early childhood experiences and that it can be conquered. Shyness can be turned around to its opposite, he suggests, by reaching out and showing concern for others. He urges shy people to go out of their way to make *others* feel comfortable and welcome.

It is well known that many actors turned to their profession to overcome shyness. The opportunity acting affords to become another person often provides welcome relief to this personality problem. Dr. Zimbardo believes that major elements in shyness are lack of self-esteem and a fear of failure. He urges parents to love their children unconditionally, without strings. In that way, a child will build self-confidence and will not be afraid to try something new. Praising a child, if only for trying, is a powerful antidote to shyness. There is an old Irish proverb, "Praise a boy and he will prosper." The Irish also know that the proverb works just as well for girls.

Gus is very thoughtful about his characters. He makes an important point, saying, "Dennis is ignorant, but not stupid." Dennis asks the Captain the kinds of questions a child would ask, disarming, well-meant questions. Dennis will say, "Captain, why does the turtle live in his own house? Every time I go near him, he goes inside." This ad-lib question set me up for an explanation about the turtle's shell.

Adults tend to forget that children are intelligent; they just have not lived as long as we adults have, and, therefore, they lack the experience and fund of knowledge that we have acquired through living. It is also true that children and adults who are in some way handicapped suffer from others' incorrect assumptions. Many such people are intelligent but, because of their handicap, are unable to communicate in conventional ways. This leads many people to assume that they lack intelligence. For example, people whose hearing is severely impaired from an early age rarely speak well; they have never heard speech to imitate. In another age, the hearing impaired were routinely referred to as "deaf and dumb," and, by inference, without intelligence. My nephew, Derry, has been severely hearing impaired since birth. Now in his forties, Derry is a college graduate who earned his master's degree and teaches the hearing impaired. I think he is more intelligent than I am, and I certainly wouldn't want to put it to the test.

Often, television executives seem to forget that children are intelligent. Children's television, particularly at the local level, suffers from poor production standards, because many television executives think that children will not know the difference. Typically, a local show might be created by management not to meet the needs of the children in the community but to meet the economic needs of the television station, especially when a local advertiser may have expressed an interest in sponsoring a children's program. In past years, a station manager might have asked a staff announcer to put on a clown suit or a policeman's uniform or a fireman's hat and do commercials between cartoons. The receptionist was often given the task of writing the program. It was not considered necessary to hire professional writers or performers with experience and knowledge in children's television. "The kids won't know the difference," was usually the attitude of the management.

For several years, we conducted a workshop on children's television for local producers, writers, performers and management. We preached our philosophy about the importance of meeting the needs of children and, using our production people and the personnel of CBS, we attempted to give local people some tools to help them serve the young people of their community. In talking to these people, I was always amazed at the different and *indifferent* attitudes toward children's programming expressed by local management. Now, with the deregulation of television, and the fact that a station's record of community service is not reviewed at the time of license renewal, there are very few local programs for children other than those designed to meet a station's economic need. Sad for our children. Sad for our communities.

Young people do know the difference between a good performance and a shoddy one. They are captivated by good writing, production standards which are high, a good set, and creative costuming. When we began "Captain Kangaroo" in 1955 we stated our aims in a simple equation—children are intelligent and we would cater to that intelligence; and children are of potentially good taste and it is incumbent on us to help develop that good taste. Parents who develop the intellectual, emotional *and* cultural faculties of a child are nurturing a complete human being. That is what the Captain's crew and our hundreds of associates in the world of arts and entertainment have been attempting through the years. Many of you, now adults, have told us it worked. We thank you.

Of course, I've had a lot of help on Captain Kangaroo's crusade. Geraldine Fitzgerald was the nicest penguin I've ever seen. Joan Rivers was the "Pickle Lady" on a quest for the perfect pickle. Celeste Holm was Mother Goose in search of a new home for all her fairy tale children. She had heard that the Captain's house was for sale. It was an ugly rumor, but who could turn Mother Goose away?

Gwen Verdon brought us her cat. Jack Gilford brought us vaudeville whenever he appeared as "Doctor, Doctor." And Edward Villela brought us dance. But he wasn't the only one. Pearl Bailey taught the Captain to dance on one show, while on another, Dancing Bear gave a few pointers to Andrea McArdle. Then Debbie Allen appeared as—what else?—a dancing teacher.

Carol Channing once joined us for a show at Opryland to play the charming wife of the mayor. Carol fascinated us off-camera, also, as she daintily ate a lunch of cold leg of lamb that she had brought to Nashville from New York. Arte Johnson, a frequent visitor, played the title role in a delightful tale, "The Emperor Finds a Son." Lucie Arnaz was the lady sheriff Marshal Max, while Andy Griffith played another delightful sheriff in the wild West setting of Knott's Berry Farm. For Loretta Swit, "Captain Kangaroo" was her first television show before going on to her "Hot Lips" smash on "M*a*s*h."

Hundreds of the great performers from show business have appeared on "Captain Kangaroo" in the last thirty years. During the sixties and seventies, many stars sought a guest appearance. We treated people very well, and our talented writers provided them with fine material that was fun to perform. Rarely does a performer have the opportunity to reach children in an intelligent and sensitive setting. "Captain" provided that setting.

Often, one of these great performers would teach us a lesson. For Eli Wallach, the writers had devised a character called "Trader Eli," a collector of old things. The rest of the world might refer to him as a junkman, but Trader Eli would not hear of it. He had a high regard for the items in his collection; he would find new uses for an old wheel, a tire, an old and bent tray; an electric lamp that no longer gave light gave Trader Eli joy. This was a subtle lesson in recycling. Eli played the character with the same intensity he brought to great roles on Broadway, a reminder to us all that our audience of children were deserving of the best performance in us.

Eli appeared on the show often, until one day he sadly told us he could no longer visit us, that his wife had forbidden it. Anne Jackson was at first curious and then jealous of the pleasure he was finding in the show. "How come I'm never invited?" she asked. With great pleasure we extended an invitation, and another fine performer reached our special audience.

Occasionally the script would call for a chicken to be played by someone wearing our uncomfortable chicken costume. Gus Allegretti hated the costume and he would always protest that it must be somebody else's turn. He got his way when the great soprano, diva Roberta Peters of the Metropolitan Opera, was scheduled to appear. The writer of that show, to my consternation, wrote Roberta Peters into the script playing a chicken in the infamous chicken suit! It was a day I thought seriously of staying home, but I made my way to the studio, ready to tell Roberta that I fully understood her reluctance to appear in a chicken suit and that I was prepared to ad-lib a different show with her. As I entered the studio, I saw the great soprano encased in the chicken suit with only her face showing. She was beaming, flapping her wings and gaily singing, "Isn't this fun, chirp, chirp, isn't this fun, chirp, chirp?" The great lady gave a fine performance and set a good example for us all.

One of the most popular regular characters on "Captain Kangaroo" is the Dancing Bear. There has been speculation and rumor about who is "inside the bear." To this day Jeanne Keeshan will say to an insistent stranger, "I'm sorry, you're wrong. I am not the Dancing Bear." The stranger often corrects her, "But I read it in the paper."

We made a record album a few years after the show went on the air with a song about a dancing bear. We tried to think how we could provide an interesting video production of the record, and one writer said, "How about we get this big bear suit and . . ." All eyes in the room turned to Gus.

After some genuine resistance, Gus agreed to try it. The suit was fashioned, Gus climbed in and performed to "The Dancing Bear." That was nice, we all said, and forgot about it. Then the postman rang once, then twice, then once again, and the mail poured in. People loved that bear. More songs and some skits were written for him, and Gus found himself with another hot character, in this case, literally. It is very warm in that bear suit. Try it. You won't like it.

In the riddle at the beginning of this chapter, I refer to Gus as an etymologist. Gus has a fascination for words, their meaning, history and appropriate use. It is an interest that goes beyond the *New York Times'*

Sunday crossword puzzle, though he is very good at that. It is really a reverence; Gus values words and language and is offended when they are misused. This is something else we share.

In the early eighties I did a daily three-minute radio show on the CBS Radio Network called, "The Subject Is Young People." It was about young people but was directed to adults. One of the eight hundred programs we did in a three-year period was about language and the epidemic of "ya knowism" running rampant in the land.

I started by saying, "Many people are showing concern, ya know, for the way young people, ya know, are misusing, ya know, or not using, ya know, the English language, ya know?"

I pointed out that in virtually every interview with a sports figure, especially after a great victory on field or court, the speech was buried in "ya knows." I apologized if I seemed dull or stuffy. "But nothing could be more dull than a string of "ya knows" surrounding and smothering whatever meaning the speaker is attempting to convey.

"Our language is what distinguishes us from other earthly creatures. If we do not communicate with precision we will become linguistically impotent and without power of invention and creativity. We will uninvent the wheel and abandon fire. A 'ya know' is dangerously close to an animal grunt."

We have an obligation to our young people to pass on the true heritage of language. Even in this day of television, a visually oriented generation will find that precise communication skills are the foundation for accomplishment. Every word in our language, like every human being on earth, is unique and deserves the respect accorded uniqueness.

Ya know?

Chapter 18
Bow-Wow, Tweet Tweet
and Roar Roar

At some point, almost every child approaches his or her parents with an urgent plea for a pet. Thinking of the expense and effort, parents may refuse, believing that this fascination with animals will fade soon and the child will go on to something else. But what parents may not know is that such a request also demonstrates the child's desire to give love and affection to something dependent. These are powerful feelings for a young child. Because a pet is one of the few things that truly *needs* a child's attention, taking care of one fosters responsibility and a generous spirit. And generosity is, I believe, one of the most important attributes to develop in a young person.

Many parents consistently warn children that others are trying to take advantage of them or misuse them. As a result, a child can become suspicious of everyone, friends as well as strangers. This makes the development of a generous spirit virtually impossible. To be a kind and caring human being, respectful of the needs and rights of others, requires generosity. It is quite the opposite of the "me first" attitude which has burdened so many adults and made them unable to enjoy the benefits which accrue from being thoughtful, considerate and kind in close relationships. Trust and love and benevolence are all rooted in generosity, and a child who learns this can look forward to happiness.

Whether or not to get a pet can be a difficult decision for a parent because so much emotion is involved. A child should be old enough to understand the responsibility involved in caring for the pet and emotionally mature enough to keep the pact. Deciding on the kind of pet has much to do with family circumstances. It is not considerate to leave a puppy alone for eight or ten hours a day, so a puppy may be inappropriate in many contemporary homes, single-parent households or two-parent working households. While this may be so, instead of abandoning the idea, consider hamsters, fish and parakeets.

My daughter Laurie loves cats. She acquired her first kitten at a birthday party for five-year-olds, and appropriately named it "Happy Party Debbie." (Guess whose birthday party it was?) Her love through her older years was a beautiful long-haired white gem of a cat called Snowflake. That cat had great affection for Laurie and would fall asleep in her arms. In law school, she acquired a cat which she named after the degree she was pursuing, J.D.

My son Michael likes cats but, as a parent, has been tested by a cat his boys love. As a kitten, Eleazer constantly soiled the house and was the object of Michael's great unhappiness. His son, Britton, then six, telephoned his grandmother, Jeanne, and tearfully appealed, "Gama, can Eleazer come live at your house? Cats get treated better there."

Most children would do anything for animals. The appeal of animals for children seems to be natural, and has been proven by the success of animal television shows and movies. Lassie, for example, has been loved by generations of children, first in the movies, then on television. In my childhood, the movie serials were very popular. In each serial, cowboys, detectives, or space heroes would appear in a "to be continued" story ten to twenty minutes long. We would sit in the movie house for two hours or more on Saturday mornings as a string of these serials were flashed on the big screen. I remember clearly that the ones that always got the best cheers and screams from the kids around me were those featuring Rin Tin Tin, that fabulous German shepherd, who could rescue a child dangling over a waterfall on his way to herding the bad guys into the hands of the grateful waiting police. From *Benji* to *National Velvet,* children have loved animal stories.

On my local noontime clown show, Corny's dog, the sandwich-stealing Pudgy, was very popular with the audience. From time to time we had other animals come to the park and meet the children. On "Tinker's Workshop" animals appeared even more often. Tinker had a macaque, the type of monkey which, in the early part of this century, accompanied the organ grinder and held his cap out for coins. In planning "Captain Kangaroo," we knew the appeal of animals and planned to make them an important part of the program.

One of our goals on "Captain Kangaroo" was to teach children about animals, from pets to wild creatures. In the days before we took mobile tape units to zoos and other animal habitats, most of the animals on the show were found and "auditioned" by Ruth Manecke. More than two thousand varieties have appeared on the program, most of which were handled on the air by Lumpy. We had very little trouble with any of them, although it was possible to see birds still flying in the rafters of the studio days after they had appeared.

We never forced an animal to perform or do anything that was not part of its natural behavior. Of course, this meant that the animals did mostly what *they* wanted to do—and this led to some scratches and bites for Lumpy and me, as well as some interesting moments. On one occasion, Lumpy stood completely still while a young python methodically wrapped himself around the farmer's body. As Lumpy quietly, and in great detail, told the children about the snake, its Burmese habitat and its propensity for crushing its victims, I watched off-camera in fascination. Lumpy calmly continued to explain and the python calmly continued to wrap, around and around and around. When Lumpy's voice seemed to be constricted, I knew I had to act. Absent the Greek Apollo to slay the serpent, I casually walked on set and began to unwrap the python from around Lumpy's body. It was not easy for me because I was quite put off by the reptile, but I pressed on, only to have the python let go of Lumpy and begin to wrap itself around me! This is the place where a show usually goes to a commercial. We did.

Lumpy had great compassion for the animals. On the Saturday morning show we once had an old vaudeville animal act in which a dachshund would jump from a tub onto a seesaw, causing a rubber frankfurter to sail through the air. Opposite the seesaw was a second dachshund sitting atop a ladder. As the frankfurter sailed into the air, it would pass the ladder and the second dachshund would catch it in its mouth. The dogs were quite old, as was their trainer, and we dispensed with the usual rehearsal. Our director, Peter Birch, set the camera shots for air and we allowed the animals to rest. But what we didn't know hurt us.

On air the first dachshund jumped upon the seesaw and the frankfurter flew toward the top of the ladder. Peter cut to a tight shot of the dog on the ladder just in time to see it duck as the frankfurter flew, untouched, through the close shot. This was repeated several times while everyone in the studio laughed hysterically at the ducking dachshund. What we had not known was that the old dogs were without teeth and had sore gums. It *hurt* the poor canine to catch that frank, and it was ducking to avoid the pain. When we found out, Lumpy was outraged, and, of course, he was right.

As you can see, things can easily go wrong when animals are around. Fortunately for all of us at "Captain Kangaroo," we had Ruth Manecke to remind us that these were wild animals.

I first met Ruth in 1953 when I had just started "Time for Fun." It was Ruth who was responsible for some of the live animals we had on "Time for Fun" and "Tinker's Workshop." Ruth had grown up with her own private little zoo on the grounds of her childhood home. She'd always loved animals and learned to train them and rear them at an early age. In college, she majored in zoology, then took a job in the education department of the Bronx Zoo when she graduated. Just about the time I started working for WABC-TV, Ruth was doing her own show for the station called "Animal Fun Time," which ran every weekday opposite "Howdy Doody." Through her numerous contacts in the business, Ruth had access to all sorts of interesting and exotic creatures. I decided to invite her on "Time for Fun" as a guest, and she appeared on that show many times as Miss Ruth, the Pet Shop Lady.

Later, on "Tinker's Workshop" and then on "Captain Kangaroo," Ruth brought animals on but didn't appear on camera. Instead, she prepped me or Lumpy carefully, told us everything about animals, what to do, what *not* to do and said, over and over again, "Remember: these are wild animals. They are *tamed* but not *trained*."

Once Ruth arranged for a seal to be our visitor. I was inside my Treasure House telling the boys and girls that Mister Green Jeans had an interesting animal in the garden. I started to walk to the garden when I was given a frantic signal by the stage manager to "pad," delay my move, something was wrong. I swung into a riddle game. "What kind of animal claps and goes, awrrh, awrrh? Can you guess?" Then I started to walk. No! Not yet, signaled the stage manager. "An elephant, you say? Noooo. An elephant doesn't clap. Think. You know. Let's go see." NO! Now frantic, the stage manager was dancing. "Who said duck? No, a duck doesn't clap and he goes quack, quack, not awrrh, awrrh. Let's look."

This time, there was no stopping me. I opened the door to the garden just in time to see a black seal whirl by me and around and beside the set, followed by Mister Green Jeans. "Yes, I said, a seal, that's the answer. Could you see him? He'll be back." And he was, in another flash, whizzing by me on flippers and tail, with Mister Green Jeans in pursuit. I fell into the garden rocking chair, my professionalism vanished, in hysterical laughter.

"Here he comes again," I laughed. Whoosh! He came and went, followed by Mister Green Jeans and this time by his off-camera trainer, now on camera. "And look," I said, "Mister Green Jeans is being helped by Mister Barton the Bus Driver!" We never did get a good look at the seal, but we had created a new character for the show, Mister Barton, the Bus Driver.

Our producer, Al Hyslop, recently reminded me that the seal had been awaiting its entrance in the Gents bathroom, and the soap opera stars who had their studio on the same floor were not too pleased. I guess they never worked vaudeville.

As funny as that incident was, I hate to see things go wrong on the show. It destroys illusions, and is never as amusing to those at home as to those in the studio. Today, such things continue to happen: animals run amok, stagehands walk across camera, cameras are out of focus, actors and actresses forget lyrics or lines. But with tape, we are able to stop and start again, saving our audience and our self-respect. On "Captain Kangaroo" we deal in illusions, live in a special world, a place of fairy tales and special fun. Some children are jolted into reality by adults who cannot abide the world of the imagination. We like to preserve illusions which, all too early, fade away.

Lumpy and I hope that the introduction of many animals to our audience has engendered a love, even a compassion, for animals. Many of the animals who appear on our program are in big trouble. Gorillas, orangutans, tigers, and birds are being pushed by humans from their natural habitat; others are being poisoned into extinction by people's inconsiderate use of chemicals. We are shocked at the thought of chemical warfare, yet we have carried on our own chemical warfare, all too successfully, against nature.

There is hope, however, and if programs of protection and regeneration continue, the planet may be a safe place, after all, for some of the world's wild creatures. Adults can help directly in these efforts to develop a respect for animals by talking to their children, even very young children. If the next generation is more considerate than those past, there is hope for our world.

Programs to regenerate the California condor and the peregrine falcon have brought encouraging results, for example. And zoological parks have been making significant contributions. The outstanding San Diego Wild Animal Farm does wonderful work. Many other such places are also helping in the fight to preserve endangered animals.

The Bengal tiger, a magnificent creature, is being pushed from his natural Asian habitat by the intrusion of humans. But zoologist Peter Gross is only one of several successful breeders of the Bengal in captivity. We once taped a large litter of Bengals bred by Peter, and then went on to tape the Bengal in other situations. One such taping resulted in one of my favorite songs, composed originally for "Captain Kangaroo." In the scene I'm in a long boat, powered by an outboard motor, skimming along the surface of a lake. I am seated in the stern, steering the boat in a wide circle. Forward of me in the small boat is an enormous Bengal tiger, looking much like a huge bowsprit as he put his nose high into the wind. The song?

"Me and My Pussy Cat," of course.

Chapter 19
Boys and Girls—Girls and Boys

Not too long after "Captain Kangaroo" went on the air in 1955, someone pointed out that all the live characters on the show were male. This was before the women's movement, and most men were not sensitive to such things. I *was* sensitive, and aware that we had no female role models. But the presence of two strong males, Mister Green Jeans and Captain, was quite deliberate.

In the present generation of parents, fathers often take a day-to-day role in the nurturing of infants and small children. Many men are also in the ranks of preschool and early childhood educators, though women still predominate. In my generation, however, this was not as common. When the Captain first went on the air, almost no men were teachers of young children. And almost every other program for very young children, from "Ding Dong School" on NBC to the local kindergarten programs, was presided over by a female. A father working outside the home and mother working in the kitchen and caring for the kids was the predominant family structure. For very young children, strong male models were few. The casting of Gus and Lumpy and me in the show was to fill specific roles—the farmer (Mr. Outside), the Captain (Mr. Inside), Grandfather Clock and a bunny—and I felt they balanced the lack of strong male role models in the lives of young females and males.

"Snips and snails and puppy dogs' tails, that's what little boys are made of." I remember hearing that rhyme when I was very young and attempting to make sense of it. Like so many young children, I accepted the words literally and attempted to search for the snails and puppy dogs' tails within me, which led only to a juvenile confusion.

Boys of my generation were prohibited from openly expressing feelings. "Men don't cry," was a commonly used expression. It was okay for my sister to cry because she was of the "weaker sex," but certainly crying or otherwise displaying emotions was a weakness not permitted to men.

I don't know what happened to me between then and now, but today I'm a sucker for tears. I can cry when moved by a well-written line read well, at a good movie when the hero or heroine dies, when my children or grandchildren make me proud, on almost any emotional occasion. I'm often given to tear-filled eyes and I certainly don't view the condition as a sign of weakness.

According to Dale Carlson, author of *Boys Have Feelings Too,* boys grow up with the freedom to function, but never the freedom *not* to function. Ms. Carlson outlines the modes of behavior expected of boys, explains how their feelings are shaped, and talks of the pressure that may result by following such prescribed roles.

In our culture, boys have always been expected to be successful, strong, capable and unafraid. These are fine aspirations, but they can be hazardous when a young man is out of touch with his own feelings and desires. What his world expects of him may not be what he wants for himself. We all know that achievement without satisfaction can be both meaningless and dangerous to our mental health.

The male-female conditioning process starts at an early age, and on "Captain Kangaroo" we attempted, from the beginning, to address the issue. As common as they were in 1955, we never used phrases such as "boys don't cry," or "act like a man." Such expressions have been part of the culture for generations, but adults would do well not to use them in dealing with children. We may say them in a casual manner, but a child will find them a new experience and will look for their meaning, one we probably do not mean to impart.

Consider the case of a young child who has a feeling toward water quite common to youngsters—fear. A father, in attempting to teach his son to swim, may fail to be sensitive to this fear and adopt a firm attitude toward the boy's reluctance to follow instructions. "Come on, any son of mine will love it." Clinging to the side of the pool and overcome with fear, the boy may begin to cry, only to be told, "Oh, stop it. Crying is for sissies!"

Now, the child's fear of the water is compounded by shame. He has let down his hero, his father, and he cries even harder. At four years of age, the child has had his manliness put to the test and found wanting. Such a swimming lesson may have unexpected and long-lasting negative results.

When I was a child of six, I went to camp in the Catskill Mountains, a place of great beauty. My brothers had been campers at Camp Acadia and, by the time of my arrival, were senior counselors. Every young camper soon learned how to swim. I was certain I would, also, in good time. I had absolutely no fear of the water, but the lake was so cold I was not enthusiastic about getting wet. After a few weeks of this, my big brothers became impatient. Taking me to the end of the dock, Jack took my left arm and leg, Bill, my right. Swinging me back and forth as I giggled, they let go and propelled me twenty feet off the end of the dock. I hit the cold water and sank; my forty inches were covered in seven feet of water. I rose to the surface, sputtering and screaming. I'm certain it was less than a minute that I struggled to remain on top, but it seemed like forever. Jack and Bill dove in and pulled me to the dock, in disgust. I had failed them, I felt ashamed, and I developed a fear of water that I did not overcome until I was more than thirty years of age. I was, to my knowledge, the only World War II Marine, out of over five hundred thousand, who failed the swimming test. The instructors gave up on me and falsified the records in their frustration. Please don't tell the Commandant; I'm not certain the statute of limitations has lapsed.

When I was thirty-three years of age, we built a swimming pool for our children, and at night, out of their sight, I slowly overcame my fear and taught myself to swim. I am now a strong swimmer and a lover of the water, but I missed many years of pleasure as I lived with a fear born in a cold Catskill lake.

Many parents, particularly fathers, feel reassured when their children display traditional male/female attributes. A girl hugging a doll, or a boy playing a war game, seems to contribute to the security of some parents. Actually, it is the insecurity of many parents that makes them yearn for traditional role-playing in children. A boy playing with a doll can send shivers through some parents. I think this play is great. A young male displaying and learning nurturing skills is a good sign; here is a young man preparing to be a modern father. Parents' insecurity about their son's masculinity is a *parental* weakness. A young girl with a good hook shot beating her brothers to the hoop is okay, too. Magic Johnson wouldn't feel threatened; parents shouldn't either.

My son Michael would often join his sisters in play in their great backyard playhouse. Today, he is a warm and wonderful father. He must have picked up some of his many nurturing skills in the play of his childhood. Britton and Connor are fortunate to have such a fine father and terrific mother. Watching Michael and his wife, Lynn, with their children is one of those things that can moisten my eyes. I am very fortunate.

My daughter Laurie liked dolls, but she was a Davy Crockett for a while, too. I wonder if she still has her coonskin cap, which she often wore with the tail in front, over her eyes. It was rumored that there were some neighborhood boys who were in love with her and terrified of her, as well. I can understand that; she was very lovable, but she also had a mean right hand. As a teenager, Laurie was very competitive on the tennis court and in the classroom. If you wanted Laurie to do something, you only had to tell her she was incapable of it; it would only be a matter of time before she had done it. Forty years ago law schools had quotas for admitting females. Laurie did not face discrimination and good thing, too, for the law schools of the land. She would not have accepted it. She took her law background to broadcast journalism, and her show garnered an Emmy, at a younger age than her father was when he won his first "lady." When I see Laurie and her husband, John, nurturing their daughter and son, I can get emotional, too.

My youngest, Maeve, was her daddy's very best friend. She followed in my footsteps as a toddler and smiled a lot. She was a big player with dolls and more relaxed about each day than her sister. But when Maeve wanted something, she could not be stopped. She liked to sail but, during race week, I always thought she had her eye on more than the finish line. That showed in the scoring, but she certainly was social, and very happy. Maeve and Hans have two great sons in Derek and Alex. I get teary over them, too.

My children's childhood was pretty relaxed. Jeanne and I expected them to do things well, but we never asked the impossible. In my generation, families often gave greater financial and emotional support to the boys of the family and then helped girls with whatever resources were left. My girls always knew they were on an equal footing with their brother; we never made much of it, but they knew from the beginning that they could pursue any path, traditional or nontraditional, with our support.

Neither Jeanne nor I came from families where women were expected to follow traditional paths. We had limited economic resources in my family, but my sister, Catherine, knew she could pursue any educational or career route. Jeanne was an only child from a family that encouraged her best performance, and there was never any question of her not going to college. Even when she earned her college degree and decided to marry an actor, her family did not stand in her way. Now, that's being open-minded and supportive!

It might be valuable for parents to do a survey of their own "stereotyping index." A discussion between parents may turn up some attitudes which can lead to developmental obstacles for children. Candor is appropriate here; after all, we are not responsible for attitudes acquired in the past. But we are responsible for how we address those attitudes in the present and how they affect our children in the future.

In the early years of the "Captain Kangaroo" program, we were sensitive to stereotypes at a time when that did not seem very important. Times were changing, and it was obvious that the American family was undergoing change. Family structure could no longer be thought of in traditional ways. Mother could not be viewed traditionally, either. For the first time since the end of the War, mothers in large numbers were leaving home to go to work. Children of such mothers, watching the program, would be made to feel different if we addressed Mother only in her traditional role. We made it clear to all children that mothers can assume different roles, and that a mother who worked outside the home was not less of a mother.

I can remember a song often used about mothers, in which we portrayed the many roles they were assuming. We showed Mother as a mother, as well as a nurse, physician, lawyer, businesswoman, office worker, crane operator, telephone line worker, police officer, firefighter, and railroad worker. Today, women are common in all these occupations; in those days such activities were not as common. "After all," we said, "that pole worker may be somebody's mother."

It was surprising to me then, when we received some letters from traditional mothers showing resentment of our support for mothers in nontraditional roles. But we also received many letters from mothers and fathers thanking us for helping to broaden the attitudes of children toward these activities.

It is through language that we often display stereotyping attitudes; and it is through language that many parents destroy their children with emotional abuse. As I previously mentioned, I am a director of the National Committee for the Prevention of Child Abuse, an organization that has caused significant change in the attitudes toward child abuse in this nation. The media gives coverage to the many cases of sexual abuse and nonsexual physical abuse of children. This attention helps educate the adult community and, along with the many legal changes of the last decade, helps prevent the abuse of children. Another form of child abuse exists, however, that is less well-known by adults and often not recognized as abuse by the community. This abuse is emotional abuse. No bones are broken, no bruises raised, but a child can be crippled by emotional abuse, and the results may bring a lifetime of failure and misery.

Many parents engage in emotional abuse as a style of parenting, unaware of the immense damage they cause a child. Emotional abuse is often verbal: "You dumb kid. Put that down, you know you'll only break it." I have no confidence in you, says this message. "You call that a report card? You idiot. You're not my son. I wish I had never seen your dumb face. I'm ashamed of you!" This is personal degradation. The child's problems in school are not addressed; his lack of value is the subject, and the contempt of his parent for him is openly expressed.

A parent might say, "Mary, you are home late. Could you please explain why?" This is reasonable and addresses the issue of Mary's lateness. But an emotionally abusing parent will say, "Hey, stupid, look at the clock. Can't you tell time? No, I guess not. You can't do anything right, can you? You dumb jerk!"

Many parents emotionally abuse their children casually and routinely, unaware of the immense damage they are causing. The bedrock upon which we build an emotionally stable child is high self-esteem. But in this abusive style of parenting, the child is denigrated by the most important person in his young life, the parent. If Dad says so, it must be so; I am stupid, I am bungling, I am incapable of accomplishment, I am of no value. Dad says so. It must be true.

A companion to emotional abuse is emotional neglect. A child, like any human being, needs signs of love and respect. A parent may not be overt in emotionally abusing a child but may withhold signs of affection. This is often a result of the lack of affection the parent experienced in his or her own childhood. Such people have been emotionally crippled. A child quite naturally feels the need for expressions of love, touching, holding, hugging, patting, kissing, but when such physical signs are withheld, the child feels deprived and neglected. Recent clinical studies have shown that withholding physical affection from infants may result in emotional damage at that early age, restricting healthy emotional development.

Emotional abuse and neglect may be the most dangerous forms of child abuse because they are so difficult to identify and, therefore, often go undetected and untreated. Unlike the physical abuse of children which usually shows in bruises and broken bones in the hospital emergency room, emotional abuse and neglect can simmer in darkness for years. By the time the results show in a child—the failure to achieve, withdrawal, a complete lack of confidence—it may be too late to treat and overcome.

A great tragedy of emotional abuse and neglect is the lack of awareness on the part of the parent. Parents who beat their children are aware of the damage they are doing. Parents who denigrate their children, withhold love and neglect their children's basic need for affection, are usually unaware of their failure and the implications of their words and actions. They may only be repeating what their parents did to them.

Every parental action, every parental word weighs heavily with a child. That is why the language of sexual stereotyping, even casually spoken, can have a serious and lasting effect. That is why the language of denigration can destroy a child's confidence and self-esteem, leading to a lifetime of unhappiness. That is why parent power should take the form of "Hey, I like you, you're okay." "Don't worry about it. Give it another try. You can do it." "Did I remember to tell you I love you?" That language of parent power will make a child bloom, and bloom prettier than the most beautiful hothouse orchid.

Chapter 20
Our Rose of Texas

It was Gus who knew her best. He would spend hours in the studio, patiently listening to her tell of joy, tell of sadness. He remembers, as we all do, her great talent and her sweet, sweet nature. Her name was Debby Weems. She was a young and vivacious performer who had made her way from Texas to the lights of Broadway. When our producers saw her in *Godspell,* she was invited to perform as a guest and ended up staying on as a member of our family in 1973.

We had been looking for a young woman to join our cast and Debby seemed a natural from her first visit. She had a poignant voice which came as much from her soul as from her vocal chords. She played herself, as well as dramatic and comedy characters, in various skits. There was a childlike quality to her that was not acting; she genuinely adored her moose and rabbit costars. When she giggled at Mr. Moose's ad-lib jokes, it was an eighteen-carat giggle, warming and charming.

It is not an easy thing to join a group of actors who have been working together for almost two decades and become part of the family right off, but Debby was able to do it. We embraced her completely, for she had earned our love and our respect. Her off-camera personality was gentle and loving. But she also had a quiet side that turned out to be darker than the darkest night. When, on Washington's Birthday in 1978, she threw herself out a window to her death, something died in all of us.

People say that time heals all wounds, but I don't believe it. More than a decade later, I feel an ache when I think of Debby and the mystery of her tragedy. I have been left with a question as common as the tragedy of suicide—why?

We associate youth with freedom, a time unfettered by the onerous

The Captain and a lamb, enjoying the sunshine in the Treasure House Garden. *(CBS, Bob Stahman)*

The Captain, Mr. Green Jeans, Bunny Rabbit, and Mr. Moose in 1959.

Bunny Rabbit doing what he does best—tricking the Captain out of another carrot. (CBS, Jerry Urgo)

Mr. Pennywhistle and
Bernard.
(*CBS Photography*)

More than two thousand
varieties of animals, most
of which were handled
on-air by Mr. Green Jeans,
have appeared on the
program.
(*CBS, Bill Warnecke*)

Lumpy Brannum as a clown and the Professor.   *(CBS Photography)*

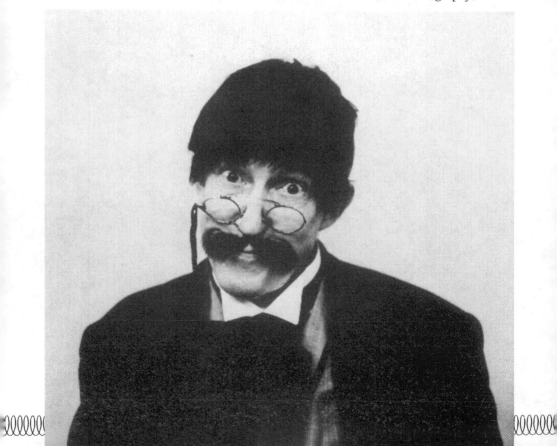

Cosmo "Gus" Allegretti gave life to many characters, including Mr. Moose and Bunny Rabbit. But his "hottest" was the Dancing Bear. (*CBS Photography*)

Introducing a lion cub to Bunny Rabbit. *(CBS, Mario Ruiz)*

The children in our audience join Captain Kangaroo and Mr. Moose in learning a language.   *(CBS, Ira Lewis)*

The Captain is once again showered with Ping-Pong balls. Some things never change.   *(CBS, Karen Epstein)*

aspects of the workplace and untouched by the heavy responsibilities associated with maturity. Youth is joy, youth is delight, youth is vigorous, fresh, vital. We think of youth as a time of supreme optimism, a time to anticipate and revel in the joy of living. Yet too many of our young people are shrouded in a darkness that smothers optimism and takes away their choices, until only one is left, the decision to take their own lives. Suicide is the third leading cause of death among people between the ages of fifteen and nineteen. More young women than men make the attempt, but males are more successful, mostly because they usually choose more violent methods, such as guns, while women usually choose ways that are more reversible, such as sleeping pills.

Like many other young women, Debby was troubled. Apparently, she was despondent over a recently failed love affair. Not enough reason, it seemed to us, to explain why she had taken her own life. She had everything to live for, it seemed, but obviously we were not seeing all of her. There was more to it, but what?

Debby had suffered more than we had known. She had gone for help and had been institutionalized for a number of months during a period when we weren't taping. On a trip home one weekend she had made the final and irreversible decision.

Afterwards, we blamed ourselves for not having done more; we could have been more attentive, we could have helped to prevent the tragedy, we thought. I recalled the times Debby asked me how she was doing, whether I thought her work was good. She had to be kidding, I remembered thinking. She has to *know* how great a performer she is. So, as is my nature, I usually teased her about her questions. I just didn't know that she was serious, that she really needed to hear what I felt, because she was not self-confident enough to know that she was doing a great job. I should have recognized that need and stroked her now and again.

Something must have gone terribly awry in Debby's childhood and created a tragic flaw in the development of her personality. She must not have felt worthy; she must not have felt loved enough. Like everyone else, children need to feel good about themselves, to feel in control, in order to handle the daily crises involved in being alive. Rarely do adults think of children as feeling in crisis. Surely, these children cannot be facing problems of any consequence, we say. We don't take seriously the seemingly petty problems they wrestle with but, to them, there is nothing petty about the issues they face.

Children and adolescents need to know they are loved not solely for what they accomplish, but because they are trying to accomplish it. It is, once again, a question of emotional nurturing or abuse. "Mary you're home late. Could you please explain why?" This is a reasonable way to address the issue of lateness, and a stable adolescent will be able to handle such questions. But the denigrating abuse which is found in, "Hey, stupid, look at the clock. Can't you tell time? No, I guess not. You can't do anything right, can you. You dumb jerk!" is difficult for the most stable adolescent to accept. Children and adolescents should be criticized for their *actions,* but not for themselves. The personal denigration of a child is the path to tragedy and, perhaps, to the ultimate tragedy, suicide.

By the time Debby entered the tumultuous and difficult teen years, it is likely that the foundation had been laid for the path her life would take. Even if Debby's life had not ended in this way, there was, sadly, little anyone could do who knew her toward the end of her life to compensate for the deprivations she had suffered earlier in life.

In *The Family Book of Adolescence,* Dr. John Schowalter and Walter Anyan conclude that two recent changes in the way we live have contributed to the reasons some young people might opt for dying. First, there is the abuse of drugs and alcohol. These substances can alter perception and deepen an existing depression; the world can appear gloomier and grayer through a drug or alcoholic haze. Second, there are the great changes in family structure and in family life. After witnessing the hostility and pain of divorce and separation, for example, many children are growing up in single-parent homes. Usually, there is cruelty between parents during a divorce and after the fact. If parents seem cruel, couldn't the whole world be filled with such animosity? It is estimated that at least one third of all adolescent suicides are children of broken homes. With so many of our children residing in such homes, this is not a comforting statistic.

In addition to drug abuse and family instability, other environmental variables can trigger depression—unrealistically high parental expectations, a lack of acceptance by peers, and poor academic performance. Heredity may also be a factor.

Parents and other adults perform an important function when they serve as listeners, observing children and adolescents for signs of emotional difficulty. We are a very busy society and often we do not have time for children. We expect them to function independently of our lives, not to intrude upon our limited time. A parent with this attitude may well miss important signs of emotional disturbance.

Withdrawal, a drop in school performance, a sudden involvement with drugs or alcohol, a rejection of friends, a desire to give away prized possessions, and talk of joining a dead loved one, are all important warning signals of emotional problems. Sometimes a depressed child may hide behind a show of aggression by being belligerent and argumentative or perhaps by getting in trouble with the law. Overeating or strenuous dieting, psychosomatic complaints such as stomachaches and headaches are also common red flags. In retrospect, many parents have said, "It was almost as though my child was shouting to me, 'Help! Help!' and I was too busy to hear the plea." None of these symptoms should ever be ignored or taken lightly. It is a myth that people who talk of suicide don't really mean it.

In the last decade we have become increasingly aware of the danger of teen suicide. In most communities there are counseling services available to parents and teens who are suffering from emotional problems. Parents and other adults familiar with a troubled child should never ignore adolescent problems. It is far better to be safe and seek professional assistance than to be sorry if a tragedy occurs without it.

Depression is common in younger children as well. Parents should take note whenever a child talks of feeling sad or expresses guilt about an experience that happened a long time ago. A pet may have died and the child may feel overly responsible. It may seem ludicrous, but a child may feel that because he or she failed to feed the pet on schedule or walk it on time, he or she contributed to the pet's demise. It may not be rational to an adult, but it makes great sense to a young child.

A young child of divorced parents may feel responsible for the separation. If only he had been a better child, not have misbehaved so often, his parents would still be together. This attitude is sometimes unconsciously fostered by the parent who, through his or her actions, says things like, "Please, can't you see I am alone? I can't do everything. If you had behaved better, I might not be in this fix." It may seem an innocent remark to the parent, but it is confirmation to the child of his guilt.

Dr. Puig-Antich, former Director of the Child and Adolescent Depression Clinic at Columbia Medical Center in New York, states that few children attempt to kill themselves before puberty. "But," he says, "this is not because they don't *feel* like doing it. It's because they don't yet have the maturity to know *how* to do it." He recalls the incredible case of a nine-year-old boy who attempted suicide on three occasions. "Each time he tried hanging himself from a shower head with a wet towel which, fortunately for him, is impossible to do." Today, as a result of medical care, the boy's depression is under control. He is free to be a child again. Doctors can do much to help such young depression, but early detection is of vital importance, and in order to do that, parents must be aware.

Parents are the key. It is always better to bring family and personal problems out into the open. With family understanding, depression does not have to lead to despair. Though not easy to live with, it can be treated. Professional intervention is required, but parental recognition of a problem must come first.

There's a story about a child of three who had never spoken a word. Physicians of every discipline were consulted, but they found nothing wrong with the child. Still, he grew to five years of age without speaking. One day, at the age of six, as he stepped into his evening bath, he said, "Oooh, that water is very hot!" "You can speak! How come you haven't said anything before?" his joyful parents exclaimed. "Oh," said the boy, "up until now, everything has been okay."

Children will send verbal and non-verbal signals when everything is *not* okay. Parents have but to listen.

Chapter 21
It's About Time

The early "live" days of "Captain Kangaroo" were grueling; thank goodness I was so young. To get six hours' sleep I would have to be asleep by nine each evening. But it was hard getting used to such a wacky sleeping schedule. I would toss and turn a lot before finally dozing off. I set three alarms to wake me, and we had a telephone service call me and everyone else in the cast. Gus was the toughest; he really detested early morning hours. If Gus didn't answer his phone after twenty rings, the wake-up operator would call a production assistant who would taxi to Gus's apartment on Irving Place and bang on the door. I guess that made him popular with the neighbors.

The hosts of today's early morning network shows are whisked from their homes to the studios in limousines. That's more than luxury; it makes sense. I remember the day when my car broke down halfway to Manhattan from Long Island. I arrived at the studio five minutes before eight and frantic. I had to say, "Good morning, boys and girls, and what a nice day it's going to be . . . ," off-camera because I wasn't quite the Captain yet. The children didn't see me for the first two minutes of the program, while I got my make-up on. Hugh Holt, my longtime costume handler and good friend, got my costume on at the same time, quietly cursing while he tried to get each of my arms into the proper jacket sleeve.

Ad-libbing desperately, we made a game of it with the audience. "I'm playing hide-and-go-seek. See if you can find me. I'll tell you if you are getting closer by playing 'hot and cold.' " The camera panned to the garden door. "Oh no, you're getting cold." Pan to the hat tree. "Warmer but not hot." Offstage, my arm was in the correct sleeve, finally, and the make-up complete. The camera panned to the stairs. "Oh, you're very hot. You found me. You win!" Down the stairs I came and went on with the show as planned. I'm certain some people thought, "What a clever way to have the children participate in the program."

When the "Captain Kangaroo" show first went on the air in 1955, I would arrive home at about 4 P.M. and want very much to spend some time with Mike, Laurie and Maeve, before they toddled off to bed. Of course, Jeanne hadn't seen very much of me either, and she would be full of questions about my day. Sometimes she would get upset when I was too tired to answer her.

"Later, later," I would say, but somehow later never came. The last thing I wanted to do was relive the details of the day. However, I was happy to leave show business in the studio and in the office. Home was, for me, the place reserved for family life. Jeanne soon came to understand and appreciate this.

There are performers who crave the spotlight and would be happy in front of an audience all day and all evening long. I know singers and comedians who are disappointed when the lights are dimmed and the audience goes home. They visit nightclubs while on vacation and love to be recognized by the master of ceremonies; they adore being invited to perform on their nights off. For such people show business is a need.

I like to leave it all behind me and enjoy my private life. If I spend an evening in a restaurant without being recognized, I'm quite happy. I understand that being recognized, signing autographs, and answering questions, even when they border on being silly or rude, is a price entertainers pay for success. I pay that price willingly, but I am no less a private person who appreciates the opportunity to be with family and friends without the hype of show business.

Home is a refuge from the travails of the workplace for most working men and women, as it should be, but it worries me to hear parents talk about how the kids just won't let them alone when they get home. They push the children away so they can have some solitude, not understanding that their children need them as much as the parents need their solitude.

There was a popular musical production that the Captain performed to the lyrics of *Cinderella*. Dressed in an apron and head topped by a blond wig, the Captain rushed about, following the commands of the lyrics. "Go up and do the attic, the cellar needs some sweeping, the stars above need dusting. . . ." Poor Cinderella, the mean stepsisters used every minute of her time, and even when she went to the grand ball, she had to watch the clock.

It often seems as though we are all modern day Cinderellas, putting off midnight. We attempt to squeeze so much into our lives that often the process squeezes children out of our day. We watch the clock and try to race ahead of it to do all we can do, at work, at play, often leaving the kids in the dust.

"Oh! the Duchess, the Duchess," worried the White Rabbit in *Alice in Wonderland,* "Oh! won't she be savage if I've kept her waiting!" Time-saving products are advertised with those intriguing phrases: "in just minutes . . ." "in just seconds . . ." The stores and markets are stuffed with products to save us time, from microwaves to Minute Maids. Society seems to be in a timesaving frenzy. But what to do with the time saved? Why, squeeze more out of life, of course. And what about the children?

Time is an artifice, a construct dividing the day. A child's day is measured differently than an adult's, however. When we vacation, one of our great pleasures is in removing ourselves from the constraints of time and schedule. We allow our bodies to tell us when to eat, when to sleep, when to read, when to wake to a new day. Return to work, and the routine of daily life disturbs this natural, relaxing rhythm.

We press our children away from these natural rhythms into artificial time constraints. We schedule our own day so tightly as to leave little leisure time. We eat in fast-food restaurants. (My mother would be puzzled by that term; she would ask, "Is it the opposite of slow food? Does it taste better?") Such restaurants are a blessing for busy parents, but hardly the place for the family roundtable conversation of my youth. Conscientious working parents complain of feeling fragmented and of having no time for themselves or their children. Life, for them, is a treadmill of work, chores and sleep.

The imposition of time constraints on a child has another potentially negative effect. Introspection, or daydreaming, is an important function, particularly for a child with an artistic bent. In my childhood I remember quiet hours spent lying on my back on the grass, staring at the clouds or at the night skies. I was doing more than staring, of course. I was engaged in an introspective process, a concentration on my inner life, a procedure of self-discovery. Now many people refer to such times as "quiet times," or "lazy hours," implying disapproval. Others come right out and say they're a waste of time. Quite the contrary—such "lazy hours" are a vital process in the development and growth of the human being. Unfortunately, our modern lifestyle, with its imposed, tight schedules, has all but eliminated the opportunity for this activity that is so important to the growth of a child.

When I was young, my mother was always home and cooked every meal for me, my siblings and my father. There were no fast-food places around the corner or at the mall; in fact, there were no malls. Restaurants were for the wealthy or for great celebrations such as an anniversary or a significant birthday. Restaurants were not for most children. The local diner, the "greasy spoon," was for the unfortunate bachelor store clerk upon whom everyone took pity.

In retrospect, what was most important about that family dining room was the opportunity it afforded for conversation. The meal was pleasant, but the conversation was what was important. That dining table brought me in contact with my brothers and parents and, from talking with them freely and informally, I acquired a wealth of knowledge. That coming together of the entire family, on a daily basis, is unusual in the American family today.

Like most other women of her generation, Jeanne also chose to stay home caring for her children, and it was not until they were grown that she relaunched her own career at fifty-one. She was fortunate that she had developed interests that have made her valuable to many community institutions and a help to many individuals. But early on, it was her children who received her attention. She and they were lucky that staying home was an option open to her. Except for the bare-cupboard days following my "Howdy Doody" demise, I have provided for my family well, and it was not necessary for Jeanne to work outside the home.

This is not an option offered to most women today. Even if a young mother might desire to stay home with a baby, two salaries are often necessary for the financial well-being of the family. For an increasing number of American women, motherhood versus career is a conflict that can make them feel torn in two. "Someone asked me why I bothered to have a child if I intended to return to work," a young mother once told me. "I told them it's not so easy. I like to work. I like my job *and* I love children."

In 1979 Dr. Martha Zaslow, a former research psychologist at the National Institute of Child Health and Human Development in Bethesda, Maryland, began a study of sixty families in the Washington, D. C., area. She and her colleagues tried to determine "significant differences" between employed mothers and nonemployed mothers. Their findings were revealing. One of the biggest differences seems to be in what Dr. Zaslow calls "reunion time," when the family reunites again at the end of the work day.

"In families where the mother was the full-time care giver," Dr. Zaslow reports, "she was often literally waiting at the door to turn the baby over to the father. It was seen as *his* time with the child." But when the mother was away all day at her job, it became a different story. "That reunion time was seen primarily as hers."

It is too early to say if the many changes in family structure and in the American economy over the last thirty years will have significant effects on our children. It is clear, however, that careful and attentive parenting remains the prime need in the American family. The family may have changed, but the needs of children have not. Children still require caring, loving, attentive, responsive parents who are willing to give the time to meet their needs. That was probably true in ancient Rome and will always remain so.

Some studies indicate that working parents elevate their rates of interaction with their children and pay a great deal of attention to finding the time to meet their children's needs. They seem to communicate more with their children, as if to compensate for the times away.

I believe I did that with my three youngsters, and I was gratified to hear my son Michael reminisce about our special times together when he was interviewed by Kathy Cronkite for her book about the children of celebrities, *On the Edge of the Spotlight.* "The deal was that my two sisters and I would each get to take one trip [a year] on one of his 'Fun With Music' concerts," he told Ms. Cronkite. "I liked it very much and I traveled around most of the states when I was a child. It was a good chance to spend time with my father. . . ."

· · ·

We began taking the Captain on the road early on in the show's life. Most of our work was in a television studio without a live audience, and it was stimulating for me and the producers to meet fans, hear their reactions and feel their affection for the Captain.

We developed the "Fun With Music" format because we felt it was complimentary to the work we were doing on the television show.

The "Fun With Music" format provides for participation by the audience. During Rossini's "William Tell Overture" the children "ride" their "horses" to the Western sky. During Leroy Anderson's "Sleigh Ride" the children reach out for imaginary reins to control the horse while, onstage, the Captain progressively adds pieces of clothing to warm himself against the cold. Before Rimsky-Korsakov's "Flight of the Bumble Bee" we search the orchestra for an instrument that can create the bee sound. The children decide against the timpani because it sounds more like a walking elephant, but the strings receive a resounding "yes" because they can sound like a bee in flight. The audience conducts the orchestra in the "Stars and Stripes Forever," and meets the instrument families, including the buffoonish trombones. Many symphony orchestras wisely look to the future and plan programs that will bring young people, their potential audience, into early contact with the orchestra. During "Fun With Music," the Captain did not instruct in any formal sense. As when we perform with orchestras today, our purpose is to introduce very young children to the sight and sound of the symphony. I figured that why Beethoven wrote the "Choral" Symphony, or the role of Handel in the development of the symphony, could come later, in the more formal Young People's Concerts given by most orchestras. It is only important that contact between the child and the orchestra be made at a very young age, setting the stage for a closer and more intellectual relationship as the child matures.

One year we used a part of Gershwin's *An American In Paris,* which we produced on stage with the Captain playing a caped gendarme directing traffic. The "traffic" was composed of young children driving down the "boulevard" in cardboard boxes painted like the autos and buses of Paris. Mike drove an auto early in that season and told his sister, Laurie, about the experience. She enjoyed being a bus a few weeks later and told Maeve about her experience. Maeve was very excited about being an auto until it came time to go on stage. Then she applied the brakes, and her show business career came to a rather sudden stop.

The children traveled with me not only on concert trips but also on family vacations. One such trip to Disneyland with Jeanne and the children cost me a few anxious moments. We stayed at the hotel on the grounds of Disneyland and were leaving our room for breakfast one morning, when we were surprised to find the corridor filled with police. One plainclothes officer, wearing a badge on his breast pocket, stopped me and began asking questions. It seemed a man in the room adjacent to ours had been found by the maid, apparently murdered.

"Gee, Dad," Michael chirped cheerfully, "I guess that was the noise we heard last night."

"Quiet, please, Michael," I said.

"Noise?" asked the detective. "Tell me, sir, where were you at nine o'clock last night?"

"In my room, of course," I answered.

"No you weren't, Dad," said Michael.

"Oh?" asked the detective, eyebrow raised.

Gulp, I swallowed.

"You were with me on the balcony watching the fireworks," said Michael.

"Oh," said the detective with eyebrow lowered. "Thank you for your cooperation."

"Let's have breakfast, Mike," said I, taking him by the hand and moving faster than I usually move with small child in hand.

Chapter 22
I Can Do It Myself

I enjoy leading a private life not only because I am, by nature, a private person, but because it affords my children and grandchildren an opportunity to live a conventional life. When my children were young the community in which we lived was kind and no fuss was made about my being on television. Picture stories about me would appear in *Life* or *Look* or *TV Guide,* and nary a neighbor would be heard from. Once *People* magazine wrote an article on me, accompanied by a picture of Jeanne and me with our good friends, Roger and Kate Healy. No one mentioned the story to us, but Roger and Kate heard from just about everyone they knew. People were very kind in protecting our family. This was great for my children, who certainly did not need that extra baggage to carry in growing up. I often say that I could have been an airline pilot or a corporate executive, and their life would have been essentially the same. The children benefited from this treatment and grew to be very fine human beings.

Anonymity came more easily when I was younger. I started "Captain Kangaroo" as a twenty-eight-year-old with make-up needed to make me look sixty. Now it can be said that I've grown into the part; my dark brown hair has turned white, I now wear a real mustache and, especially when I speak, I am usually recognized. Also, I have been in mufti much of the last two decades, speaking on behalf of young people. Now, I appear as myself in public more often than as the Captain.

Occasionally, in the past, my children would be taunted by their peers with silly innuendos about Mister Green Jeans or Dancing Bear or even the Captain himself. Once, when he was in high school, Michael was asked when his father was going to grow up and do something serious. Their close friends never made such remarks, but that didn't take the sting out of them.

In the end, despite our best efforts, Jeanne and I came to realize, as all parents must, that we could not always be there to protect our children. It is not an altogether comfortable reality for a parent to accept and, unfortunately, some parents never do. A newborn infant is totally dependent on her parents, but as she grows she will attempt to do things on her own. While it's important for parents to meet the needs of young children and give them guidance, it is also important to allow them, at appropriate stages, to function independently. It may seem ironic, but one of the principal goals of parenting is teaching a child to do without parents. We all know of overzealous parents who "kill with kindness." Their overprotected children often become adults who are unable to cope on their own. Those parents simply did not heed the words spoken by all children, "I can do it myself." Permitting a child to develop as an independent adult is a principal achievement of successful parenting.

A parent can begin to encourage decision making in even a young child, and it's important to start as early as possible. In this way, a child can be taught to feel confident in making decisions, and even learn the consequences of them. Encouraging a child to try something, even when he or she is making a mistake, will enhance the ability of that child to make independent judgments in later life.

With a young child, decision making can be fostered by offering choices. My daughter, Maeve, allows her children to choose clothing each day. Derek, seven, the older child, is doing very well in picking out his own outfits. Alex, only three, often decides on mismatched colors and designs. So Maeve negotiates a bit, reducing the number of choices, but still allowing Alex to choose an outfit pleasing to him and acceptable to his mother. It may take a few extra minutes, precious morning time in many families, but it is a very worthwhile investment. If a busy parent cannot afford this time in the morning, the decision game could be played out the evening before.

I was at a restaurant recently with my son Michael, his sons, Britton and Connor, and their mother, Lynn. Lynn asked the boys to choose a dessert. Connor, almost three, wanted ice cream and, pressed further, chose chocolate. When the ice cream came, however, he decided that what he really wanted was vanilla, like the ice cream his brother Britton was thoroughly enjoying. He was very unhappy that he had to settle for chocolate, but he had just taken an essential step in a long process in which he and other two-year-olds come to appreciate that decisions bring consequences.

Psychologists have long recognized how necessary the breaking away process is and how difficult it sometimes is for parents to let go. The late etiologist, Jean Piaget, warned that unless given the appropriate freedom, a child cannot grow emotionally. Dr. Piaget also taught us that a child will only develop into a truly moral person if allowed to assume responsibility for his or her own actions.

As parents we find it difficult not to interfere; we are so wise, have lived so long and have learned so much. "No, that's not the way to tie a shoelace. Here—let me show you." But human beings learn from experimentation and from mistakes, and if never given the opportunity to make those mistakes, we will never learn. The most casual, ordinary experiences are learning opportunities for children. That is why a trip to the supermarket can be so rich an adventure for a child.

I have sometimes watched in horror while a parent fights, slaps and pushes a small child in the supermarket. "No, put that back! Keep your hands off the shelves or I'll take you out and throw you in the car." This is not an uncommon sight. The child is young and only needs to learn that we cannot take everything from the shelves and put it in our basket. But personal debasement and the threat of physical isolation are not going to teach the child these consumer skills. Such threats will, however, have other consequences.

It may extend the time it takes to shop, but try asking your child's advice in the selection of items from the shelves, and you will create a marvelous learning environment. It will not be long before your child takes pride in being part of the decision making process. Your guidance is needed, of course, but the family shopping chore can become a rich educational experience.

Whenever I take a drive with my grandsons in the back seat (wearing seat belts, of course), I ask them, in their own neighborhood, to guide me. "Tell me where to turn and in which direction to turn, please," I say. They love the powerful feeling of informing me that a left turn at the next corner will bring us closer to their house. Occasionally I will be told, "Turn right, Granddad, at that corner we just passed!"

Jeanne and I have tried to give our children the capacity to make independent, if guided, decisions from early in their lives. They made decisions about pets, music lessons, Scouting, and academics, among many others. They also made some mistakes. We own a piano that everybody was enthusiastic to play. Several years and several children later we came to the conclusion that we probably could have saved the expense, but their musical learning experiences were rich even if we eventually ended up with flutes and guitars, rather than the piano.

When he was in the seventh grade, Michael decided it would be nice to go away to secondary school. We were able to afford it, and he seemed enthusiastic, so we investigated until we found the Cranwell School in Massachusetts. He did well on his tests and was accepted. Then, in his last year in elementary school, we visited Cranwell on a fall football weekend. Mike remained enthusiastic, but I think he was also overcome by the place and the thought of being so independent. I could see that he was troubled and took him aside at the playing field to talk to him. He displayed some insecurity and I assured him that it was his decision to make; it was not too late to change his mind.

"Yes, Dad, I know, but you've made the deposit and now I have to go."

"No, you don't, Mike. The decision is still yours. Forget the deposit. It's not worth having you unhappy for four years. If you decide not to go, that's okay."

Mike gave it serious thought, and by the next week he wanted to go as much as ever. He went to Cranwell and thrived. He remembers the school today as one of the best decisions he ever made.

In the process of fostering independent decision making, it is critical to respect a child's wishes. If you tell a child she can make a determination and then overrule her without a reasonable explanation, you are debasing the child's ability to make independent choices. If the child's decision is to do something unhealthy, dangerous or immoral, of course you must intercede, but with a reasonable explanation. If your decision to overrule is whimsical, such as *"You* may want to wear blue but I want you to wear yellow," then the child will never trust herself to make decisions. She has learned that you have not given her the authority, and she will never venture to decide matters for herself. She will remain dependent upon you and emotionally stunted. Have faith in a child and show it.

Learning to make independent decisions is part of the process of developing trust between parent and child. As I mentioned earlier, the psychologist Piaget believed that a child will only develop into a *moral* person if allowed to assume responsibility for his or her own actions. It should be obvious to parents that they will be unable to follow their children through life to protect them or to assure that they will maintain the values that their parents have transmitted. It is only by giving the child the tools for independent decision making and the trust to make the right decision that a child will be able to truly practice the values and morals instilled by his parents.

My daughter, Laurie, arrived on the Dartmouth campus in the fall of 1973, after the trustees had allowed women to earn degrees there. Not only were men and women now taking classes together, they were also living in the same dorms, where they were running around in their bathrobes and their pajamas. Some of my friends were shocked when I told them about dorm life and wondered how I could "trust" Laurie in such a "permissive" setting. I pointed out that her brother, Michael, had been running around the house in his shorts for years. It was not the same thing, they said. "There's all sorts of hanky-panky going on in those places."

I was very serious when I replied, "We trust our children. They have a set of values which was pretty much theirs by the time they were twelve years old. Laurie is now twenty and I trust her."

Before going to Dartmouth, Laurie was at Smith College. In her sophomore year one of the women on her floor invited her boyfriend, who was not a student, to live with her in the dorm. This very much upset the other women at this all-female school, who would not accept this breach of conduct. Through social isolation they made this woman aware of their disapproval, and in less than two weeks the boyfriend had packed his stereo, guitar and jeans and departed. These women had a code that they were intent on living by. Without official intervention or other adult intercession, they upheld their values.

In my day, I do not believe we were any more or any less virtuous. We might have been a bit more sneaky, because we had to be. We were not as trusted as the present generation is trusted, and, therefore, our transgressions were more hidden from view. Anyone from my genera-tion who does not believe this is either short on memory or long on imagination. I like the openness that is possible today, it keeps lying and deceit to a minimum.

As important as teaching independence is, much of our society is geared to penalizing such independence and rewarding compliance and docility. Our schools, generally understaffed and burdened with bureaucracy, rarely reward the student who is inquisitive and who makes independent decisions. The blue ribbons are usually given to the docile, "easily managed" student who is quiet and unquestioning. This occurs because, in most school systems, there are not enough teachers to teach, and those who are there are kept busy with record keeping and testing. Teaching the inquisitive, curious child is often not possible in today's American schools. Quite rare are those communities which have insisted on providing all the essential resources for education and the enlightened administration to meet the challenges.

What parents and educators, and, indeed, the total adult community, are trying to do is to socialize our children, to give them values and set a certain standard that they will act upon independent of us. We can't follow them around all the time telling them what to do; standards of behavior must become internalized. That's what socialization is all about. If the values don't stick, then we have failed; or something extraneous has intervened, some outside influence beyond our sphere, something we cannot prevent.

If we have been successful in teaching independent decision making and engendering the trust of our children, then we can say we have achieved a great goal: teaching our children to get along without parents. And as most parents quickly learn, being rid of their parents is also the goal of most children!

Chapter 23
Who, What, Where, When and Why?

Jeanne thought it was axiomatic: when the children made friends it was always with a child from the farthest end of town whose mother did not drive. Most suburban mothers know the story; enough hours behind the wheel to qualify for the Indy 500. However, the time is usually not wasted. I have often thought that more questions are asked in station wagons than in classrooms.

The car is a splendid environment for answering questions and is particularly suited to informal lectures, the kind children walk away from in freer situations. Michael has said that, as a child, he admired his mother for volunteering to be the driver so often. Only in retrospect, and after having children of his own, did he realize that she was engaging in some pretty sophisticated brainwashing.

Jeanne learned something about me in the station wagon, as well. She was driving the children to Manhattan to attend a "Captain Kangaroo" concert at Carnegie Hall that I was doing for the local CBS station. I had done similar concerts for stations in Robin Hood Dell in Philadelphia, McCormick Place in Chicago and the Hollywood Bowl in Los Angeles. Carnegie Hall, now celebrating its one-hundredth anniversary, was endangered at that time. Most of New York's musical institutions had moved to the splendid new Lincoln Center. Halfway to Manhattan the radio reported that Governor Rockefeller had approved legislation creating a commission and the funding to preserve Carnegie Hall. From the back seat, Mike piped up, "See, Mom. Dad just saved Carnegie Hall!" Powerful guy, this Captain Kangaroo.

. . .

A parent bringing children to school or child care should use the time spent in travel as a valuable opportunity for answering questions or engaging a child in discussion. Urban parents, who don't usually drive, can use travel time on the bus, train, or while walking for the same purpose. Regardless of the circumstances, questions and conversation between parent and child are very important. Surely, there are days when the parent of an inquisitive child does not know whether to read *The Guinness Book of World Records* or submit an entry. Inquisitive children can be a delight and, sometimes, an annoyance. Children don't store questions in a "memory bank" to be released at a time convenient for parental consideration. When they ask a question they want an answer, now. Persistence is a quality in curious children. They display the same singlemindedness as a wild animal foraging for food.

A parent is a child's greatest resource for finding the answers to life, answers critical to that child's development. A child of school age soon discovers that, as one of many in a classroom, he does not have the "right" to ask too many questions. It's not practical to expect a teacher to give an inordinate amount of time to one or a few inquisitive students. This may lessen opportunities for learning, but it does maintain order. The parent of an inquisitive child must understand that such a child relies upon the parent as the principal source for answers.

Most children are naturally inquisitive. If, over months or years, a parent has discouraged questions, however, the inquiries will become fewer, eventually being reduced to utilitarian questions like "What's for dinner?" A parent who does not respond to the questions of a child from an early age stifles the development of that child intellectually *and* emotionally. The process, the conversation, that occurs in answering a child's questions also contributes to the parent-child bond and helps to build trust.

It is often necessary for an adult to figure out the real question *behind* the question being asked. A baby-sitter arrives, and the child asks, "When will you be back?" The question is a security-related question and means more than simply "when?" The real question is "Are you coming back? Do you love me? I'll miss you, will you miss me?" Some very basic needs are being put on the line with such a simple-sounding question. More than a verbal answer is needed; a display of affection and a hug or kiss are in order, reassurance that a child is loved and that "Yes, I will be back."

Children can display their own special reasoning. I know a three-year-old who asked his mother how she fit into the tiny telephone when she called him from work every day. The mother went into a long scientific explanation of the working of the telephone, an explanation that might have baffled Alexander Graham Bell. When asked did he now understand, he replied, "Yes, but how do you crawl out?"

The educator Jack Blessington told me of a particular classroom experience. He had been explaining some elementary arithmetic to a young student. He was explaining numerators and denominators and the manipulation necessary to find the answer to a division problem. His attention was called to another student, but he overheard a classmate explain to the child, "Look, you take the top number and the bottom number and you flip them. . . ." Sometimes we get too fancy.

Parents who are very good about answering a child's questions, who thoughtfully explain, who research when necessary for the sake of accuracy, may live in terror of the day when a child asks THAT question: "Where did I come from?" Children think about reproduction and therefore ask questions from an early age, sometimes two or three. Because many children have younger siblings or a new baby has arrived in the neighborhood, wondering about where the baby came from is quite natural. Without a suitable answer the question never goes away, even for someone as clever as the Scottish author and minister, George Mc-Donald, who coined the lyric, "Where did you come from baby dear?/ Out of the everywhere into the here."

In a technologically oriented age, at a time when men and women think of themselves as "liberated," parents still duck behind the birds, the bees, and the gangly stork. Maybe babies are made in workshops, like Pinocchio. Wow, that Geppetto is a busy guy!

There are *no* good reasons for ducking the question. When young children ask, "Where do babies come from?" they are in search of their origins; it is *not* a question about sex. Many brave adults, however, decide to answer with a full and complete lesson on sex. They are somewhat disappointed when the young child looks at them with that

"Are you crazy?" look. And they still want to know where they came from.

Children, even toddlers, should be given correct information about their origins complete with simple information about body parts, leaving nothing out. If the genitals are omitted, children may feel that something is wrong with them. Correct information, early in life, becomes a foundation which you can add to at appropriate ages of maturity and understanding until the child has built a frame of knowledge given by you in love and trust. Then peer gossip, the school yard slang, the fantasies built from ignorance will find no home in the mind and heart of this child. Reproduction, sex, love and trust will be bound together in a repository of knowledge and understanding to be drawn upon throughout life.

I believe strongly that teaching about reproduction and sex ought to begin with parents, so that such information can be coupled with the values and moral implications which are an integral part of such knowledge. It should also be a part of the school curriculum. If a child has been given a good foundation of knowledge, along with the understanding of the role played by love and trust in a relationship, the teaching of sex in the classroom should hold no fears for parents. For children who have not been fortunate enough to learn from enlightened parents, sex education from school or other sources is especially urgent. It would be nice to believe that all parents give their children accurate information about sex, but that is simply not so. And without this knowledge our young people are at peril.

It has been charged that teaching about sex is implicitly condoning sexual activity. This, of course, is not so. Adolescents in today's society have many opportunities to be sexually active. If parents have transmitted their values successfully, the adolescent is going to handle these situations in an appropriate and moral manner. If the child is without such values, sex education is not likely to trigger a sexual experience. But if the child has not benefited from sex education, the results of sexual activity may be more than he or she or society would wish.

One of our greatest social problems, and one which is generally ignored by society at large, is teenage pregnancy. Children who are sexually active and ignorant of consequences are a great social and economic problem in large cities, suburban towns, farm villages. A teenager who becomes pregnant is bringing radical change to her academic and social life. The baby of such a child may be in physical jeopardy, and a new single-parent household may result. Many cases of child abuse result in such homes, simply because a baby is being cared for by an adolescent who is not yet emotionally mature. Misery is the companion to teen pregnancy. It is a condition that very likely could be avoided with knowledge that could come from sex education in the schools.

With teen pregnancy, divorce, and dual-career couples so prevalent in modern America, the family structure is very different from that which was typical only a third of a century ago—Mother at home with the kids, Dad in the workplace and grandfather, grandmother, aunts and uncles just around the corner ready to lend a helping hand. The definition of family is not very easy today because it has many forms. It was Ogden Nash who said, "A family is a unit composed not only of children but of men, women, an occasional animal, and the common cold."

Most of us know single parents, usually employed outside the home, trying hard to be mother, father and everything else to the child. That's one family form. Both parents working outside the home and relying heavily on day care and after-school services comprise another form. The traditional unit with Mom at home and Dad out working—or vice versa—can also be found.

It was in college that Jeanne first met Kate Healy, and for many years the Healys have been our closest friends. We spend a lot of time together but make no demands on each other, as is usually the case with the best of friendships. The Healy family is like any other family except in one respect: there are a lot of them. Roger, who is a successful builder, and Kate have fourteen children, from the oldest, Maureen, to the youngest, Elizabeth. There are a dozen more between these two, ten boys and two more girls. For some people in the community it is a game to name the fourteen Healy children in order of their age. If you can accomplish that, remembering the Seven Dwarfs is a cinch.

This is the nicest of families because of the love and manners displayed in the house. Oh, they are far from perfect; count on Edward or Justin or Michael to be up to something, although young Roger and Eugene and Terence have outgrown that stuff. John, Christopher, Joseph and Kevin can also be pretty interesting, at times. And Kathleen and

Mary broke many a heart on their way to growing into lovely young women. I include myself in that group.

When they were younger, Jeanne would telephone Kate and, when she wasn't home, leave the message with the kids, "Tell her the White Rabbit called." She said this for years until one day the voice on the other end replied, "Okay, Mrs. Keeshan, I'll tell her."

"How do you know this is Mrs. Keeshan?" asked Jeanne.

"Oh, you're the only White Rabbit who calls here!"

The Healys are well-educated children; they're all in college or through now, except Elizabeth, who starts this year. Brown, Trinity, Lafayette, Villanova and the London School of Economics are among the institutions that have taught them. Every time I wrote a tuition check myself, I thought of Roger and multiplied.

A family can have one child or many, one parent or two, support from grandparents and family close at hand, or only an occasional telephone call from distant relatives. Yet the best definition of family for me is that it is a nurturing place, a nest where we protect our young and teach them to fly. Perhaps we give much thought to the process, or perhaps we do it as the birds do, by instinct. There is something to be said for doing a little of each.

What is important today is the recognition that the family has changed and that there are many families with few of the traditional support systems. That is why everyone must assist, give aid and support to help raise the children. We have to be nurturers of *all* of our children as a society. I'd like to think that we would do this out of compassion, because we like kids and want to help them. But if not out of compassion, we must do it in our own self-interest; when a parent fails to nurture, we all pay the price, the social and the economic cost. It pays for us to see that parents are successful in nurturing children.

I have enjoyed myself doing something few people do, performing on television and on stage. However, I have derived the most pleasure from doing something many people do, parenting. I have survived the critical years with my children, and I am now thrilled, watching them parent their children. I am also enjoying the great rewards of being a grandparent. It has been said, with some accuracy, that parenting never ends.

My daughter Laurie married John almost a decade ago, but somehow, being far away in the Midwest, she didn't manage to clear the house of all her possessions. After waiting eight years, I telephoned her and suggested that her husband meet me in Indiana at Maeve's home, the halfway point, in four weeks. I wanted to turn over a van filled with her possessions. On the appointed weekend, I rented a van and loaded it up on a Friday evening. I was on the road well before 5 A.M. and greeted the sun at the Delaware Water Gap. I stopped for gas somewhere in central Pennsylvania. As I was climbing back in the van, a nice man, about my age, asked where I had rented the van. I gave him an 800 telephone number, and he explained that his car had broken down—filled with his daughter's possessions, which he was transporting from Missouri to New York. I explained that my van was filled with my daughter's possessions, which I was transporting from New York to Missouri.

He beamed at me with a most cherubic smile, ear to ear, and said, "Aren't fathers wonderful!"

I couldn't agree more.

Chapter 24
Romeo, Juliet and the Kids

With love's light wings did I o'erperch these walls;
For stony limits cannot hold love out,
And what love can do that dares love attempt.

And so, with Romeo's tribute to the great powers of love, we hear the sweeping crescendo of strings, woodwinds and horns of a Tchaikovsky serenade. Poet, composer, author, artist, sculptor, every artist and everyman praises love, and every human of any age requires the nutrition of love for growth and survival.

Love finds a great fulfillment in the deep affection between man and woman, a love which often leads to an alliance, an attachment, a marriage. They become linked together as one, a couple. They may think of themselves, in the most romantic way, as being in heaven. As the song goes, ". . . and baby makes three, in my Blue Heaven."

It is the stuff of fairy tales. Cinderella slipped her foot into the glass slipper and moved into the palace. Snow White accepted the kiss of her prince and lived happily ever after, sharing that happiness with all her "adult children," from Doc and Grumpy to Bashful and Dopey and the three in between.

As "Old Blue Eyes" sings, "Fairy tales do come true." But, despite the occasional lifelong fairy tale, true love does not always last enough to live happily ever after. The palace is mortgaged and the prince works hard and, today, the princess is working outside the palace, too. Along come the darling little princess and the darling little prince, but they grow up asking questions and making demands. They need child care while the true-loves are at work, and that puts another strain on the royal treasury. The golden threads tarnish, the royal chariot has a broken wheel, and it soon becomes known that love hath not all the powers claimed by that incurable romantic, Romeo.

In the last few years, the American divorce rate has climbed to half that of the marriage rate. In many of these divorces the couple had a child or children. Does that mean that "baby makes three" is now "baby makes two"? Divorce creates a single-parent household, but the baby, or child, has *not* been divorced from a parent. The ties that bind parent and child ought to remain tied to *both* parents. Unfortunately for children, battling parents often don't permit a nurturing relationship between their children and their "ex-spouse." The children may become just another battleground, a means for inflicting hurt upon the other partner, with little thought given to the potentially cataclysmic effects upon the children, who are in need of the love of both parents.

Recently Mr. Gallup sent forth his legions to poll Americans on the most important qualities of life and came back with the answer that "having a good family life" is very important to the vast majority of young people in this country, a result indicative of the desire of young Americans to feel rooted and secure. And yet, in the family feud that is the residue of so many divorces, parent pits child against parent, cutting roots and bashing security.

As an adolescent I laughed when the radio humorist Henry Morgan asked the question, "Do B-47s consume their young?" A ludicrous notion, thought I, but based on an event which occurs in some species in nature. An even more ridiculous notion is that parents of the human species would consume their young, but the abuse done to children by many parents is just as destructive.

We are the most "attached" species on the planet, requiring and enjoying the protection of our parents into young adulthood. This need for warmth, unconditional love, understanding and guidance does not change when parents change their feelings for each other and separate. Indeed, these changes increase these needs, whether a child is eight or eighteen.

When parents decide upon divorce, it is important to tell the children before they learn about it in some other, perhaps confusing, way. Honesty is vital in telling children about divorce. It should not be an occasion for spouse bashing. A parent may be a former spouse but is never a former parent. In an honest, open relationship with children, the discussion of circumstances leading to divorce should not be a problem. It is important that children be reassured that they are not in any way responsible for the divorce.

Small children are very self-centered, and it is easy for them to conclude that their actions precipitated the problems between their parents. "I was a bad boy and left my tricycle in the driveway and that's why Daddy is going away" is the type of thing a small child might think. A ten-year-old I know recalls his mother saying to him, "This has nothing to do with you," a statement he found bewildering when it was clear that his whole world would be affected by his parents' divorce. Only later did he realize his mother meant he was not to blame.

Parents themselves sometimes believe that the children are responsible for the breakup of a marriage. "Things were so good between us until the children came along. Then we had to stay home to care for them and money became tight. The good times went when the children came." Unfortunately, children are sometimes given this message explicitly or implicitly.

Adults can spare a child emotional difficulties in a divorce or in any other stressful situation if they understand that the development of a child is a *partnership* between parent and child. A child relies on both parents to help with his development and is hindered in this development when one or both parents fail to fulfill their role in the partnership.

Along with the other problems of a divorce also comes the dilemma of custody. Custody is a legal term and, unfortunately, it implies ownership. I believe that much of the maltreatment of children, both physical and emotional, arises from an embedded concept of children as property. Not very long ago in our history, children were a valuable asset, particularly when we were largely an agricultural economy and they were needed to work the fields. Even today, our public school schedules reflect our roots. The school year, in what we think of as agricultural states of the Midwest and the South, is geared to the planting of spring crops. In industrial states, the school year ends later and begins later.

Because of their economic value, children were legally viewed as "property." If children failed in their work responsibilities, their father could beat them, and no interference from outside the family would be tolerated. "A man's home is his castle" meant that what went on inside the walls of that "castle" was nobody's business. And woe to the mother or sibling who interfered with a father's exercise of his "rights" over his child.

This concept of children as property, although almost eradicated in the law, remains in the American psyche to some extent. Until a decade ago, it was rare for a neighbor to "interfere" with another household. A child's screams from next door went unheeded. Bruises on a child went unquestioned. Only recently, largely because of media attention, have neighbors recognized that the abuse of a child is not a parental privilege and have intervened by calling the authorities.

The American Society for the Prevention of Cruelty to Animals has been protecting domestic animals in this nation for a hundred and twenty-three years, successfully lobbying for legislation and aggressively protecting dogs, cats and horses from human neglect and cruelty. Recently, lawmakers have begun to show the same compassion for children. If we work conscientiously, we may soon afford children complete protection from human neglect and cruelty.

Children are no longer an economic asset but, in fact, an economic liability requiring a great monetary investment in food, clothing, medical services and education. Many divorced fathers take advantage of the fact that custody is most often awarded to mothers, abdicating their emotional and economic responsibilities as fathers, and leave the parenting to Mom. Many children in families on public assistance rolls are there because men have refused to support the children they fathered. Recent legislation may force errant fathers to recognize their economic responsibility to their children. Unfortunately, no law can force fathers—or mothers, for that matter—to understand and fulfill their emotional obligation to their children.

As a single parent, almost always employed outside the home, a mother can have a difficult time meeting the needs of her child economically and emotionally. This task becomes more difficult if she is far away from her own mother, father and other relatives. She leaves work tired, swings by the child care center and picks up Junior, who may be cranky or questioning or both. She has little time, energy or inclination for the warm nurturing this child craves. Arriving home to an empty house, with no spouse to share the chores of parenting, she feels the need to talk to another adult. But her parents are an expensive long-distance telephone call away. In despair, she's had just about all she can take, and the situation is ripe for the emotional or physical abuse of her child.

Divorce need not be a disaster for children. If both parents are responsible and loving to the child, splitting up may be positive when compared to maintaining a home in which the parents stay together "for the sake of the children." In such homes, where no real love or security exists, a child can be deprived of the love and nurturing needed for growth. In a divorce where both parents recognize that a child continues to need the love of both parents, a bad situation can be made workable. It is not divorce per se which causes damage to a child but the parental arguing during and after that has the potential for much emotional harm.

Parental stress, whether in a single- or dual-parent household, breeds the emotional maltreatment of children. Many parents were neglected and abused when they were children and are unable to function as loving and tender parents. This experience causes them to reject their children, and to make their few displays of affection conditional. "If you love me, you'll clean your room." Only a child who is obedient gets a hug or a kiss from these parents. Children should be loved for just being, but many parents are unable to give love on those terms.

Parents who are in any of these circumstances should seek professional help; counseling can release feelings that they are unaware exist. Parents can be assisted in finding ways to give the emotional support their child needs in a manner that will make parenting a joyous and rich human experience.

Parenting requires energy, time, love and compassion, but parenting does *not* require perfection. Adults make mistakes—and that includes parents, who make mistakes in the nurturing of their children. An adult who is very nervous about parenting transmits this nervousness to the child. Even a newborn infant is able to sense anxiety in an adult. Parenting ought to be a relaxed, enjoyable job, and one in which we are allowed mistakes. Children are resilient and no reasonable error made by a parent is going to have a lasting effect.

From the beginning, Captain Kangaroo was never exactly competent at everything he did, and he still isn't. When he is on stage with an orchestra, he makes mistakes. He takes the baton from the conductor, who "has been doing nothing but waving his arms in the air in front of the musicians." Concluding that he can lead a symphony orchestra as well as the next fellow, he politely nudges the conductor off the podium and gives the downbeat. The chaotic and cacophonous result delights the audience. The Captain has made another mistake, but he has also demonstrated that talent, study and knowledge do an orchestra conductor make.

Children delight in the gullibility of the Captain when their surrogate, Bunny Rabbit, makes off with another bunch of carrots or when a large-eyed, innocent-appearing Mister Moose lures him beneath another thousand Ping-Pong balls. If children realize that grown-ups are fallible, that they too make mistakes, it is easier for them to accept the mistakes they themselves make in exploring their environment. It also makes it easier for them to accept advice and guidance and to work cooperatively in the effort to achieve the ultimate goal, self-discipline.

Much has been written about the testing of children, and our schools do spend much time in testing children, but little has been said about the testing of parents by children. Children test their parents from infancy, probing, searching for guidelines, fences, rules. Watch a toddler waddle to a coffee table and pick up an object. Almost always, her eyes will look up to her parent. "Is this okay, what I'm doing? Am I allowed to pick this up?" Her parent gently takes the object from the toddler and returns it to the table and sternly says, "No." The toddler stares at the object, at the parent. Again, the toddler tests her parent by picking up the object. Her parent, again, gently takes the object from the toddler and replaces it on the table with a "no." What patience parenting requires!

That parent could have slapped the child's hand or bottom and this would have probably led to tears. The lesson of what is out-of-bounds on the coffee table would have been obscured. The testing toddler would be less secure about the parent's love and no lesson would have been learned. The coffee-table object would have been safe, for the moment, but might be assaulted another day.

Children do need firm guidelines. They do require the "training that strengthens," which is Webster's definition of discipline. Discipline and punishment often go hand in hand, but they are very different. Discipline is training, the teaching of control. Punishment is a penalty which is often used to effect discipline.

As parents, we socialize our children, teach them the rules of life by which we must all live to be accepted in civilized society. A parent who fails to teach discipline is crippling a child, making it impossible for that child to be accepted. The patient and often tedious process of socializing will, eventually, be internalized by the child, who will then be able to impose a self-discipline. This will promote the type of conduct that will enable the child, as an adult, to find happiness in secure relationships with other adults.

I am generally opposed to the corporal punishment of children because I don't believe it works. A young child may find it difficult to relate corporal punishment to the offense. For all children, it is emotionally degrading, and that is too high a price to pay, whatever the desired result. It is a shortcut for impatient parents, achieving the immediate results, but not teaching a lesson. Corporal punishment is counterproductive and, all too often, a venting of parental anger which can lead to very unexpected and undesirable results.

In thirty-nine of our states corporal punishment is permitted in our schools. Here too, it is a shortcut, because it treats the symptoms, not the underlying disease. An unruly child in school is misbehaving for a reason. We ought to be prepared to find out why a child is misbehaving and deal with the causes. Beat children, if you will, but they will be back misbehaving tomorrow, because the reason for their disobedience, their cry for help, has not been addressed.

Discipline in the classroom is essential if a learning environment is to be provided for all students. Treat the causes behind the child's misbehavior and discipline will improve. But corporal punishment is a practice which rates an "F" on the school report card. It is also emotional abuse of children *and* their classroom peers, even when the punishment is inflicted out of their sight.

Courts have upheld the right of school officials to practice corporal punishment, even when parents have sued to prevent the punishment of their children. By law, a health professional must report a suspected case of child abuse. In a recent emergency-room incident in which an eight-year-old was treated for a severe beating, the social worker, called in by the emergency room physician, told the child's father, "If you had done this, I would have you in jail right now. But this was done by the boy's teacher and he is protected by the law. He has a legal right to beat children."

Children can be very successful in breaking the will of their parents by employing the "last straw" method, and many parents are severely tested. Comedian Dom de Luise once said in an interview that when he reaches the boiling point he tries calmly to say, "I am very, very angry with you. I love you, but I must tell you that you must never do that again." But instead, it always comes out, "Go to your room!"

Professionals advise angry parents to "take the count." Count to ten and beyond before striking the child in anger. This may be the best advice yet.

Like corporal punishment, breaking a promise you have already made to your child is always an inappropriate punishment. "I was going to buy you a bike, but you were bad, so no bike." Children are smart enough to recognize that such promises are created to serve a purpose. This is a cruel form of manipulation by adults, and serves no purpose but to make children feel powerless in the shadow of adult authority.

Eventually, repeatedly breaking promises will cause a child to distrust *all* promises. A promise, after all, is a contract of sorts, and such contracts should be honored. A child who is regularly subjected to broken promises comes to accept failed hope as a condition of life. That may be more punishment than any parent would wish to inflict upon a child.

You can be very effective in enforcing discipline by involving your child in selecting an appropriate punishment. It is very important that the punishment be related to the offense in the mind of the child and that it not be too harsh or too lenient. Letting the child help choose his or her punishment can assure that both these objectives are met. Most children will select a punishment too harsh, thus affording a parent the opportunity to show compassion.

On one of the nine thousand or so "Captain Kangaroo" broadcasts to date, Mister Moose lied about hitting a baseball through Mrs. Barton's kitchen window. He blamed Bunny and Miss Worm, the Banana Man and the Man in the Moon. Finally, with his back to the wall, he took responsibility for the kitchen-sink home run and felt ashamed that he had lied and implicated others. I asked him if he thought he should be punished and, if so, what punishment was appropriate. "Send me to the South Pole to spend the rest of my life feeding the penguins," he replied. "No, that's too good for me. Send me to the zoo to wash the elephants, the big ones and the very big ones and the very, very big ones and the very, very, very big ones. . . ."

"Mister Moose," I interrupted, "how would it be if, as a punishment, I took away your Ping-Pong balls for a week?"

He fainted. I revived him. Panting, he said, "A week, a whole week?"

"A day?" said I. "An hour?"

"Sold! Make it an hour."

No Ping-Pong balls for an hour. But for the rest of the show Mister Moose popped up every thirty seconds demanding, like any child would, "Is the hour up yet?"

Chapter 25
Way to Go, Gama!

When Laurie graduated from Dartmouth, she decided to take some time off from the classroom and think about her future. She returned to New York and went to work as an assistant to the incredibly talented Charlie Osgood and other correspondents at CBS Radio News. Kindly nurtured by Charlie, Dallas Townsend, Doug Edwards, Morton Dean, and other good people, she developed a love for broadcast journalism that holds her to this day. After two years, however, she decided to study the law. Perhaps this was genetically related to her father's desire to do the same thirty years before.

Laurie enrolled at Washington University's School of Law in St. Louis and commenced a rigorous routine of study. There, she became acquainted with a fellow student, John Sullivan, who was a year ahead of her, and after graduation she married him. I well remember Laurie's last semester of law school. I sat down to write a check for that last period's tuition with some ceremony. Since Michael had left for prep school, I had been writing tuition checks for my three children for a dozen years. Prep school, college and graduate school—it totaled twenty-nine years of tuition. At last, it was coming to an end; I wrote the check and carried the envelope to the post office with the joy of knowing that I had given each child the advantages of a fine education.

When I arrived home, however, Jeanne smiled at me and said, "You'd better sit down. I'm going back to New Rochelle to study for my master's in gerontology."

So, our days of mailing tuition checks weren't quite over yet. At the time, I was Chairperson of the Board of Trustees of the College of New Rochelle and, in a silly mood, it occurred to me to act in an official capacity and welcome her back to the institution on behalf of the board and administration of the college. Instead I said, "Well, nowadays, you can use your MasterCard."

I was very proud of Jeanne. She returned to New Rochelle exactly thirty years after earning her bachelor's degree, and she worked hard to earn her master's degree. The drive to and from New Rochelle consumed more than two hours several days a week. I was impressed and respectful when I would come upon the kitchen table piled high with research papers and texts.

Her commencement occurred two years later, just as I had retired as Chairperson. But I was seated on stage with the academic party as she came across it for her diploma. Our president, Dorothy Ann Kelly, was kind enough to hand me her diploma and, as I presented it, I picked her up and whirled her around while her son, Michael, seated in the audience with his family shouted, "Way to go, Gama!"

The fact that more people than ever before are interested in continuing their education has been a remarkable phenomenon of the last few decades. In addition to the increased numbers of traditional students attending college, adults of all ages are to be found on the nation's campuses. Many of these older students are seeking credits for career advancement, but a significant number are studying for self-improvement and for the sheer joy of pursuing interests denied to them in their younger years.

At New Rochelle, I presided over a commencement at which a woman almost ninety years old was presented with her bachelor's degree. At a reception afterwards, I asked about her plans. "Why, I'm headed for New York University to study for my master's in fine art," she replied. I would not be surprised to learn that at the age of one hundred and two, she became the curator of an outstanding collection.

Many mothers who elected to stay at home to raise their children now take jobs and pursue a career when the children have left home. This can be disturbing to their children. I know a mother who converted her adult daughter's bedroom into an office so that she could bring work home. "How could you do this to me, Mother?" asked her daughter. She felt her room should always be there for her to come back to. Besides, mothers are not supposed to change. And fathers are supposed to re-main the same, too, frozen in time.

Many children leave home to strike out on their own, then find that the style to which they have been accustomed is unaffordable on a modest starting salary. For some, the answer is to move back home. Living at the old home means that these adult children can afford to spend more on clothing, more on entertainment and more on expensive vacations. Many of these young people have come to expect an unrealis-tically high standard of living. This often leads to a clash in life-styles, and the parents, who are enjoying a new life-without-parenting, are sometimes resentful of this intrusion.

On the other hand, many parents don't want their children to be deprived in any way. This sometimes leads to a level of generosity that also creates an unrealistically high standard of living for their children. Lavishing material goods upon a grown child is not always a good idea. Sooner or later, that child will have to break loose and become finan-cially independent, and those gifts may make it harder.

But you can run into the same problem even if you don't overindulge your grown child. I remember, as an undergraduate, hearing a colorful lecture given by a professor of sociology. "I have a washing machine and dryer and a dishwasher and a nice car and a nice home. My daughter is getting married, and she expects the guy she's marrying to give her all these things. But I'm sixty years old and it has taken me forty years of work to get all that stuff. How can she expect the poor slob she's mar-rying to give her all that at twenty-five? It's not fair to him to have such high expectations. She could do the dishes by hand, but then, she's always had the dishwasher. It's not fair!"

It is difficult for children and adolescents to understand the stages of life. It often escapes all of us that each of us is in a perpetual state of change. Parents expect children to grow, but they often forget how rapid that growth can be. All too soon, years have passed, and their little baby is off on a life of her own. It is hard for many parents to adjust and often even harder to "let go" of children, to allow them to live their own lives. There comes a time when the ordinary daily routine of parenting ends and children must be allowed to make independent decisions, even if they are decisions with which their parents do not agree.

There also comes a time when children must let go of parents and act independently, as well. While they were maturing, their parents were also changing. Children must allow parents to live a new life-style, should they choose to do so. Whether they remain at home or return to the nest, children cannot expect the level of "service" that was in place when they were less able to care for themselves.

It is true, however, that parenting never ends. A parent and child who have developed a warm and close relationship will remain close, and those parents will continue to be that child's resource for guidance and information. But there is a difference between being close and being dependent. My children call us frequently, keeping us up-to-date on their households and often asking questions and seeking advice. But there is no question that they are fully independent. They often visit us with their children, and as an extended family we spend some very good times together. The time I have spent with my grandchildren has given me the greatest of pleasure.

I am careful not to overstep my bounds with the grandchildren. I know that my children want to raise their children in their way. I seldom disagree with what they do, but I also never forget that, should I disagree, they are the parents. Grandparents would do well to remember their role and enjoy being grandparents.

Grandparents may have changed since my childhood. My maternal grandfather, James Conroy, was the only grandparent I knew. My father's parents died in Ireland before my birth, as did my maternal grandmother. I have nice memories of my grandfather. In the 1930s there were still some horses and buggies and horse-drawn delivery wagons left on the streets of New York. James Conroy had a stable on Manhattan's West Side off Central Park West, where he cared for some of the horses who had not yet been nudged aside by the gasoline engine.

The great day of every year for us children was Thanksgiving Day. The wonderful Macy's Parade would move south on Central Park West, and we would move east to west from a side street to my grandfather's stable. Inside, we would warm ourselves in front of a huge coal burning stove situated on the badly worn broad wooden planks alongside the hay-strewn stalls and then, warm and cozy, rush back the half block to watch the clowns and the floats. I thought Grandfather was the greatest, and I was proud he was remembered in my middle name, James.

He seemed a quiet and stern man, but then, men of that era rarely had much to say to small children. He had a kindly bearing and his occasional pat on my head with his huge hand made me feel as though he had placed a crown upon me. He lived in the Bronx with my step-grandmother, and the Sunday visits to their home were a joyous time. The fragrance of Sunday dinner cooking and the warmth of family remain with me. We lived in Queens and, in an age before bridges spanned Long Island Sound, we drove our sleek black Buick, complete with running boards along the sides, onto the College Point ferry. It was quite a trip, especially in rain or fog. For a youngster with a keen imagination, it was akin to an ocean crossing.

In the summer of 1933, my father did take us on an ocean crossing, home to Ireland to show us where he had grown up. It was almost like visiting my grandparents because, though they were gone, the family homestead remained. My Uncle Ned and Aunt Maggie, brother and sister, had stayed behind to tend the farm. Some chickens scratched in the dirt beside the thatched roof cottage, squealing and smelly pigs dug in the mud beyond, and across the road, the cattle grazed on Carrick Hill.

A climb to the crest of Carrick Hill was like a journey up Everest for a small boy, but my reward was the cool water drawn from the rock-enclosed well on top. We would lower a bucket, raise it, and then scoop the water in a tin cup which sat upon the rocks. It was a long time ago, but not since have I tasted water so cool and refreshing.

The family had the contract to maintain the roads in and around Roscrea, County Tipperary. I was taken in a pony cart along with Uncle Ned and the hired hand to the peat bog where, with a sharp, long-handled tool, squares of the peat were cut and piled in the cart. The poor pony strained under the weight of so much peat and a small boy to boot; the men showed enough charity to walk. When we came upon a hole in the road, the men dropped in a square or more of peat and tamped it down with a long-handled tamping tool. It was a crude maintenance program, but good enough for a road used by only four or five autos a day. There was no gridlock in Roscrea in those days.

When the long day in the fields or on the roads was complete, we snuggled around a peat fire in the small cottage. That fire was the heat in winter and the cooking place all the year, as such fires have been in Ireland throughout the centuries.

On the ocean voyage home, I was shown to be a cheat. There were deck games on the S.S. *Manhattan,* and I entered the potato race in which a potato was picked off the deck and carried on a large spoon to the finish line. The black-and-white movies shot by my brother Jack clearly show me illegally holding the potato on the spoon with my other hand. Shame! Will I ever live it down?

These childhood memories are an important part of my "root structure," an important asset for any child. Grandparents are one of the means of enhancing that root structure. A child is fascinated with the notion that Granddad is his or her parent's father. Young children, especially, find it very difficult to picture their mother or father as a child. Maeve's youngest, Alex Keeshan Ashbaugh, giggles when I talk of his mother as having been my little girl. He thinks I'm kidding, of course. When I first told this to Maeve's oldest, Derek, he thought I was kidding, too. His father, Hans, didn't help by also expressing astonishment.

Michael's youngest, Connor MacNary Keeshan, spent his second year being "Granddad's boy." He would follow me everywhere and reward me with the broadest grin anytime I spoke to him. He would laugh at my lines whether they were funny or not. That's a child with a future.

My oldest grandson, Britton Conroy Keeshan, reminds me of myself as a child. Watching him at play, I see a dark-haired boy of fifty years ago. I have a picture that shows me sitting on our front stoop, a photo which could have been taken of Britton. He has my peculiar sense of humor, also.

When the older boys were very young, I would talk to them on the telephone and tell them that the ducks had wandered in off the lake and taken up residence in the kitchen. I would hold the kitchen phone out and ask the ducks to say "hello."

"Quack, quack, quack" went the ducks to laughter at the other end of the line.

Subsequently, the ducks would visit on the phone, now and then.

Not too long ago I phoned Michael's house and Britton answered.

"Hello," said Britton.

"Quack, quack, quack," said I.

"Oh Granddad," said Britton, "I don't want to talk to a bunch of ducks!"

The kids are catching on. I need new writers.

Perhaps when Laurie's Kaelan Devon and Connor Matthew begin to speak on the telephone we can, once again, drag out the old "ducks in the kitchen" routine.

.   .   .

Grandparents are a great resource for children, and a strong relationship between them should be encouraged. In these days of the transient
family, a strong bond is often difficult to achieve. When Grandmother is
only a voice on long distance, the development of a close and warm
relationship is almost impossible. The generations should be brought
together as frequently as possible. It is a great investment in the root
structure of the children.

I have read accounts of grandparents who have taken legal action to
gain visiting rights with their grandchildren, children whose parents
have divorced. Just as a parent never becomes an ex-parent in divorce,
so a grandparent is never an ex-grandparent. Children need the very
special nurturing of grandparents, and a divorced parent who refuses
this access is stealing precious experiences from those children.

As a gerontologist, Jeanne has seen some fine programs which bring
the elderly together with children. It may be a school class visiting a
nursing home or a child care program merged with a senior citizen's
program for a morning or afternoon. Such intergenerational programs
provide huge benefits for the elderly and for the children. The synergy
between the generations is wonderful to watch.

Grandparents and their relationship with grandchildren have
changed over the years because the world has changed. My grandchildren know that they have an unusual grandmother. As Jeanne, known
to her grandchildren as "Gama," expresses it, "Some grandchildren
have grandmothers who sew for them, some grandchildren have grandmothers who bake cookies. My grandchildren have a grandmother who
boogies!"

She dances for them as they giggle in delight. "Way to go, Gama!"

Chapter 26
Please Leave Quietly

Often at one of my lectures or other appearances, an adult of thirty years or so, will say, "Captain, I saw you on public television the other day and it really brought back memories. I saw Bunny, and I saw the Ping-Pong balls fall on your head. But I always thought your jacket was blue. I was surprised to see it is red. And where are Grandfather Clock and the Magic Drawing Board and Tom Terrific and his Wonder Dog, Mighty Manfred? And what happened to the music, dah, dah, dah, dah, . . . dah, dah, dah-dah, dah, . . . deedee, deedee, deedee, dee, dee, deeeee . . . ?"

As I have said, we are all in a constant state of change. I have had adults show great displeasure with me because their old Treasure House is not there today. In the seventies, it became the "Captain's Place." Grandfather is now in a back room and the Magic Drawing Board is a memory. Tom and Manfred were in black and white and not suitable to today's very colorful Captain. Change is essential because, in television today, with all the high-tech effects that children have now come to expect, the old Captain and his Treasure House would not be accepted. These changes are almost totally cosmetic and technological in nature, however. Beneath the changes reside the Captain of old and a philosophy toward children that is virtually unchanged. We merely express it differently.

In the fifties, I thought that the movie, *The Treasure of Sierra Madre* was the greatest movie of all time. I clung to this idea for years. Recently, I had to admit it is showing its age. The story remains moving and the acting superb. But we are not accustomed to seeing movies shot that way. We have been conditioned by today's motion-picture production techniques. It has little to do with content; it's the style that's different. The Captain remains philosophically the same, but today's "Captain Kangaroo" is produced using today's production techniques. To many thirty- and forty-year-olds, that is trifling with their fond memories. But of course, today's Captain is being produced for today's child.

When we first appeared in American living rooms in 1955, there was no videotape. Tape made life a bit different in the late fifties, but we were essentially taping a live performance; editing was difficult, time-consuming and expensive. As editing of tape became easier, we were then able to remove mistakes or redo material we did not like. We soon were able to add special effects and many post-studio production techniques. It was like magic; the production standard of the program was greatly improved. We started to spend large sums of money on musical productions and comedy pieces and fairy tales. We could justify the added cost because this material was placed in a library to be used again. The cost was divided by three or four or more plays and thus was made affordable.

We went to color in 1965, but didn't change much on the set or anything in the way of costumes. In 1971, however, we could abide the dull set and costumes no longer. We gave the Captain a bright red jacket and placed him in a colorful set. Some stations were delaying the time of broadcast and, therefore, Grandfather Clock was not giving the true time; so into the back room he went. Producers Jim Krayer and Jimmy Hirschfeld, who oversaw the changes, said it was akin to bringing down the walls of Jericho.

The original theme music was wonderful, but to a generation of youngsters conditioned by Elvis and the Beatles, something more contemporary was needed. Writer-composer Bob Brush wrote a new one, keeping a thread of the old, and then, a few years later, a completely new theme. The public television show plays what is our theme song number four, "Here Comes Captain Kangaroo!"

Following the death of Debby Weems, we added the greatly talented Carolyn Mignini. Carolyn, who plays Kathy and ten million other characters, can sing, dance, act, be funny and anything else you ask of her. She has been a great member of our family. Another new addition, Kevin Clash, has been playing with puppets in a most professional way since his childhood in Baltimore. He has worked with Jim Henson as a puppeteer. For "Captain" he has created puppets, acted as a puppeteer, and after much arm-twisting, Kevin came out from behind his puppets to act many characters on screen. He is very talented and very young. It was sobering to me when I realized that this young man of such talent now working on "Captain Kangaroo" had grown up watching the program. We had been on the air several years when he was born.

Many celebrity guests also added something special to the show. Tammy Grimes dropped by with her delightful daughter, actress Amanda Plummer. Hermione Gingold, James Broderick, Theodore Bikel and Walter Slezak graced us with their fine performances. Carrie Fisher was kind enough to baby-sit for Mister Moose, and that was not an easy job. Andy Williams brought his bear and Estelle Parsons was regal as a queen in a fairy tale. Bobby Vinton played a frog who kissed Miss Frog and was transformed into a prince; type casting, again. Mister Green Jeans invented a machine to make cloth from carrots, and Phil Donahue came by to tape this extraordinary news for his show. Much to our embarrassment, our clothes turned to carrot greens in the middle. Paul Sorvino played a visitor from space and Kaye Ballard was a delightful, if zany, Tooth Fairy.

Mike Farrell and Lola Falana were great as contestants in the Great Kangaroo Games. In addition, real sports figures were always prominent on the Captain's show, from Frank Gifford, Willis Reed, Walt Frazier, Earl "the Pearl" Monroe, to Bruce Jenner and Rosey Greer, who showed up with his needlepoint, making still another point.

Chita Rivera was a favorite of the Dancing Bear and we took the "Wicked Witch of the West," the gracious Margaret Hamilton, and turned her into a kindly and warm Fairy Godmother. Edie Adams was "Little Red Riding Hood," and Dudley Moore dropped by to play the piano and be, well, . . . Dudley Moore. Bob Denver was a part of the Great American Circus while Tommy Smothers nearly broke his neck trying to be a circus acrobat. James Whitmore and his lovely wife, Audra Lindley, tried to rescue the "Hotel Splendid" from the wrecker's ball and show our young people a respect for the architecture of another age. Clifton Davis helped Mister Moose to be a prince, and Irwin Corey was Irwin Corey. Allen Funt was candid and Lyn Redgrave was lovely. Phyllis Diller played a lady who adopted every animal in sight, and Imogene Coca played a silly lady who meant the reverse of what she said. Paul Dooley was the zaniest professor I ever met; John Ritter was a New England ship's pilot, continuing his family's relationship with the show.

John's father, singer Tex Ritter, had recorded many of the songs heard on the early "Captain Kangaroo." Jerry Stiller and Anne Meara were frequent visitors, and Bill Cullen was cast in an unusual role, a game show host.

The sixties and seventies were very healthy years for "Captain Kangaroo." There was not as much competition from shows on local stations and almost no competition from cable television. Sponsors had flocked to the program and, because we were relatively inexpensive to produce, CBS made money from the program. But always present was the notion that they could make more money.

If a newspaper has a heavy advertising or news day, it is able to add four or eight or twelve or more pages. A television station or network does not enjoy that advantage; God made each day with only twenty-four hours. The money has to be made within that finite time period. If the Captain is on the network between 8 and 9 A.M., that means that a news program or game show or soap opera cannot be broadcast in that hour on that network. The game in the network executive suites is to make hay while the sun shines and when it does not, in twenty-four hours, no more, no less.

The "Captain" is a children's program and, despite large audiences and a modest budget on CBS, could not demand the high commercial prices that an adult program could. That irritated network executives for years and years and years. One executive once said to me, "I like what you do, it's nice. But, I don't like you because you are the one show on this network I cannot cancel. I don't like that." No network executive enjoys limited powers.

The program was protected as long as government regulators held television stations accountable for the service they were rendering to their communities. That meant that each station was obliged to serve the needs of minorities and special audiences. It was a system that required community service of those who made a lot of money using a publicly owned asset, the airwaves.

When network executives would ask the local stations, "How about if we give you something for grown-ups at eight o'clock? Some news, for instance?" The stations replied, "The Captain is valuable to us. It is the way we serve children in our community. He protects our license. Leave him alone." Some of the stations even said the program was doing something for the future by nurturing our children, and that was more important than money or a third news program just for the sake of competition.

The deregulation of broadcasting became a *fait accompli* when President Reagan appointed Mark Fowler as chairman of the Federal Communications Commission. Former Chairman Fowler was doctrinaire, literally one who attempts to put abstract theory into place without regard for practical difficulties. As Commissioner Henry Rivera said, "Get out of the way, here comes deregulation." Fowler was unconcerned with results. He said, "The marketplace will take care of children." I never thought Mark Fowler had much of a sense of humor, but that was a funny line, if somewhat ironic. The marketplace has taken care of children by removing network and local programs of value. Saturday morning network programs hardly pay lip service to the needs of children.

Meanwhile, in England, France, Germany, Italy and Japan, broadcasters were and still are meeting the needs of children. The Soviet Union, whose television message we may find distasteful, uses the medium to educate young people. The Soviets are wise in recognizing the power of television and its potential to inform and educate. In the United States we use television to sell to children.

In the early eighties, I knew it was only a matter of time before there would be no room for a "Captain" at CBS. The news division was hot to prove that it could run rings around the "Today Show" and ABC's "Good Morning America." If only they had the entire two hours, they thought, they would show who could get audiences, they would bury the competition. Gene Jankowski, the CBS Broadcast Group president, liked that idea a lot.

Gene and I had one of our many executive suite lunches one day in the early eighties and Gene then ushered me into his office for a friendly chat. "What am I going to do, Bob?" There was more than a question in his voice, it was a plea. He could have come right out and said, "Won't you go away quietly, no embarrassment, please?" I had played some poker in my day and I knew enough not to feed Gene the lines.

"I want to be number one, Bob."

"You are number one, Gene. CBS has been number one in serving American families with the 'Captain' for years."

"I mean, I want to be number one in the ratings. I want to cream the competition." He slammed his fist down on the glass tabletop so hard I was in awe. I knew there was no stopping this man.

    I had been eyeing public television for years. When "Captain Kangaroo" went on the air in 1955 there were six so-called "educational" television stations. Now, there were almost three hundred. While there was no home in 1955 for a Captain in public television (because it barely existed), now was the time for a move. On public television, teaching and entertaining children were more important than selling to them. I had been feeling that way for a long time. "He places the needs of the children ahead of those of the advertiser" was the inscription on my first Peabody Award in the fifties.

    I knew that the news division wanted that additional hour, and, with the deregulation of broadcasting, it was only a matter of time before they moved their things into my time period. I also knew that CBS did not want me to make a fuss and a noisy exit. What I wanted was time to build programming in order to make the switch to public television. I agreed to move to a very early morning time period in exchange for a few more years in which to build that programming. I also agreed to make the move quietly.

    After a year in the early morning, the voracious appetite of the news division had not yet been satisfied; they wanted my new time period, as well. They got it, and I moved again to Saturday and Sunday in October 1982. Fewer stations carried the program and of those that did, many aired it at five-thirty or six in the morning. I commented to the press that asking children to watch the Captain at that early hour was akin to cruel and unusual punishment.

    Added to what I had in programming from 1980 forward, the new shows gave me four hundred hours of material to be re-edited, added to, and built into shows for public television. At the end of 1984, I tossed it in and the Captain said goodbye to CBS, nine months short of thirty years.

    Meanwhile, the news division had been unable to cream the competition, as they had expected to. They found they couldn't attract much of an audience; usually their ratings were less than the "Captain" had been earning. They were also spending over thirty-five million dollars a year, more than ten times the "Captain Kangaroo" budget. So much for the wisdom of the executive suite.

After I left, I was quoted in a New York newspaper as saying that television executives sometimes display arrogance in making their decisions. My good friend, Tom Leahy, who was the number two Broadcast Group executive at the time, took offense. This caused me to examine the word "arrogance" more closely. I was ready to admit I had misused it, but I concluded it was the proper word to describe such actions. There is a sense of superiority displayed when an executive decrees that audiences *will* watch a program; it is a command to American audiences. The answer of the audience, in this case, is on the record.

In my many years in commercial television, I would often look to the people working in public television with some envy. How fortunate they were to be able to spend their time on creative matters with no concern for advertisers and their agencies. I have been very shocked since moving to public television to find that most of my time is not devoted to creative matters but is spent seeking funding and underwriting.

After three seasons on public television, I have come to the conclusion that the system will never reach its potential to serve Americans as long as we fund it in a meager and haphazard manner. There are many creative people in public television who are unable to unleash their talents because of the constraints of inadequate funding. Yet special audiences, children included, can only be served by public television, now that deregulated commercial television looks to the marketplace and profits in making programming decisions. Cable television serves little more than half of the nation and those in need of television most, the poor, cannot afford cable programming. Public television is where America's special needs can be met. But as long as funding of it is scanty, the system will be unable to meet those needs.

"Captain Kangaroo" has successfully met the needs of young people for over a third of a century. Those needs are greater than ever in contemporary America. To produce new programming, to address such present-day issues as substance abuse, new family structures, child care and others, we need more funding than has been available to us. Thus, while I would prefer to be spending time creating programming, I am spending most of my time looking for funding for that programming. I have a dream that, someday, American citizens and American business will recognize the very special place public television occupies and will make it possible for the system to realize its potential.

American children spend more time watching television than they spend in the classroom. If my dream for public television comes true, this influential medium will be augmenting the American family in giving values to children, making them feel good about themselves and passing on the information they need to grow to be literate, useful and happy citizens. That's a dream for a very bright future, a new nation of great possibilities. That's a dream we all ought to work to make come true.

Chapter 27
Thump, Thump, Thump
Went My Heartbeat

On July 11, 1981, I was scheduled to talk to a convention of Parents Without Partners in Toronto. The talk was to be given that evening, but I had booked an American Airlines flight at eleven-thirty that morning. In retrospect it doesn't make much sense, but I decided to carry my luggage aboard rather than wait a few minutes to claim it at the terminal. When we landed, I lugged the baggage, at a fast clip, several hundred yards to the immigration area. I don't know why I was hurrying except that I always seemed to be in a hurry. I was living by the motto "hurry up and wait," as we once said in the Marines Corps.

Out of breath, I arrived at the end of a line of people waiting to be passed through by the Canadian officials. As it turned out, I was never required to speak to them because I was carried past them. Arriving on line, I had begun to feel dizzy. I looked up to see the ceiling circle round about me, then all went black. I was having a heart attack.

Gilda Radner had been on the airplane with me and was standing close behind me on line. A few weeks later, Gilda told me I scared her half to death by collapsing in front of her, enough to cause her to take a CPR course upon her return home, which is a very wise thing for anyone to do. She was very concerned and felt helpless. Years later, Gilda won admiration for her fight against cancer. Although she died in May, her courage demonstrated for us all that we humans have within us the power to overcome great obstacles in the celebration of life. The knowledge of this power is a great gift for a parent to give a child. Gilda

Radner will always remind us of the potential of this power in each of us.

Fortunately for me, there was a meeting of cardiologists in Toronto that July day, and several physicians were also on line, one of them carrying a defibrillator, the device used to control the erratic beating of the heart muscle. Along with the physicians was a nurse from the Coronary Care Unit of a local hospital, who was returning from holiday. Someone in heaven above had me wired.

I remember not a thing of all this; later I was told many conflicting stories about what occurred as I lay on the floor of the airline terminal. I know I was successfully defibrillated by the physicians, may God bless them, and was taken to the Etobicoke General Hospital, where an hour later I awoke in the Emergency Room. I looked around and realized what had happened to me. I am now embarrassed to recall that the first words I spoke were, "Oh no. My work is not finished yet." They sound like the words of a prophet about to be martyred, but I never spoke more spontaneously. I fully realized, at that moment, how much there needed to be done for the children of this nation, and how much more I wanted to do.

I determined that I was going to change the way I lived and give myself a chance to continue working. I had smoked once but had given it up in 1964. I was overweight and did not exercise much. I have since managed to correct that, but I cannot do anything about two nice people, my parents, who both compiled a lousy cardiovascular record. However, I can give my heart every other break within my control.

Stress plays a large role in heart disease, and I'm in a stressful business. I think I'm pretty casual and laid-back, but I know that things do get to me. Shortly after my coronary, "Saturday Night Live" did an outrageous sketch in which Captain Kangaroo was stressfully beaten into a heart attack by a television network executive. I don't think there was a straight line from the CBS executive suite to the Toronto airport, but the stress of the previous few years certainly played a part in bringing on the coronary event.

When I was leaving the hospital to return home, my cardiologist expressed some concern. "I know you," he said. "In no time you'll be back in the studio, in front of the cameras. Please, relax a bit. Why don't you take some time off to play golf?"

"Doctor," I said, "every so often you may be asked to go on television, perhaps a cable show, to talk about cardiology. You know your subject but you can't help what happens to you. The cameras move in and the stage manager throws you a cue and your blood pressure moves up a notch or so. It's stressful. For me, a television studio is like my living room. I'm at home, relaxed. But ask me to go out on a golf course and address a small ball at the first tee with ten people watching how I hit . . . Doctor, that's stressful! Don't make me do it."

The people at Etobicoke Hospital had a great impact on my life after saving it. They practiced medicine as both the science and the art that it is. I'll never be able to thank them enough, but then, I know that they do it because they are professionals. I owe a great debt to them and will always have a special feeling for the Canadian people. They treated me very well indeed.

When I was a child, a large appetite was considered the norm and was thought to be very healthy. The diet of the United States was, no doubt, affected by the collective experience of the many cultures which had gone into the melting pot of American society. Many of the peoples who came to the new land were fleeing a poor economy, among other things, often a life on the edge of starvation. This was certainly true of my ancestors. The great Irish migrations to the United States followed the potato famines. Beginning with the great famine of 1845–46—which alone saw the death of five hundred thousand Irish and the emigration of over one million—recurring famines caused the emigration of millions of Irish over the next half-century. Most of these Irish came to the United States and brought with them the memory of starvation and bad times in their native land.

It is not surprising, then, that these newly arrived first- and second-generation Americans regarded the cornucopia on most American tables with joy. *"Essen, essen! Mangia, mangia!* Eat, eat!" were universal commands from mothers, custodians of the immigrant tradition. And they ate and ate.

As a modern parent might say, "What did they know?" And she would be right, what did they know, indeed? Eating large amounts and developing the robust to corpulent figure that resulted, were considered healthy. The roots of the American banquet were in the insecurity of the undernourished immigrant experience and the bitter homegrown American experience of the occasional depression. Even the doctor said, "Eat." Many a mother heard the friendly advice, "Put some meat on her bones." To be thin was to be sick and unattractive. To be plump was to be healthy and sexy.

To a very large extent, these parents and grandparents of ours were wrong. Science has since turned the American diet in a new direction, virtually one hundred and eighty degrees from a generation ago. Many modern parents relate more to Oprah Winfrey and her new slimness than they relate to immigrant insecurity.

But the old diet had already done its damage to many of us. The number one killer in the United States is not on the FBI's most wanted list. The big, bad killer of so many Americans is heart disease. Like me, no one can do anything about heredity, but we can improve our chances in other ways. Diet is high on the list of protective measures. What we know can help us.

Unlike his professional ancestor, today's doctor is urging us to play it smart when we sit down to eat. The "clean plate club" still has its virtues for children, but a parent can help by loading that plate with healthy foods. We acquire lifelong dietary habits in childhood and, once acquired, such habits are hard to break. If, with parental permission, we learn to love the foods we should hate for the sake of our health, we are setting ourselves up for trouble, perhaps fatal trouble.

The American Academy of Pediatrics recently recommended that physicians test cholesterol levels in all children two years old and older who have a family history of high cholesterol or premature heart attack. It is recommended that children with high cholesterol levels be counseled by experienced registered dieticians, so that their fat intake is decreased to within normal limits, but not so drastically that growth might be retarded. As in anything else, moderation and common sense should play a role in juvenile dietary decisions. Our mothers knew, instinctively, that food fueled growth in a child. What they did not know was that some foods can set a child on a lifelong course toward poor health.

Another bad habit which seriously lowers our chances of prevailing against heart disease is smoking. The Surgeon General has told us that smoking is addictive, among many other things, which means that once you start it's difficult to stop, as with any other substance abuse. I already knew that because I had gone through it.

Peer pressure is a dreadful monster. When I was a late adolescent and serving in the U.S. Marine Corps, I wanted to be just like all those other tough Marines. I washed my khakis till they were bleached "salty." I drank 3.2 beer at the post exchange, bellying up to the bar in imitation of all those old salts recently returned from the Pacific. And I bought cigarettes at the post exchange for three cents a package and coughed my way through three or four packs until I felt I belonged to the real Marines. Some old-timers referred to them as "coffin nails," but surely they were wrong. I believed it was a relaxing and necessary habit for those going off to war.

Twenty years later, Dr. Luther Terry, then the Surgeon General, released the first report on the effects of smoking on health, and it was pretty damning. Any reasonable person could understand that there was a causal relationship between smoking and certain diseases. Shortly thereafter, I was going into the hospital for some minor surgery. A few days prior to my admission, a friend of mine who was also a surgeon pointed to my cigarette at a social gathering and said, "You won't be able to use those while you're in the hospital. It might be a good opportunity for you to break the habit." It was good advice, if somewhat ironic; he was puffing away while dispensing the wisdom. I gave up cigarettes while in the hospital, though many of the physicians were smoking before and after making rounds.

I wish all those I love and respect would break that dreadful habit, and I feel the same way about people I don't know. I don't like to see people suffer and, as a taxpayer, I don't like paying the price we all pay to provide the health care costs of many smokers. I also don't like its effects on American business; poor employee health and absenteeism is costly to us all. But I am not a leader in the no-smoking campaigns. Hooked adults are old enough to be entitled to make their own decisions, even though they are costly to me and to other taxpayers; I don't make a big deal about it. I also don't make a big deal about the non-smoking areas in public places. Smoking offends me but I am too embarrassed to ask a smoker to show some consideration. But reaching out to children and influencing them to take up the habit is where I draw the line.

I have testified before Congressional committees several times in opposition to the tobacco industry's sponsorship of rock concerts and athletic events. The industry denies that it attempts to influence young people through these activities, but clearly such sponsorship does reach young people with a positive message regarding smoking. If the tobacco companies don't believe that, why do they sponsor such events? Their ads in many magazines appealing to young people are designed to show how "cool" smoking is. In addition, the industry attempts, through sponsorship of rock concerts and photos of handsome athletic, healthy, young people in its ads, to present smoking as "healthy by association." That's my opinion, and I express it to protect the health of young people.

I am not in favor of banning the sale of tobacco products and certainly would not be first in line in urging other restrictive legislation, but I wish the tobacco industry would self-regulate and refrain from sponsoring activities for children and adolescents. While an adult has the right to make decisions regarding tobacco, I don't believe young people are capable of making an informed decision. Appealing to them with sports heroes and rock figures is, in the end, unfair. Furthermore, it is in the self-interest of the tobacco industry to distance itself from the youth of America. It would show wisdom in what, for the industry, are very precarious times.

I have said that adults are old enough to make decisions about smoking. However, for parents, part of that decision making process should take into account the effect of their smoking on their children. I am not talking about the "secondary smoke" effects, although recent evidence shows that this can be quite a health hazard. I am most concerned about the modeling of a behavior that most parents would not wish their children to copy. Smoking is a very difficult habit to break, I know, but perhaps its effect upon children will be an incentive for a loving parent. Besides, parents will be needed by their children for years to come; poor health should not interrupt or terminate the relationship.

In a routine medical exam in July of 1987, (July must be my lucky month), my cardiologist, Joe Lambert, told me that an arteriogram, the old tube-and-dye-in-the-heart-muscle routine, revealed a good case of gridlock in the arteries supplying my heart. The next day I was on a plane to Houston with Jeanne tightly gripping my hand. In the splendid Methodist Hospital, the Baylor medical team took me on. Dr. Stanley Crawford, pride of Alabama, performed a triple bypass, and the blood began flowing to the muscle as it should. Thump, thump, thump went my heartbeat, and I felt terrific.

I won't kid anybody by saying it was easy or that I enjoyed the experience. The postoperative period constituted the worst three days of my life and, in some ways, it was cruel punishment. Threatening bypass surgery as a judicial sentence could definitely reduce the crime rate!

Four weeks after surgery I was on a stage in Champaign-Urbana, Illinois, doing three stage shows. I didn't do much dancing but I didn't shuffle too much, either. I felt great. I read some of the literature, both popular and medical, about people who have had this procedure and was intrigued to discover that many people suffer severe depression following bypass surgery. Given good medical results, I would think anyone would be greatly encouraged, but apparently this is not always so.

I raised the subject with Joe Lambert, and he said that, in his experience, "You come out the way you go in." I know that is a simplification, but Joe was saying that it helps to be an optimist. I am an optimist and I feel great. Besides, my work is not finished yet!

Chapter 28
Anarchy Begins at Home

We do not usually associate stress with children, but children of all ages are often subject to it. In fact, preadolescents and adolescents suffer the effects of stress in much the same way adults do. The reasons that older children feel stress may seem trivial to adults, however, so they are taken lightly or escape notice. Yet academic and social pressures in particular are as serious to an adolescent as job insecurity or economic disaster are to an adult. As with adults, children need help handling anxiety. Because adolescents are capable of resorting to harmful escape measures, their problems with stress should be taken very seriously. If not, they may cause great emotional or physical damage.

Recognizing stress is vital if the condition is to be addressed. Children, particularly young children, will not articulate their feelings. A three-year-old is not going to face Mother and say, "Mom, I'm feeling particularly stressed with that new baby you've brought into my house. Let's discuss this." But the child may regress in behavior, by bed-wetting, soiling clothing, crying, having temper tantrums and showing other signs that parents may not readily associate with the stress of a new baby. The child sees the attention given the baby, attention once exclusively his, and will revert to babylike behaviors in an attempt to regain parental attention.

As in the case of a new sibling, anxiety in a young child usually results from an interruption of routine—an illness, a new job for a parent, a move to a new house, anything that destroys set patterns. Children are secure when routines are in place. Anything that interrupts routine can result in stress to a young child.

. . .

I recently saw a bumper sticker, "Anarchy Begins at Home." That sticker carries great wisdom; the breakdown of law begins with the breakdown in family routine. Systems of governance are critical if each of us is to be secure and safe in our community, but many of the smaller rules and laws of society are routinely disregarded today. Much of that disregard begins at home.

We are organized in society by laws, both minor and major. We have misdemeanors and felonies. We have traffic laws and environmental laws. We seriously offend when we commit burglary, robbery, assault, rape, incest, murder and other felonies. The minor and major offenses are connected as a ladder has steps; the breaking of the law is a progression beginning with indifference, a disrespect for the law.

In many places today, perhaps because of budgetary restraints, we rarely prosecute the minor offender. As a child, I remember gazing upon the sign in a New York subway, "Smoking and Spitting Prohibited Under Penalty of the Law." I swallowed several times lest some saliva accidentally escape my lips and make me a lawbreaker. Today, passengers smoke and spit and commit other unlawful acts under the eyes of police officers and are rarely cautioned, much less officially charged with offending.

If we do not routinely observe the small laws of society, it will be quite impossible to expect observance of the major laws. The major laws of our society have their underpinning, their foundation, in the order and routine of the family. The observance of household rules instills a respect for rules—for laws—in a child; the child internalizes this respect and becomes socialized.

Teaching respect for the symbols of the law is also important. I was taught, as a youngster, that the police officer walking the beat was a friend, deserving of my respect. Today, many adults express a disrespect for the police officer in many ways, both in words and by action. The parent who drives the freeway with an eye for the highway patrol gives a message to a child. The parent in the supermarket who slaps a child and says, "Behave or I'll call the policeman and he'll throw you in jail" is also teaching that child. Wow! That's the way to give a gross of negative messages in under twenty words.

We grow to understand that not all police officers are worthy of respect; there are bad police, as there are bad lawyers and doctors who should not be practicing. But we must instill a respect for the symbols of authority as well as for the laws, major and minor, that those authorities uphold on our behalf.

Despite our establishment of routine, things change, from new baby to new job to new house. Young children are stressed. Regression in behavior patterns may be misinterpreted by a parent as plain, old-fashioned misbehavior. The stressed child is calling for help. But the parent misreads the signs and resorts to punishment, and the child becomes more anxious. Run up the foul-weather flag!

As I have said before, children must be interpreted; the words they are speaking may not be what they are saying at all. If this sounds confusing, it's because I want to convey that children and their means of communication can sometimes be the closest thing to chaos under the sun.

Parenting requires full concentration. When I am driving my car, I must be careful not to get too wrapped up in what Charlie Osgood is saying in his morning report. If I do, I may miss my turnoff or brake later than I should. Driving, like parenting, requires full concentration.

It's easy not to concentrate. There are so many distractions in our daily life that children sometimes become background noise, and we stop listening to them. Much of what they say may seem like idle chatter; not all of it is. We have to listen to what they say and interpret it. A few chapters back, a child asked a parent, "When are you coming home?" But the question really was *"Are* you coming home?" At one time that child screamed and cried when the baby-sitter arrived. Now, the child has accepted the parent's need to leave, but is still insecure. An understanding, an interpretation, of the child's reaction will help to deal with the stress the child is feeling at the departure of the parent.

Understanding that, in a young child's behavior, regressions or other apparent misbehaviors are a sign of stress will help a parent react in a reassuring manner and get the child back on the security track. With an older child, communication is easier, but it is important not to trivialize the reasons for preadolescent and adolescent stress. They may be mountains in the road to maturity for the child. Understanding and real help are appropriate parental reactions. Don't hesitate to seek professional assistance in this area.

Often, communication with adolescents proves difficult for adults. If a good relationship has been established in younger years, teen-adult communication should be easier. But there are times, even in the best of parent-teen relationships, when the teen does not wish a parent to understand. Teens often speak a peer language which may drive adults to distraction; it is impossible to understand what they are saying. That is because they do not *want* adults to understand what they are saying; peer language is designed to exclude those not in the peer group.

Though they may think they are doing something unique, peer language has been around as long as there has been a need for it. When I was a kid, I went through the ixnays of pig latin and its many derivations and, at an older age, we used good English words given a different meaning which only our peers understood. Parents and grandparents who spoke a language other than English used the native tongue to exclude children and others from hearing things they were not supposed to hear. Jeanne found fault with the work of some contractors in our house, and they cursed her in a foreign language. She admonished them. "The Irisher speaks German!" they exclaimed. She responded, "If you'd said something other than a curse, I wouldn't have understood." In her childhood, her German family members had spoken naughty words in German to protect the ears of baby Jeanne!

Peer language is part of the bond that unites adolescent peers, a union of those who "understand." Children can give great comfort to each other in very healthy ways. They share experiences and thoughts and notions that they cannot share with adults, especially parents. This peer bonding is natural, but some parents feel hurt by the exclusion. Teens are progressing along a road every child must travel, the road to maturity. Parents should understand that this means that the child is placing a distance, a natural one, between herself and her parent. Remember, successful parenting means teaching a child to get along without parents, to be independent.

As reluctant as some parents are to see children mature and grow independent, other parents, usually well-intentioned, rush their children to adulthood. On playground park benches and in pediatricians' offices it is common to hear conversations concerning how to get a child into the best nursery school. Some parents are willing to try anything, from putting books into the crib in order to instill a good feeling for reading to buying a computer to give a three-year-old a head start. Push, push, push. Some parents seem terrified that they will fail to provide the tools and develop the drive to get their children accepted by Stanford or Harvard before they blow out the candles on their sixth year birthday cake.

Some parents seem impatient with childhood, not understanding that it is a critical stage of human development that cannot be hurried without risking great harm to a child. Kindergarten is well named; it is a children's garden, a place for play, for you must remember that play is the serious work of children, through which they learn. Childhood is a garden in which we plant seeds, the seeds of love and the seeds of good feeling, we hope, that will grow into the flower of maturity. Did you ever try to grow a daisy in fewer days than nature prescribes? We can carefully provide food and water, light and warmth to assist the plant, but the daisy will take its sweet time and will bloom only when it's ready, when its time has come. So it is with children; they will grow at a natural pace and mature when ready. Rush them and you risk harm.

Some parents are consumed with a need to have their children read early in life. This places a great stress on the child who may not yet be ready to acquire the skills needed to read. I recently met a child who, at age seven, said, in a rather precocious way, "I can't read yet. I guess I'm a flop in life."

Recent research gives some indication that forcing a child to read before he is ready may not only be nonproductive, but counterproductive as well. This research indicates that ability to read well may be *hindered* by pressure.

Many parents also seem impatient with the outward signs of childhood and feel that they can advance maturity by dressing their children in the clothing of adults, engaging them in adult conversation, inviting them to adopt adult practices. In his book *The Hurried Child,* David Elkind observes that children "are growing up too fast, too soon. They are being pressured to take on the physical, emotional and social trappings of adulthood before they are capable of dealing with them."

In the 1940s and 1950s, says Dr. Elkind, "Middle-class parents were afraid of repressing their children, making them neurotic through too much discipline." They were also reluctant to accelerate their children's academic skills. But in the 1960s all that changed. The new belief was that if children weren't taught at a very young age, a golden opportunity would be lost forever.

Several decades ago emotional precocity was considered undesirable.

It was unheard of for young girls to wear makeup, for example, or for preteen boys to ask girls out on a date. Children have always clomped around in Mom and Dad's clothing. I can remember in my halcyon childhood days, putting a lovely Strauss waltz on the old windup Victrola in the basement. My sister, Catherine, would parade about wearing her mother's hat and scarf and high-heeled shoes. I would wear an old felt fedora belonging to my father and some fancy white shoes, the pride of my brother Bill. (They always found themselves back in the closet before Bill's return home. In retrospect, I lived dangerously!) Catherine and I enjoyed our musical masquerade and our wonderful disguises. But we always knew they were just that—disguises. We never deluded ourselves that donning adult clothing bestowed maturity beyond our young years.

There are now what are called "children's cosmetics" on the market, and parents and grandparents are buying them for youngsters. A child is only four, but Dad buys her a makeup kit so she can imitate Mom. The package states that the makeup is safe, so what's the harm?

The harm factor lies in how the child sees herself in relation to the "play" makeup. Experts point out the way these products are often advertised on television. If these kiddie cosmetics are designed to promote the image of a young temptress, ask the experts, are little girls being asked to mimic Mommy or to *compete* with her?

Dr. Francis Palumbo, associate professor of pediatrics at Georgetown University Medical Center in Washington, D.C., raises the question, "Why would anyone *want* to sell cosmetics to little girls?" He comes up with a simple answer, "Money." And the fact that a market should actually exist for these products sheds an uncomfortable light on the status of present-day childhood.

Young parents often feel bewildered by these pressures, pressures that reflect our society's attitude toward children. It is an attitude that says it's never too early for a child to become an achiever, for a child to compete either academically or socially. But pushing a child to academic or social achievement can boomerang and seriously hinder a child's naturally paced development.

Some parents "manage" their children's lives so completely that a child has little opportunity to make decisions about small or important things. This removes the opportunity to plan life, beginning with a single day. When finally asked to take over, such children are incapable of decision making; they've never had to do it before.

When I was a child I enjoyed playing baseball. The way we played the game might have shocked or delighted baseball's inventor, Abner Doubleday. We did not always have eighteen kids to play so we made the best of it; if there were eleven of us, six played on one team and five on another. That made covering the outfield a job not even our hero, Joe DiMaggio, could handle. But who cared? We had fun. When someone slid into second base, whether he was safe or out was a matter of negotiation, and usually a lesson was learned from that negotiation.

I am not opposed to organized juvenile sports, but at times it does seem to get pretty serious. The adult officials are on hand to make that call at second base, and the teams are splendidly organized and uniformed by adults. Many teams are now computerized, and a young player's batting average is posted after each game. Heaven help the kid whose average slipped twenty percentage points in the last few games. Such organization is fine if we are trying to develop athletes for college and professional baseball, but it's not play, so please don't call it that.

Childhood must be a time for a child to learn about the world, to love, to enjoy being loved, to satisfy curiosity, to gain confidence and develop self-esteem. These activities are critical to the natural rhythm of development. To rush it is like asking a musician to play Beethoven's "Choral" Symphony in double time; it's not very pleasant to the ears. Life's rhythms are carefully planned, and a parent is like a symphony conductor, trying to lead the many facets of a child's personality, uniting them in a pleasing way. The parent/conductor must be careful to respect the music as written. Rushing it will bring very undesirable results.

I once narrated Sergei Prokofiev's lovely *Peter and the Wolf* with Leopold Stokowski, the great and very colorful conductor. Because I am so lacking in musical talent, I had not the foggiest notion when to "enter" with each line. Maestro Stokowski was asked to cue me carefully each time. At rehearsal, I stood next to the podium, eyes riveted upon Mr. Stokowski. My gaze did not wander for a second, so fearful was I of missing a cue.

Stokowski was having trouble with the orchestra, and he stopped several times to tell the musicians that they were entering at "letter G too early. Please watch me."

Again he started the orchestra and again he stopped, displeased with their performance. Finally, at the fourth stop he looked with great displeasure at the orchestra and said, "People, you must watch me, you must watch me. May I point out to you how carefully the Kangaroo is watching his conductor!"

Chapter 29
All in the Family

In school I learned many of the laws of physics. Objects in motion tend to remain in motion—a good reason for wearing a seat belt. Objects at rest tend to remain at rest—a good reason for having an alarm clock.

There are laws in the social sciences, also. Most people tend to resist change; we are comfortable with the familiar. If Mother stayed home to take care of us as children, that feels comfortable to us. Then we get caught up by the winds of change. We discover the fact that it takes two paychecks to provide the same things that one paycheck provided twenty-five years ago when Mom was in the kitchen. We may not be comfortable with the unfamiliar, but we know that unless we are willing to lower our standard of living, Mother is going to have to leave the baking to Duncan Hines and become part of that growing army, the working mothers of America.

Aside from the economic need, many woman wish to work and, the last time I looked around, it was considered plain un-American to get in the way of someone in the pursuit of happiness, including economic happiness. The American family is a different sort of creature than in the past. Instead of bemoaning change, we ought to get on with the task of nurturing our children in this different world.

The duties of fatherhood have changed in the last few decades, and today fathers are nurturing children in ways that were quite uncommon only a few years ago. When I would mention to the guys on the train that I fed the baby and changed diapers, I was regarded as an oddity. Some men would even change seats to distance themselves from me, as though my strange notion of caring for infants were a communicable disease they might catch. Today, most fathers take an active role in raising their children from their earliest days. My son Michael's wife, Lynn, works at moving numbers around in budgets and reports for her employer, a large food-manufacturer. She is very good at it and valued. Occasionally, Lynn will find it necessary to travel. It is at such times that her sons, Britton and Connor, find themselves nurtured by "Mister Mom." Michael is a big part of the nurturing system in his home at all times. He's very good at it, too.

The traditions of "woman's work" and "man's work" have all but disappeared in most modern families, and sharing household and nurturing chores is fairly commonplace. So, the family itself has made some adjustments in recognition of changing times. But usually this is not enough. Most modern American families are not nearly as self-sufficient as the families of fifty years ago were. Today's family needs outside help to plug the gaps in our nurturing system.

Upon hearing the words "outside help," many people can work themselves into quite a lather about "interfering" in family affairs. Politicians especially like to talk in eloquent terms about "the sacred family, basic unit of our society" and "let us not allow government to do what the family is entrusted to do." I could not agree more. I believe the family is the basic and most critical unit in our society's structure. I am also opposed to government interference in family affairs except where appropriate, such as in cases of child abuse or neglect, spousal abuse, illness or other family crisis requiring intervention for the safety of family members. I also believe that the family has a job to do, including acting as the nest where children are nurtured and socialized to become happy, productive, and considerate adults. I believe that, because the structure of most American families is so changed, this function cannot take place successfully in most families without some help from all of society, including you and me. The contemporary family needs backup assistance from all of us to do the job we have charged it to do.

I like to think we all like children and feel compassion for them, as most of our "apple pie and mother" hype and image would suggest. But I learned some years ago that many adults cannot abide children and would not give a small finger of assistance out of compassion. Perhaps such people could be persuaded that *not* assisting the family is a very costly mistake, a mistake paid for in tax dollars by both individuals and American businesses, and costly to society because of the conditions that result. Illiteracy, malnutrition, ignorance, abuse, neglect, and crime are among the costly conditions that come about because some families fail to nurture successfully. If we can plug those holes, assist the family, and prevent bad results, we taxpayers will save a fortune. And our economy will be vigorous from the input of well-educated workers and consumers. It could be like living in Japan.

Almost fifty years ago, at the University of Pennsylvania, Franklin Delano Roosevelt said, "We cannot always build the future for our youth, but we can build our youth for the future." It is wise public policy to assist the family in preparing our youth for the future. Few would argue that it is wise policy to charge a police officer with foiling a robbery attempt by a youth with gun in hand. I would argue that it should also be public policy to assist in nurturing that youth so that he would never pick up that gun, to nurture him to be learned, compassionate and a gift to society, to prepare him for our future.

There are many actions that we, as a society, can take to assist the family in successful nurturing. I will cite a few, but my list is not all-inclusive. I am certain any observant citizen can add to my list. We ought to recognize that we have some out-of-the-mainstream subcultures in our society. Let us not waste time on rhetoric as to why such subcultures exist. They are there because, despite our claims of compassion, we have effectively excluded many people from the mainstream of American society. This has resulted in millions of Americans who feel alienated and cynical, citizens who often do not act like good citizens, who have developed a value system quite different from the mainstream, a value system that often results in actions that shock our sensibilities and destroy our property and occasionally harm or destroy our person. Some good citizens like to mumble about those "no-good so-and-so's" and "why should I care about those lazy. . . ." Everyone ought to care, if not out of decency, then simply because "those people," those outside of the mainstream, are smoldering like a stick of dynamite in a school yard. We must, as a society, work to allow all Americans the opportunities of the mainstream.

We probably brag about ourselves more than any people on earth and we have good reason to be proud of our accomplishments, but we are far from perfect. In what we refer to as the greatest nation on earth, we are the only modern industrial nation to have made children its principal underclass. It is not our glory but our shame that fourteen million American children live in poverty. That represents twenty percent of our future, one in every five kids, and that is going to mean big trouble if we don't act fast. Poverty is the ultimate violence, as Gandhi said.

Poverty is not a statistic to a hungry child; malnutrition is a daily experience. Many of us have never experienced malnutrition and hunger but their effects can be seen in classrooms across the land. In a 1987 Carnegie Foundation survey of twenty-two thousand teachers, more than two thirds said undernourishment was a problem in their schools from kindergarten to high school. The school lunch program served eight percent fewer children in 1988 than a decade before, despite rising enrollments. This decrease resulted from public policy and budget cuts. For many children this school lunch is not only their best meal, but their *only* meal of the day.

Kids coming to school without breakfast are well-known to most teachers. These are the kids who are nervous, irritable, uninterested. Sometimes an empty stomach causes dizziness, nausea, headache and fatigue. And we expect these children to learn? They fail, they grow to be illiterate, they soon are on public assistance rolls. All because we saved the modest cost of breakfast and lunch. We're not too bright.

Children living in poverty often don't get routine medical and dental care. Deferred maintenance doesn't work with an automobile, and it certainly doesn't work with a child. I have met, at personal appearances, children with decayed teeth, disease and deformation. Why, in modern America? We are a better people than that. We are a wiser people than that. Aren't we?

Child care has become a political issue in this "kinder, gentler America," and it should be. Few families can afford the cost of *quality* child care. Pure custodial care, the placing of a child with a person who provides some nutrition but no program—perhaps a television set to while away the hours—is not quality child care. Many parents must settle for such care, however, because affordable, *quality* child care is not available to them. The children may be physically safe, although not always, but they suffer in many ways in a purely custodial-care situation.

Quality child care is provided in a *safe* and *stimulating* environment. *Quality* child care is a *structured program* administered by educated people and by teachers who are qualified educationally and by temperament. The program should not be meant to "push" the child into early intellectual development but should be designed to emotionally develop and reassure the young child, to make her feel good about herself, to aid in the building of self-esteem. If an individual child shows that she wishes to undertake some aspect of intellectual development, the program ought to be able to recognize this and provide the stimulation.

Quality child care is a partnership between teacher and parent. The parent must be a participant, understanding the objectives and goals of the program. The teacher must be trained to recognize problems, no matter how slight. For example, a withdrawn, overly quiet child may have a problem. The teacher can be a person who communicates with the parent and assists in problem solving, even when the problem originates outside the center. The teacher should be able to refer the parent to sources for assistance and counseling. Successful nurturing is the objective of *quality* child care.

I so want to interest American business in undertaking child care programs that I founded a child care company of my own, Corporate Child Care, Inc., of Nashville, Tennessee. Under the tax laws, American companies can afford to provide quality care for the children of their employees at a modest cost. In fact, when I speak to chief executives, I make it plain that I am not talking about charity, but a good business program that comes down to the bottom line in black ink. In dollars and cents, businesses can offer this employee benefit and *save* money doing so. Quality child care helps companies retain employees (thus saving on training new employees), reduce absenteeism, get an employee's mind on his or her job and off worrying about his or her child, attract new employees in a low-unemployment market, and build employee loyalty. Put all of that together and child care as an employee benefit is plain old bottom-line business sense.

Business taking care of its own is a start, but such programs will not completely meet the needs of American families for quality child care. Government, the churches, private child care companies and small independent centers will all be needed to meet the huge demand. Public policy ought to assure that quality, affordable care will be accessible to every American family.

A particularly urgent need is felt by the single mother on public assistance who is unable to work because she cannot afford child care. Often, she needs to be trained to acquire job skills. She can't go to school to gain these skills because she can't afford the tuition and can't afford child care while in school. For such people, life is the cruelest Catch-22. Some states have instituted programs in which the mother learns job skills while the child is safely cared for. When she finishes and gets a job, the child care subsidy continues until she is up the ladder enough to stand on her own. Ultimately, the government saves money on public assistance to the mother and to the child, and the mother becomes a productive member of society paying taxes. This is intelligent public policy, a good example of what we can be doing to nurture our children by assisting the family, whatever its structure.

Because our schools are locally administered, we all have an opportunity to affect public policy in education. We ought to plead with our school boards to make our schools places for teachers to teach and for children to learn. Because of local administration, there exist many differences in American education from place to place. Therefore, I risk generalizing. If the points I make do not apply to your school system, please understand.

In general, we spend too much time in the administration of our schools. Organization and standards are necessary, but often they seem to be the reason why people in education come to work each morning, while teaching children is put aside until the business of administration is satisfied. I served on a school board in a growing suburban school district for five years and I am far from unsympathetic to the problems of school boards and administrators, but I also know that it is easy for them to forget why the schools exist. The schools exist for children, not for school board members, not for administrators and not for teachers alone. Whatever gets in the way of education should be pushed out of the way.

Teachers ought to be relieved of excessive administrative burdens— including testing designed to relieve administrative insecurities—and be allowed to teach. Good teachers ought to be rewarded accordingly, and poor teachers should be reassigned to duties more compatible with their talents or urged to adopt a more appropriate occupation. Teaching is a high profession and no child should be burdened with poor teaching; learning is a difficult enough task for a child. Everyone in the community should respect and assist good teachers and good administrators.

Let us see that the failed practice of corporal punishment is removed from all of our schools, as it was a half-century ago in our more enlightened systems and almost everywhere else on earth, including the Soviet

Union. Instead, let's train intelligent, compassionate teachers to recognize the unruly child and other children with problems—train them to identify children crying for help and refer them to outside sources for counseling and aid. Then our teachers will not only be teaching, they will be saving young lives for all of us.

We also save lives when we intrude upon the smashing and bashing of children. Little children should not be subjected to the outrageous blows of unruly or out-of-control parents. Parents who are close to abuse, tried by the rigors of a cruel society, need to seek help. A parent who is anywhere near this stage ought to call the many 800 numbers offering assistance and real help to distraught parents. The white pages of the telephone directory may contain a number for Parents Anonymous, a fine organization founded to help parents in need.

Like physical abuse, the sexual abuse of children is a dreadful occurrence and public policy should protect children and identify and deal with abusers. The counseling of an abused child is a critical component in any program dealing with the sexual abuse.

As I have said, the most common form of child abuse is emotional abuse. Yet it may be the most difficult type to identify and treat. Awareness on the part of all adults that denigration and insult are not appropriate behavior would be most helpful. It takes courage to confront anyone engaging in such behavior, but it is a kindness to the child and to the adult who may be unaware of such behavior and its consequences.

The list of the many ways in which we can support the modern family and assist children could go on. Please add to the list from your own observation. If we see to it that public policy is truly supportive of the American family, then children will more often be successfully nurtured, and our failures will be fewer. We will save money and we will save lives for the future.

The family is the basic unit of society and the future will be only as good as the quality of nurturing done by that family today. Quality nurturing is something every one of us should work to achieve. Make yourself a member of every American family, and the family you save will be your own.

Chapter 30
Wish List

In the preceding pages I have chronicled many of the events of my personal and my professional life. Those of you who grew up with the Captain as part of your nurturing system shared some of those events on television. I am very grateful that those experiences proved to be a positive influence upon so many young lives. That some of you are able to look back and, with the judgment of an adult, confirm the benefits of spending some precious time with the Captain, is most pleasing to me. I love to read letters, especially those from today's adults, yesterday's children, telling me about the intergenerational aspects of "Captain Kangaroo."

"My husband is twenty-eight years old and has watched the Captain since he was a child. Now, we have a one-year-old and they both watch the Captain."

"Dear Bob, I feel I can call you that because you have been so much a part of my life for so many years. Although this letter may seem kind of silly, it's just to let you know how much admiration I have for you and the wonderful things you do for all children. My eight children are almost all grown, and now there are two grandchildren, and I am hoping they will come to love your program as the rest of us have over the years."

"I have had the pleasure of being one of your millions of fans since I was a child. Captain Kangaroo, Grandfather Clock and Mister Green Jeans are a

part of my upbringing. Now, with children of my own, I enjoy sharing our 'together time' watching you and your beautiful show."

"As a teacher, I can spot your kids in the first week of school. They are comfortable with themselves. When I mention your name, they smile and eyes sparkle."

"I was born October 3, 1955, on the Monday morning that "Captain Kangaroo" first came on the air. From the Captain, I learned about music and dancing, all about different kinds of animals, how flowers grow, how little children all around the world were different from me, yet very similar, and much more."

I am very grateful for the response and it encourages me to continue. Never before, in my experience, have families and children been in greater need of friends and helpers. I have something of a "wish list" which suggests some ways in which I can be of help to families and children.

"Captain Kangaroo," remains at the top of my wish list. Because of changed family structures, television is used by families more than ever before. I want to see quality programs like "Mister Rogers," "Sesame Street" and "Captain Kangaroo" available as part of the nurturing system. In public television, where the Captain now lives, that means underwriting. The John D. and Catherine T. MacArthur Foundation has been very generous in affording us the opportunity to produce new programming. The public television stations have made the broadcast possible with the generous support of local underwriters and members —that's you, I hope.

There are so many needs "Captain Kangaroo" could address—substance abuse, new family structures, the continued building of self-esteem. This will be possible only with corporate underwriting, and that is why I spend so much time asking for the support of business. It's not charity, it's a good media buy. The program viewing is shared by grateful adults who write letters such as those above. Even smaller local businesses can become involved by underwriting the Captain on local stations; it's not much money and children will benefit all year long. Call your local public television station. If I have the proper underwriting it would be my wish for "Captain Kangaroo" to serve children on television forever.

I would wish to continue meeting children in concert halls with symphony orchestras. Such programs are stimulating for me—I enjoy the interplay with the children and their parents. It builds a future for the orchestra and brings many children to the experience of classical music, an experience they might not otherwise enjoy.

I enjoy lecturing because I like to communicate with adults about young people, and the question-and-answer sessions that usually follow such events are especially helpful. I am always impressed by how clearly most adults think on children's issues and how frustrated many of them feel with a system that is apparently unable to respond to children's needs in an appropriate and direct way.

Because the needs of the contemporary family are so great, I would wish to reach more adults with the information necessary to help them meet those needs and nurture their children. To do this, I would wish to continue my rounds of the talk shows, and perhaps return to a radio series and a newspaper column.

We are a nation very much concerned with family values. For good or bad, one of the most effective conveyors of those values is television. I would also wish to continue to use the medium to show positive values to children and their parents. I admire the work that Bill Cosby does in this regard with his splendid program, and I would like to make a personal effort to reach the American family with entertainment that presents wholesome values, particularly those which relate to the increasing numbers of older family members. This could be done through a situation comedy or another entertainment format.

One of these days, I am going to bring back the "old" Captain in a special for today's adults who grew up with him. I would include some nostalgia, like Tom Terrific, Mighty Manfred, the Magic Drawing Board, Lariat Sam, Grandfather Clock, the Banana Man and so many old friends, sights and sounds which were part of growing up in America.

Most of all, I would wish to be effective in everything I do for young Americans. I hope that some of my comments here will lead young parents to more effective parenting and will help all adults to understand that all of us must be a part of the nurturing system. I like that because it's good for the future but, also, because I enjoy children. They are very likable creatures.

Children are unpredictable. I remember bringing my three young ones to the circus in Madison Square Garden. I was certain they would enjoy every last bit of it, but I could not predict what they would like best. As it turned out, the girls most enjoyed the funny clowns, especially those with the shovels who followed the elephants. Michael insisted on buying, with his own funds, a small flashlight attached to a lanyard. What could he possibly want with a flashlight in well-lighted Madison Square Garden, I speculated? Then, the lights went down and a great high-wire artist began his precarious foot-over-foot progression across a tiny wire high in the air. He was, we were told, the fourth generation of tightrope walkers. What talent, and perhaps even genetic input, were needed to produce such a great artist. Were Michael's eyes affixed on this great artist? They were not! In the darkness, Michael was twirling his lighted flashlight by its lanyard and watching ten thousand other children in a darkened Madison Square Garden as they twirled their flashlights. Ten thousand circles of light. Perhaps it was as a child, in a darkened Madison Square Garden, that President Bush first saw his "thousand points of light." The great high-wire artist reached the other side almost unnoticed while Michael and his peers twirled away. Imagine their disappointment when the lights were turned on again. A greater question for me was, what instinct prompted Michael to spend his good money for that flashlight?

As a young child Michael was invited to sleep overnight on the USS *Northampton,* CLC 1, the command ship of the Atlantic Fleet, a floating technology center with every electronic device for detection and communication then known to man. The command center had a two-story-high plastic plotting screen, hundreds of antennae, thousands of miles of cable, electronic monitors of every description. Wow! "Michael," I asked the next morning, "what did you like best?" With uncontained enthusiasm he responded, "Dad! In the galley they have this toaster that makes twenty pieces of toast at once!" Children are indeed unpredictable!

Children are curious. An infant's eyes move even before they can focus, watching blurred patches of light move above her. Growing, the child will use eyes, ears, nose, hands, feet and mouth to learn about his world. Further along, her curiosity will test the parameters of her world. "Am I permitted to do this? Let's see what happens if I pull this cat's tail." The three-year-old will turn a boot upside down, eyes peering into the darkness of the toe. A five-year-old will move sand and stone for time on end, rearranging his world.

Children are demanding. They think they know what they need and they are not shy about asking. They especially like to make demands when parents are in the shower or speaking to the boss on the telephone or about to turn over for two more minutes of morning sleep.

Children are loving. That is their nature, until it is altered. It would be a far nicer world if people did not get in the way of that natural inclination to love.

Children are adoring, of parents in particular. All figures of religious and secular power are nothing in a child's eyes when compared to a parent. If the Chair of the Board felt about you the way your child does, you would be president of the company tomorrow. Caution, such power has consequences. Use it responsibly.

Children are irritable and cranky when hungry, sick or emotionally wounded. So feed them well, nurse them to health, stroke them with kindness and understanding. Tomorrow is another day and a new child will emerge, this one all smiles.

Children like to laugh, sometimes at the silliest, most unfathomable things. Don't ever ask, "What's so funny?" Accept laughter for the joyous feeling it is. Children generally look better when they are laughing.

Children cry. They tend to overreact. That's okay. So do many adults, with greater consequences. Don't make light of it, even if you are giggling inside. To a child, tears are serious and also transient. Like the rain, they go away. Be sympathetic and find out *why* that child is crying.

Children can be angry. When they're small, it's usually not too serious, but it is designed to communicate a message. Get your antenna up. As they age, children will learn from adults to "use" anger and other emotions to achieve certain ends. You've probably seen all the tactics before, but coming from your child they can be disconcerting. Again, a message is being sent. Listen hard.

Children grow. That means new clothes, and it also means new ways of speaking and listening. Each stage of growth brings new challenges and new delights. Relax and enjoy children.

After a certain period passes, you will discover that your child has become an adult. If you have successfully nurtured, even with all those mistakes you made, you will experience a great good feeling that consumes every aspect of your being, a feeling known to only one class of human beings—parents!

Thank you for letting me share my life—and your nurturing experience. Aren't children wonderful! Let's make sure they grow up happy.

Suggested Reading List

As I have suggested in this book, children should not be placed under early pressure to learn to read. However, the development of positive attitudes toward reading and books is a process which should begin early in life. Parents instill these attitudes when they read in front of their children. If a parent assigns value to reading, that attitude will usually be adopted by the child.

Reading *to* a child is one of the best ways a parent can do this. What follows is a list of suggested books, all of which have been read by Captain Kangaroo on the public television series. Like most such lists, it's marked by incompleteness. It could be a hundred times longer and still not include all the fine reading materials available to young people. Browse through a library or a bookseller's stacks and add to these selections.

My Mom Travels a Lot by Carolin Feller Bauer
No Good in Art by Miriam Cohen
Two Ways to Count to Ten by Ruby Dee
In the Forest by Marie Hall Ets
Corduroy by Don Freeman
Even If I Did Something Awful by Barbara Hazen
Cromwell's Glasses by Holly Keller
There's No Such Thing As a Dragon by Jack Kent
Emma by Wendy Kesselman
The Ship That Came Down the Gutter by William Kotzwinkle
The Shy Little Girl by Phyllis Krasilovsky
A Zoo for Mr. Muster by Arnold Lobel
Giant Jam Sandwich by John Vernon Lord

Tracy by Nancy Mack
Make Way for Ducklings by Robert McClosky
Alligators Are Awful by David McPhail
If the Dinosaurs Came Back by Bernard Most
The Little Engine That Could by Watty Piper
Book of Hugs by David Ross
A Bug of Some Importance by Robert Sargent
Sometimes Mama and Papa Fight by Marjorie Weinman Sharmat
Gwendolyn the Miracle Hen by Nancy Sherman
Caps for Sale by Esphyr Slobodkina
People by Peter Spier
The Famous Blue Gnu of Colonel Kachoo by Mary Villarego
Most by Mort Walker
William's Doll by Charlotte Zolotow

Home Video: As Fun and Learning

Many parents are concerned about the influence of commercial television upon their child. The purpose of commercial television programming is as an advertising tool. A program which is produced to meet the nurturing needs of children may not meet the commercial needs of advertisers, and so may never make it to the small screen in a regular way.

But parents who can afford the technology of a videotape recorder can exercise more control over what their child is watching on television. My daughter Maeve calls herself "my children's program manager."

Although a VCR can be an expensive purchase, the industry is now marketing more modest machines at lower prices, such as machines without recording capability that only play tapes. Using a VCR, parents can select taped programming that meets the individual nurturing needs of his or her child, and not worry about commercials or other influences.

How do you choose among the myriad tapes available for children? It's important to pay attention to who has produced the tape. Children's Television Workshop produces many fine tapes for home viewing, as do Mister Rogers and Captain Kangaroo, both of whom offer stories which help develop a child emotionally and intellectually while entertaining. Many other producers, such as Walt Disney, also create tapes of high quality for children.

Most community libraries have a collection of tapes. By borrowing them, parents can become familiar with specific tapes, as well as the work of producers who cater to the children's market, and decide which ones to buy for their home library. Many parents also join others in building a collection to swap among many families. All it takes is agreeing to a master list and purchasing those tapes for which your family is responsible. Buying a quality children's tape is never a waste of money. Keep in mind that children love repetition and replaying a tape can have great value.

Printed in the United States
by Baker & Taylor Publisher Services